EMERSON'S
NONLINEAR NATURE

Emerson's
NONLINEAR NATURE

Christopher J. Windolph

UNIVERSITY OF MISSOURI PRESS
COLUMBIA AND LONDON

Library of Congress Cataloging-in-Publication Data

Windolph, Christopher J., 1973–
    Emerson's nonlinear nature / Christopher J. Windolph.
        p. cm.
    Summary: "Examines Emersonian naturalism from the
standpoint of nonlinearity, offering new ways of reading
and thinking about Emerson's stance toward nature and the
influence of science on his thought. Windolph breaks new
ground by exploring how considerations of shape and the
act of seeing underpin all of Emerson's theories about
nature"—Provided by publisher.
    Includes bibliographical references and index.
    ISBN-13: 978-0-8262-1742-4 (alk. paper)
  1. Emerson, Ralph Waldo, 1803–1882—Philosophy.
2. Naturalism in literature. 3. Nature in literature.
4. Philosophy of nature in literature. 5. Emerson, Ralph
Waldo, 1803–1882—Knowledge—Science. 6. Science in
literature. 7. Nonlinear theories. I. Title.
    PS1642.P5W56   2007
    814'.3—dc22   2007007349

Designer: Kristie Lee
Typesetter: BookComp, Inc.
Printer and binder: Thomson-Shore, Inc.
Typefaces: Minion and Copperplate

Acknowledgment is made for permission to quote from
"The Snow-Storm" and "Xenophanes," as the texts appear in
Essays and Poems, First Library of America College Edition,
Library of America (1996), by permission of the Ralph
Waldo Emerson Memorial Association and by permission
of the Houghton Library, Harvard University.

CONTENTS

ACKNOWLEDGMENTS

I would like to thank those at the University of North Carolina at Chapel Hill who contributed, in ways large and small but all important, to the development of this book, namely, Joseph Flora, Philip Gura, Fred Hobson, Joy Kasson, Timothy Marr, and Richard Rust. I would also like to thank Jennifer Heller, Chad Trevitte, and Amy Sweitzer, each of whom read drafts of various chapters and helped me define, refine, and solidify their keys points and themes. All writers should have such attentive and involved reviewers. In particular, I appreciate the efforts of Amy Sweitzer, whose direct assistance made it possible for me to send the manuscript of this book to the University of Missouri Press in the first place. Her generous friendship has always been my gain. Last, my gratitude goes to Catherine Gori, whose hospitality afforded me the time and space I needed to make what revisions to the manuscript were necessary before it went to print.

ABBREVIATIONS

Frequently cited works by Ralph Waldo Emerson are identified parenthetically in each chapter by the following abbreviations:

CollW   *The Collected Works of Ralph Waldo Emerson.* 6 vols. Ed. Alfred R. Ferguson et al. Cambridge: Harvard University Press, Belknap Press, 1971–2003.

CW   *The Complete Works of Ralph Waldo Emerson.* 12 vols. Concord Edition. Boston: Houghton, Mifflin, 1903–1904.

EL   *The Early Lectures of Ralph Waldo Emerson.* 3 vols. Ed. Stephen E. Whicher, Robert E. Spiller, and Wallace E. Williams. Cambridge: Harvard University Press, Belknap Press, 1959–1972.

JMN   *The Journals and Miscellaneous Notebooks of Ralph Waldo Emerson.* 16 vols. Ed. William H. Gilman et al. Cambridge: Harvard University Press, Belknap Press, 1960–1982.

LL   *The Later Lectures of Ralph Waldo Emerson.* 2 vols. Ed. Ronald A. Bosco and Joel Myerson. Athens: University of Georgia Press, 2001.

EMERSON'S
NONLINEAR NATURE

1

UNPUBLISHED BEAUTIES

I speak of the Renaissance as an evil time, because, when it saw those
men go burning forth into the battle, it mistook their armour for their
strength; and forthwith encumbered with the painful panoply every
stripling who ought to have gone forth only with his choice of three
smooth stones out of the brook.

—JOHN RUSKIN, *The Stones of Venice* (1853)

When we study Architecture everything seems architectural[:] the forms
of animals, the building of the world, clouds, crystals, flowers, trees,
skeletons. . . . Certainly in the forest, Architecture finds its analogons in
ferns, in spikes of flowers, in locust, in poplar, in oak, in pine, in fir &
spruce, and the Cathedral is a flowering of Stone subdued by the insatiable demand of harmony in man. The mountain of granite blooms into
an eternal flower with the lightness as well as aerial proportions & perspective of vegetable beauty.

—RALPH WALDO EMERSON,
journal entry dated September 28, 1836

Ralph Waldo Emerson's sense of his own vocation exhibits exuberant confidence: "I read my commission in every cipher of nature, and know that I
was made for another office, a professor of the Joyous Science, a detector &
delineator of occult harmonies & unpublished beauties" (*JMN*, 8:8). As a
professor of the Joyous Science, Emerson assessed the new sciences of his

day with varying degrees of assurance. While early on convinced that "the sciences are in our days striking out a new path for their progress towards perfection" (*JMN*, 1:347), he in time began to feel that "the first questions still remain to be asked after all the progress of Science" (*JMN*, 3:282). After many forays into mathematics, architecture, astronomy, physics, and Greek philosophy, he still felt compelled to ask, "The Idea according to which the Universe is made is wholly wanting to us; is it not? Yet it may or will be found to be constructed on as harmonious & perfect a thought, self explaining, as a problem in geometry" (*JMN*, 4:287–88). Geometrical sciences in particular continually held his attention and appeared to him to offer the most promise in his own search to "solve the secret enigmas of science by whose successive development the history of nature is to be explained" (*JMN*, 2:203). Of all the human sciences, then, geometry appeared to have the potential to delineate fully the "occult harmonies" so important to Emerson.

Indeed, for Emerson geometric thinking holds the key to understanding nature as well as to justifying spiritual ethics. Geometry provides many of the images and figures to which he repeatedly returns: "Show us an arc of the curve & a good mathematician will find out the whole figure," for likewise "we are always reasoning from the seen to the unseen" (*JMN*, 3:284). However, finding the arc of that curve—that is, the natural connection between matter and spirit—entails finding the proper perspective from which to view it. The development of Emerson's thought can be described, in sum, as a search for this enlightened and enlightening position. Achieving it was the most challenging conceptual problem he faced as a professor of the Joyous Science.

Recalling the well-known motto inscribed above the doors of the Athens Academy, Emerson writes, "It is not Plato but the world that writes 'Let none enter but a geometer'" (*JMN*, 11:40). Geometric thinking underpins all of Emerson's theories about nature. But geometry in this context must be understood as giving reference to metaphysical concerns and not simply analytical ones; when Emerson thinks in terms of geometry, he gives metaphysical weight, and not just epistemological weight, to the material properties of shape and structure. In a broad sense, it is a way of combining poetry with science. In "Works and Days," Emerson writes: "For we do not listen with the best regard to the verses of a man who is only a poet, nor to his problems if he is only an algebraist; but if a man is at once acquainted with the geometric foundations of things and with their festal splendor, his poetry is exact and his arithmetic musical" (*CW*, 7:179). But, as Franklin Baumer points out, the Romantic reaction to the Enlightenment was in part an argument over the meaning of geometry: "The romantics thought [the Enlightenment] world too narrow, because of its addiction, as they believed, to geometric thinking and the allied doctrine of neoclassicism, or else to Lockean empiricism. The geometric spirit, though metaphysically bold, tried to subject all life to reason, and thus to mechanize and demean it."[1] In this context, geometric thinking makes Emerson somewhat, though not entirely, unique among transatlantic Romantics who opposed it. But ideas about shape, structure, and materiality are so completely integrated into his thought that we must take them into account if we are to understand fully the way Emerson envisioned the natural world. Significantly, they reveal what might seem to be a fundamental contradiction: on the one hand we read about Emerson's "head bathed by the blithe air, and uplifted into infinite space" (*CollW*, 1:10), yet on the other we read, "I think we can never afford to part with Matter" (*JMN*, 7:377). Emerson is, in short, an empirical idealist. Like an architect, he seeks to make something real out of the ideal. Like a geometer, he seeks to give shape to the inner workings of the mind.

To such a man, everything seems architectural—when we study architecture. This rather self-evident proposition can be taken as a major theme in Emerson's life work. It is certainly the major theme of the present study. To study architecture is to learn to see the world, and everything in it, in a certain way—that is, in terms of both use and appreciation, for certainly architecture appeals to aesthetic sense as much as it fulfills the need for shelter. To study architecture is also to ask questions about design, the major occupation of both engineers and sculptors. In this regard, architecture and geometry may at first seem to respond to the same set of concerns, namely, form and structure. The former may be broadly construed as shape or outline, that is, what is outwardly visible and external. The latter, structure, is internal and often unseen, suggestive of quality, character, and development. And so taken together, form and structure, which geometry attempts to analyze and architecture puts to use, say something about

---

1. Franklin Baumer, *Modern European Thought: Continuity and Change in Ideas, 1600–1950*, 270–71.

results and effects but also, perhaps more importantly, about causes. To say that everything seems architectural is to ask questions not only about origins but also about futures: just as an architect's draft prefigures the building, the bud anticipates the leaf. Everything is modeled in something else.

The relationship between geometry and architecture is not quite so clear and tidy, however, because the history of European architecture is marked by two competing theoretical traditions. The more prominent of these begins with Euclid, whose *Elements,* one of the most influential foundational works of Western culture, helped establish a tradition of *measurement,* or dimension. Euclid presents to us a linear geometry, in which the forms and structures of architecture can be worked out with a compass and straightedge. We begin with a diagram, a blueprint, a mapping out, or, more literally, a measuring of the earth. Euclid prompts us, in short, to trace and not to calculate. The calculators, on the other hand, represent a similarly ancient, if not quite as influential, worldview. The numerology of the Pythagoreans systematized a tradition of *harmony,* or ratio, that was later developed by Plato in the *Timaeus.* Here, the ratios that exist between pitches of sound have their application in music but also in architecture, and certain magic—even "golden"—ratios are seen to regulate the order of the whole world. One scale governs the next such that order and harmony are preserved between them, and thus we begin not with a diagram but with a series of numbers. This system presents to us an arithmetic, an art of counting—in short, a means of working out form and structure by algorithm.[2] Euclidean geometry and architecture are indeed closely allied, but the Joyous Scientist is likewise sensitive to the mystery of the algorithm. The universe, as Emerson often suggests, may ultimately be self-explaining, like Euclid's axioms, but the buildings, clouds, crystals, flowers, trees, and skeletons of the world say something also about "aerial proportions": to study architecture is to recognize as well "the insatiable demand of harmony" (*JMN,* 5:215).

And so this study is prompted by a series of questions: What does Emerson mean by saying that nature is "architectural," and what exactly are the

---

2. The Pythagorean influence on architecture remained present in later centuries through Vitruvian theory, which prescribes numeric ratios for determining overall proportions (width, length, height) and *commodulatio,* or the scalar construction of architectural orders, while Euclid's influence survived among the masons and carpenters who preserved their practical knowledge by passing on the applied skills of their trades.

proportions and perspectives he finds to be so compelling? Differently phrased, just how are ferns, flowers, insects, and trees the "analogons" of architecture? How does their geometry help reveal the order of the whole? Such ideas are arrived at through observation, so this study begins to address these questions with the belief that the language of geometry and architecture—that is, of shape and structure, which can be found within a wide variety of Emerson's essays, addresses, poems, notebooks, and journals—reveals a persistent search for materiality that few who write about his ethics and transcendental spirituality have adequately explained. Architecture is more than just a convenient trope, and Emerson offers us much more than his own personal investment in an idea. Axiomatically: there is more in Emerson's curiosity about nature and the way in which it is organized than simply one Transcendentalist's abiding optimism that the world is well-ordered.

What is too often lacking in Emerson studies, in my view, is a truly empathetic connection to the man and his time, an appreciation for his perspective on the world—a problem caused, in large part, by a matter of historical perspective. As moderns, it is often difficult for us to look back upon the thoughts of those in other ages and appreciate, fully, what it is they intend to say. Their ideas are quite often not our own. To restate the problem of perspective in another way, many readers in the past century have been confronted with the problem of parsing the words of a man whose way of thinking about the world is almost entirely foreign to modern and postmodern sensibilities. In his 1990 essay "Nature's Book: The Language of Science in the American Renaissance," David Van Leer observes, "It is difficult, from our post-Freudian, post-Darwinian perspective, to imagine an intellectual environment in which neither of these figures is central."[3] It is a point we should not forget, nor take lightly. For example, in his discussions of mankind's relationship to nature, particularly, Emerson is much nearer to the concerns of certain seventeenth-century thinkers—who made much ado about the new problems technological advances in optics brought to bear on our ability to know the world—than he is to even his own nineteenth century. Thomas Browne, for example, argued that man's *active* sight still made him capable of beholding, in his phrase, the "types of his resurrection": even

3. David Van Leer, "Nature's Book: The Language of Science in the American Renaissance," 307.

if the world had suddenly become much larger—microscopically as well as macroscopically—human beings, made in the image of God, should still be able to see, with their own eyes, directly into nature's secret order, even if at times imperfectly. "This is that mysticall Philosophy, from whence no true Scholler becomes an Atheist, but from the visible effects of nature, grows up a real Divine, and *beholds not in a dreame,* as Ezekiel, *but in an ocular and visible object* the types of his resurrection," writes Brown.[4] The Galilean and Newtonian argument for *passive* sight, however, is the one that has prevailed: the influential claims of both ensure that today the eye is more or less only a simple device that detects wavelengths of electromagnetic radiation in the range between 4000 and 7700 angstroms. As such, sight has become in large part a comparative sense, or perception by proxy: the eye discerns a certain appearance, or superficial likeness, of the world, but of course it does not actually pierce into or unveil anything.[5] For most contemporary readers, then, the eye cannot *behold* in the way Browne understood the term: in everyday, normal circumstances, it sees only what is immediately before it, and nothing more. Thus, to speak of oneself as being a transparent eyeball and to claim nearly two hundred years after *Religio Medici*—but also some one-hundred forty after the *Opticks*—that "I see all. The currents of the Universal Being circulate through me" (*CollW,* 1:10), one must surely be speaking in anything but literal terms, right?

In each age, one finds examples of seemingly outlandish beliefs. The nineteenth century is no exception. When John Ruskin, for example, attacked "the evil principles of the Renaissance," denigrating both the Renaissance mind and its "pestilent art,"[6] we read his words with surprise, astonishment,

---

4. Thomas Browne, *Religio Medici,* 92 (emphasis added).

5. In *The Assayer* (1623), Galileo differentiates between an object's inherent, or primary, qualities (like extension, or length and breadth) and its affective, or secondary, qualities (like color, or hue and saturation). The first he inferred to be real properties, the second merely the results of an observer's response to reality—a distinction of foundational importance to Locke and Hume. Newton's *Opticks* (1704) records his experiments in diffraction, the separation of light into a spectrum of component colors. By demonstrating that even light possesses at least some of the same properties as other, fully material substances, Newton made the strongest early case for the seeming superiority of naturalistic science. But as Newton observed in the *Principia Mathematica* (1687/1713), "what the real substance of anything is, we know not. In bodies, we see only their figures and colors, we hear only the sounds, we touch only their outward surfaces, we smell only the smells, and taste the savors; but their inward substances are not to be known either by our senses, or by any reflex act of our minds" (371).

6. John Ruskin, *The Stones of Venice,* 228, 25.

and perhaps even resentment. We are, after all, products of that mind, recipients of its advancements in art, literature, medicine, science, and philosophy. In the face of all that, Ruskin sounds quaint, anachronistic, and—a pejorative in today's critical parlance, though a virtue in his—essentialist. As Ruskin goes burning forth to battle a Goliath of his own, determined to show that the Renaissance mind mistook armor for strength, it may seem to us the war is already lost. We have the words of the man who wrote, but we no longer share his worldview.

And so it is, for some, with Emerson. For example, Lawrence Buell, prefacing his chapter in *Literary Transcendentalism* (1973) on Emerson and literary form, in an admittedly fine analysis, maps out what is to my mind a less-than-ideal position from which to begin reading Emerson's writing. Speaking of them as a group, he is sympathetic to the goals of Transcendentalist thinkers, noting, "They believed . . . that the poet's approach was (or could be) metaphysically as well as metaphorically true." The phrase "or could be" signals Buell's position, however, that in the end "transcendentalist literature refuses to commit itself" to this overtly stated belief. And yet, claims Buell, this "very provocative dilemma, the complexity of which may easily be missed because we have largely resolved it for ourselves," does not lead—presuming it exists—to any difficulty for us, either "because we no longer believe in the divine authority of the imagination, or because Yeats and Joyce have taught us to suspend our disbelief as we read their work." For Buell, the war is most certainly lost. In essence, our distanced perspective on their world allows us to see above, around, and behind what it was the Transcendentalists were trying to do. Apparently, it leaves us with objectivity. Yet Buell leaves his readers, whether they recognize it or not, with a particularly trenchant dilemma of their own. "The Transcendentalists' vacillations may at first seem annoying, merely a psychological barrier that keeps them harping obsessively on the same issue and prevents them from ever finishing anything. But in the long run the best of their writing gains from this stimulus in richness and suggestiveness far more than it loses in indecision."[7] Obsession, psychological barriers, and indecision: hallmarks of a post-Freudian worldview applied to transcendentalist thought that

---

7. Lawrence Buell, *Literary Transcendentalism: Style and Vision in the American Renaissance,* 144–45.

entice us to know—yet in actuality not to know—what their "harping" is all about. Indeed, in Emerson's writing, the harp is a sign of fruitful intellectual inquiry that can hardly be called a sign of obsession. As he writes in "Fate," "By obeying each thought frankly, by harping, or, if you will, pounding on each string, we learn at last its power. By the same obedience to other thoughts, we learn theirs, and then comes some reasonable hope of harmonizing them" (*CollW*, 6:2). In contrast to the position taken by Buell—and this is the main point I wish to make—Emerson emphasizes the process, not the product. The apparent signs of indecision are best understood in this context as indications of the prolific love of harmony.

In addition to historical and interpretive perspective, our understanding of the eye itself is at issue. The eye is a central figure in Emerson's work, and sight a key sense—much debated since F. O. Matthiessen called attention to Emerson's optative mood in *American Renaissance* (1940) and "his almost exclusive absorption with seeing." As Lee Rust Brown notes in his 1990 essay "Emersonian Transparency," "Anyone who reads Emerson must come to terms with the depth of his insistence upon the paradigm of visual perception. And it is indeed an insistence, an aggressively asserted figure rather than an unsophisticated throwback to the problematics of British empiricism." For example, David Jacobson, in *Emerson's Pragmatic Vision* (1993), argues that "*to do,* in Emerson, primarily means to see, to make visible." And James Cox, in his 1975 essay "The Circles of the Eye," calls the transparent eyeball Emerson's "master metaphor," "an assertion of infinite existence in a definite image" that displays "the active spiritualizing power of language." But more than this, Cox makes of it a controlling emblem of personal identity, one, it seems, that overrides all others: "In the context of Emerson's *whole career,* the metaphor of Emerson as transparent eyeball at once released and defined Emerson's act of imagination." Has the transparent eyeball lost its biological function, as Cox suggests? Perhaps not completely. Even the browsing reader does not have to get far to sense that Emerson understands sight to be what Brown calls an aggressively asserted figure, something more than the passive signifier Cox implies. And in Brown's analysis, the transparent eyeball only becomes so "when a higher eye sees something *through* it," so that "Emersonian transparency occurs in the shift of intellectual focus, in the gesture of negation which enables the eye to pass from the visible sign to the previously hidden meaning of the sign." As such,

seeing is indeed an act of the mind, the higher eye. But it is always dependent on the biological eye. For the eyeball to be transparent, then, other stip-
ulations apply: "transparency cannot be conceived as an ideal ontological
condition, nor as a 'place' upon which the eye might dwell. It appears (or
disappears) only in the context of the shifting relations created by the intellect in its transit from old to new objects of focus."[8]

The sixth chapter of *Nature*, for example, entitled "Idealism," provides
an instructive overview of Emerson's belief in this sort of *active* seeing. In
the following passage, Emerson indicates just how he becomes the transparent eyeball for which he is so well known: "the animal eye sees, with
wonderful accuracy, sharp outlines and colored surfaces. When the eye of
Reason opens, to outline and surface are at once added, grace and expression. These proceed from imagination and affection, and abate somewhat
of the angular distinctness of objects. If the Reason be stimulated to more
earnest vision, outlines and surfaces become transparent, and are no longer
seen; causes and spirits are seen through them" (*CollW*, 1:30). And in "The
Poet," the description of earnest vision is repeated again: "As the eyes of
Lyncaeus were said to see through the earth, the poet turns the world to
glass, and shows us all things in their right series and procession. For,
through that better perception, he stands one step nearer to things, and sees
the flowing or metamorphosis. . . . This insight . . . is a very high sort of seeing, which does not come by study, but by the intellect being where and
what it sees, by sharing the path, or circuit of things through forms, and so
making them translucid to others" (*CollW*, 3:12, 15). The sense of active
seeing Emerson describes in these two passages is not original to him. What
Emerson does in these frequently cited passages, and in *Nature* as a whole,
is to recover a way of seeing championed in an earlier age—a way of seeing,
for example, akin to that theorized by Joseph Glanvill in his speculations,
from *The Vanity of Dogmatizing* (1661), on Adam's prelapsarian vision:
"*Adam* needed no Spectacles. The acuteness of his natural Opticks (if con-
jecture may have credit) shew'd him much of the Coelestial magnificence
and bravery without a *Galilaeo*'s tube: And 'tis most probable that his naked

8. F. O. Matthiessen, *American Renaissance: Art and Expression in the Age of Emerson and
Whitman*, 50; Lee Rust Brown, "Emersonian Transparency," 129; David Jacobson, *Emerson's
Pragmatic Vision: The Dance of the Eye*, 37; James Cox, "R. W. Emerson: The Circles of the
Eye," 61, 59 (emphasis added); Brown, "Emersonian Transparency," 129–31.

eyes could reach near as much of the upper World, as we with all the advantages of art. . . . It may be he saw the motion of the bloud and spirits through the transparent skin, as we do the workings of those industrious *Animals* through a hive of glasse."[9] Emerson's Poet is a straightforward refiguring of Glanvill's Adam. Both are supermen: they have intimate knowledge of the hidden order of things, and, significantly, they are possessed of a manner of seeing reserved, in today's technology-saturated world, only for the likes of Clark Kent. "Surfaces become transparent" to the naked eye, and the motions of "spirits" are laid bare.

For the modern reader, Emerson's (like Glanvill's) X-ray vision merges with fantasy. It seems too good to be "real," and today to suggest otherwise seems somewhat irrational. Yet Emerson never shies away from suggesting just that. He believes that earnest vision occurs (as Glanvill also does) without the "advantages of art": "To speak truly, few adult persons can see nature. Most persons do not see the sun. At least they have a very superficial seeing. The sun illuminates only the eye of the man, but shines into the eye and the heart of the child. The lover of nature is he whose inward and outward senses are still truly adjusted to each other" (*CollW,* 1:9). One should not undervalue the extraordinary (even *spectacular*) claim Emerson makes in suggesting that inward and outward senses can be truly adjusted to each other. *I see all:* this simple phrase denotes a conception of seeing that goes beyond even the power of language to describe. After all, "all mean egotism vanishes" (*CollW,* 1:10): before the eye becomes a sign, symbol, metaphor, or emblem of anything else—that is, before what is seen becomes psychologized—vision itself is direct and unmediated. Inward and outward senses, mind and eye, are adjusted to one another. It is in this way that "the laws of moral nature answer to those of matter *as face to face in a glass*" (*CollW,* 1:21; emphasis added)—when the object of the eye and the object of the mind are one and the same.

Or so Emerson believed. The burden here is shouldered entirely by the reader: reading Emerson, so as to understand him, means seeing like Emerson—seeing through his eyes. He clearly speaks only to those who are will-

9. Joseph Glanvill, *The Vanity of Dogmatizing; or, Confidence in Opinions . . .* , 5, 6. An Anglican apologist, member of the Royal Society, and Cambridge Platonist, Glanvill used skeptical arguments in *The Vanity of Dogmatizing* to attack the mechanism (and implied atheism) of the empirical science employed by Descartes and Hobbes.

ing to set aside preconceived notions, but this mode of reading requires a higher level of engagement than what many have thought adequate. For example, Jonathan Bishop in *Emerson on the Soul* (1964) offers a much more conservative approach, one that shifts a majority of the burden to the writer: "The reader's job . . . is plain: to distinguish the excellent moments for himself and, having distinguished, to appreciate the art of the saying he hears." Alternately, in his influential 1973 essay "The Problem of Emerson," Joel Porte departs from such passive reading in arguing that "Emerson . . . has manifestly not been accorded that careful scrutiny of his work *as writing*" that is commonly given to other nineteenth-century writers. The "problem," as Porte defines it, is not with the writer, but with the reader: "The heart of the problem seems to lie . . . in the overwhelming, indeed intimidating, emphasis on Emerson's personal authority, his example, his wisdom, his high role as the spiritual father and Plato of our race"—a problem so great that "the familiar rubrics of Emersonian thought, the stock in trade of most Emerson criticism, though undeniably there, are a positive hindrance to the enjoyment of Emerson's writing." Porte thus calls for reading Emerson with more engagement than what is suggested by Bishop, arguing that "the alert reader can discover, and take much pleasure in discovering, remarkable verbal strategies, metaphoric patterns, repetitions and developments of sound, sense, and image throughout Emerson's writing."[10] Porte shifts some of the burden back on the reader, and in so doing he takes a stance Emerson would seem to sanction: "An imaginative book renders us much more service at first, by stimulating us through its tropes, than afterward, when we arrive at the precise sense of the author" (*CollW*, 3:18–19).

However, the best kind of reading involves understanding the precise sense of the author who challenges us to see the world with new eyes: there is more to Emerson's explications of nature, and his own sense of sight, than tropes or other manipulations of language and figure—at least when inward and outward senses are still truly adjusted to each other. Active reading and active seeing supplement each other, as Emerson intended. Thus, as Jeffrey Steele notes in *The Representation of the Self in the American Renaissance* (1987), understanding Emerson requires the reader "to become the self [he] imagined"

---

10. Jonathan Bishop, *Emerson on the Soul*, 15; Joel Porte, "The Problem of Emerson," 63, 65.

because "failure to do so [leaves] one outside the hermeneutic circle [he] establish[es]." When, for example, James Cox writes, "If the metaphor [of the transparent eyeball] did not cause Emerson to be what he was, it nonetheless reveals to us, in the light of what he turned out to be, *who* he was," he very clearly places himself outside the hermeneutic circle Emerson establishes. As pointed out above, in realistic terms Cox assumes the transparent eyeball to be a failure. It is only "an expression of the essential relation between language and Nature," and nothing more—nothing more because Emerson's "overwhelming belief in language prevented him from being able to see visually. Seeing is really always saying in Emerson; perception is always thought."[11] The suggestion that Emerson was prevented from being able to see visually—almost as if he were blind—is astounding. What happened, one wonders, to Emerson's own eyes? Why exactly must we presume them to disappear?[12]

The important question is: what does Emerson mean by contrasting, in the passage cited above, what "the animal eye sees" with Reason's "more earnest vision"—has biological sight lost its literalness with this remark? Put another way, if outlines and surfaces become transparent, is Nature any longer an object of the eye? The question is highly significant, because as I have shown, how one answers determines to a great extent how one begins to read Emerson's work. Further, readings that make biological sight nothing more than a metaphor, albeit an interesting one, for something else (Reason's insight, Transcendental idealism, literary inspiration, quasi-religious faith) lead to readings of Emerson's statements on nature as nothing more than metaphors for something else, too: after all, if sight, in the way Emerson presents it, cannot be literal, his statements on what one actually sees cannot be literal, either.[13] Passionately believed in and earnest, yes; but metaphysically true, no.

11. Jeffrey Steele, *The Representation of the Self in the American Renaissance,* xi; Cox, "Circles of the Eye," 59, 61, 81.

12. Of course, Emerson *did* have trouble with his eyesight as a young man (beginning in 1825 and likely arising as a symptom of tuberculosis), for which he sought surgical treatment. These temporary failures in his vision possibly account for the acuteness of his visual observations throughout the rest of his life.

13. The temptation toward this fundamentally New Critical response is presumably great. Bishop suggests that Emerson may too easily be construed as "the hero of metaphor, the Representative Man of symbolic action." Indeed, "to a modern reader" this might be what is "perhaps almost too exclusively relevant about him" (*Emerson on the Soul,* 119). Four decades later, Bishop's estimation of Emerson's critical reception frequently still applies.

The problem I find with such sweeping demarcations is that Emerson becomes in this rendering not much more than a rhetorician. One might consider Jeffrey Duncan's remarks on *Nature,* in *The Power and Form of Emerson's Thought* (1973), as representative of glosses of this kind. Summarizing what he considers to be the central argument of *Nature,* Duncan writes, "Perception is a discovery, not an invention or an imposition, and it is grounded in language. . . . Through the order of nature we create metaphors, and through metaphors we create the order of nature, for creation is discovery, as the making of metaphor testifies." The circularity of this logic Duncan calls "paradoxical," and somehow that is supposed to rescue the point. "In effect, we create greater than we know. Thus perception—that is, reality—is a continuous process that transcends time, becoming that constitutes being and being that constitutes becoming. In the beginning *is* the word."[14] Translation: Emerson speaks in metaphors because seeing (or "reality") is merely a rhetorical device as shown by the fact that Emerson speaks in metaphors. And we go round and round from there.

Emerson does indeed go to great lengths to psychologize the perception of nature and to "read" in it signs and symbols of man's essential character. The Poet is, after all, an ethicist, too. But it is my contention that Emerson anchored his idealism so firmly and frequently into his understanding of the eye (as a biological organ) and his own direct observations of the natural world that it is worth our while to know better what kind of vision, and what kind of perspective, held sway for him. Building on a stance suggested by F. O. Matthiessen,[15] Steele's contention that "Emerson combines the practices of both psychoanalytic and religious rhetoricians" with the result that "identification with Emerson's literary voice is supplemented by analysis of that voice as a strategic fiction covering certain anxieties, weaving over them its myth of transcendent power," may do much to explain a twentieth-century reader's poststructuralist leanings, but it cuts off, all at once, the very denotative intent *(I see all)* that makes Emerson's writing so remarkable in

14. Jeffrey L. Duncan, *The Power and Form of Emerson's Thought,* 4–5.
15. Matthiessen makes the comparison to Wordsworth: "A man speaking to men first unlocked their primitive awareness of themselves—in such a conception of consciousness Emerson broke through the mere intellectualizing with which he was often charged, to at least a glimpse of the deep subconscious forces that remain buried in men unless quickened to life" (*American Renaissance,* 17; quoted in Steele, *Representation of the Self,* 2).

the first place. Instead of rendering seeing as an action unmediated by language, accounts such as Steele's interpret the "earnest vision" passage cited above, and others like it, as simple linguistic events—even when they attempt to avoid doing so. Steele posits that "Emerson's psychological mythmaking" does not lead "toward a Derridean model of deferral," and yet it is only by "*ostensibly* bypassing the dilemma of signification, the unavoidable erosion and misdirection of meaning," that Emerson "interiorizes the process of expression—thus giving each individual the means to apprehend spiritual truth directly without passing through the annoyance of unreliable signs." Ostensibility aside, still "the model of signification that follows from such a position is allegorical."[16] Steele speaks his cake, then eats it, too.

The handful of studies cited so far are intended to provide representative, not comprehensive, examples that help to illustrate the problems that arise when we read Emerson from positions—in Steele's phrase—outside the hermeneutic circle Emerson establishes. I contend that this circle inscribes a maximum of literalness: at its widest, it contains the belief that the poet's approach is metaphysically as well as metaphorically true; refined to a point, it centers on the belief that sight is biological, that it is an act of the living eye. But in trying to conceive of what it means to read Emerson from this particular focal point, readers are still faced with a range of options. First, it may be that Emerson intended for the literal meaning of his sight diction to reinforce, complement, and enhance its metaphorical meaning, at least most of the time; or that he intended the distinction to become productively blurred at times, in order to evoke the marriage between matter and spirit. Second, it may be that Emerson intended his sight diction literally, not metaphorically, because his usage consistently arises out of his own naturalist and scientific habits of mind—a perspective, for example, that seems to heavily inform Emerson's own reading of Swedenborg. Third, it may be that Emerson intended the very distinction between denotative and connotative meaning to be consistently impossible to maintain—that is, he would have denied using either literal or metaphoric language because one always excludes and/or presupposes the other as its opposite. Fourth, it may be that Emerson intended any one or a combination of these three; but we need not become the self he imagined so much as we must strive to understand its

16. Steele, *Representation of the Self,* 6, 11, 22, 23 (emphasis added).

permutations. Or fifth, given that Emerson so strongly stresses perception, we must completely set aside the inevitable blurring of language and begin to see with our own eyes the way Emerson sees with his.

As part of a fine analysis that in many respects stands the test of time, Sherman Paul, in *Emerson's Angle of Vision* (1952), notes that direct apprehension of the world is the single most important heuristic device in Emerson's work, and that language itself stands in a secondary, albeit crucial, position. The key passage deserves to be quoted in full, but certain main points adequately sketch out the core of Paul's argument:

> When [Emerson] spoke of making the word one with the thing, he meant that the word had to follow a perception of the thing, and had, as the vehicle of that perception, to evoke the sensuously felt image of the thing in the mind. . . . Correspondence as a doctrine of expression was not, as Emerson used it, the assigning of symbolic value to an object. It was, instead, the *perception* of the symbolic import of an object: a way to apprehend reality. . . . And this required for complete communication that men come into the poet's vision, share his angle of vision, and behold the universe with his eyes. And this required the dialectic method as Emerson employed it, not to convey facts, but to lead others in the path of perception. . . . For although as a doctrine of expression, correspondence led others to insight, in the history of the mind it followed from the sympathetic correspondence with nature, which alone prepared the mind to see nature as the expositor of the divine mind. . . . Language was not its substitute. Only a life in nature supplied the images, the pattern of their unfolding, and the spirit with which they could be read.[17]

It is in this light that *I see all* must be read: as a way of apprehending reality. The phrase—as well as the existential moment with which it coincides—is meaningless unless read denotatively. *Nature* is not about nature, nor about nature being a symbol-as-rhetorical-figure, but about the perception of the symbolic import of nature. It is, as Paul says, a treatise that attempts not to convey facts, but to lead others in the path of perception. There is no anxiety here, and no myth of transcendent power. Apprehension precedes language,

17. Sherman Paul, *Emerson's Angle of Vision: Man and Nature in American Experience*, 130–31.

and the eye seeing precedes both. Nature remains, first and foremost, an object of the eye.

In a remarkable passage from Emerson's journals, we see that even the whole body can become involved in the process of apprehending nature. In a manner that recalls how inward and outward senses can be truly adjusted to each other, vision becomes subsumed into a holistic act of sensory perception: "As if one needed eyes in order to see. Look at yonder tree which the Sun has drawn out of the ground by its continual love & striving towards him and which now spreads a hundred arms[,] a thousand boughs in gratitude basking in his presence. Does that not see? It sees all over, with every leaf & every blossom" (*JMN*, 8:169). Contradictorily, the declarative "as if one needed eyes" is followed by the imperative "look": we need eyes to understand the point that seeing does not require eyes (Emerson ignores the irony). More importantly, this passage does not tell us that yonder tree experiences something *like* seeing. It tells us that "it sees all over." Here, the sense of sight must be very literal, construed as the detection of light rays, but the tree is also an image of man *beholding*—spreading a hundred arms—in Thomas Browne's sense of the word. Sight is direct contact, direct experience. It is holistic. And it is unmitigated by language—even the awkward grammar of the passage suggests as much. Clarity of language, however, is not important. Clarity of vision is: the symbolic import of the *object*, not the language, is our key to understanding Emerson's vision of reality.

Active seeing also suggests that Emerson's perspective on the world is not Platonic, as many readers would characterize it, in the common understanding of the term. It is indeed true that one finds in Plato a nascent articulation of the Emersonian doctrine of correspondence, or the belief, as Sherman Paul defines it, "that the spiritual and natural universes share the same law, that although the natural is an imitation and therefore inferior world, its analogical identity with the Creator and the spiritual universe give it (and the man who lives in it) a spiritual significance."[18] Such a belief certainly seems predicated on Plato's theory of Forms. But Form, as defined in the fifth book of the *Republic,* is an object of knowledge, as opposed to an object of belief (or opinion), and is presumed to be always and everywhere *true*, which is to say, independent of human apprehension. Thus Plato

18. Ibid., 3–4.

establishes a dichotomy between materiality and the ideal, for nothing apprehended through the senses can escape qualification. Further, the geometry Plato's Form implies is abstract in character, existing in anamnesis, as is demonstrated when Socrates elicits the Pythagorean theorem (Proposition 47 from the first book of Euclid's *Elements*) from an uneducated slave boy in the *Meno*.

Emerson had a different conception of form. Form, as Emerson understood it, is "the mixture of matter & spirit," or more particularly, "the visibility of spirit" (*JMN*, 9:117). Form is, in this respect, subject to a special kind of perspectival arrangement, and its meaning is thus exposed in the act of gazing upon it. Geometry, in this conceptualization, is not abstract; it governs the life of the everyday moment, from the flow of the river to the course of the conversation. It does not exist in anamnesis but in apprehension, revealing not what always has been but what is always changing, new, and yet to be. It is, like the universe, "fluid and volatile," for "permanence is but a word of degrees" (*CollW*, 2:179). One must parse Emerson's words in "Circles" carefully here, as there are three meanings to this statement. One is literal, that is, that the word *permanence* is not an absolute term but, rather, one of a series, an idea that suggests, then, a second, metaphorical meaning, which is that the *idea* of permanence is relative to the natural object under consideration and the context in which it is observed. This, in turn, suggests a third, epistemological reading of the phrase, which argues that the permanence of the thing is, in a sense, anthropomorphic: it depends on the point of view of the observer. Such a position comes naturally to Emerson, a man who believed the existence of any thing in nature to be dependent, in part, on one's mental and imaginative rendering of it. Permanence is but a word of degrees—thus (as I discuss more fully in Chapter 3) concreteness itself is not merely a question of fixture or position in universal space, but of magnitude and declination in the visual plane. What this means is that an object is real on a scale relative to its context, and so in its very being, the object reveals an angle of vision. And "subdued by the insatiable demand of harmony," it makes open to us the "proportions & perspective of vegetable beauty" (*JMN*, 5:215).

This study is, then, in large part an attempt to rediscover a single, decisive aspect of Emerson's *practical* attitudes and beliefs, which is both grounded in the sense of sight and characterized by a full and empathetic

belief in the divine authority of the imagination—with the open acknowl-
edgement that it may be always and everywhere incomplete, inadequate, or
in danger of misinterpretation: I make no attempt to substitute armor for
strength. Decisive statements are surely rare, even for one such as Emerson.
The individual's "angle of vision"—an idea first suggested by Johannes
Kepler—applies to us all, and it is, quite literally, a matter of perspective.
Erwin Panofsky's injunction to the art historian pertains with equal necessity to the literary critic: "It is essential to ask of artistic periods and regions
not only whether they have perspective, but also which perspective they
have."[19] Only by keeping these questions prominently in mind can we more
faithfully begin to conceive and practice the open understanding, empathy,
and intuition needed in order to investigate the past.

In addition to active seeing, perspective is, indeed, another major theme
in Emerson's work in need of further exploration. Ruskin's allusion to a
young David notwithstanding (see first epigraph), Emerson to me seems
akin to one who goes forth with three smooth stones from the brook—matter, spirit, and perspective, all three awash in the flow of time—and contents
himself by concentrating on the mystery they contain. And I say this to
indicate that the image is as literally true as it is metaphorical: "Pick up the
pebble at your feet, look at its gray sides, its sharp crystal, & tell me what
fiery inundation of the world melted the minerals like wax & as if the globe
were one glowing crucible gave this stone its shape," Emerson writes. Easily
enough one understands this as the poet's question, as well as the primary
question confronting Emerson in his apprehension of nature. It delineates,
in its grandest sense, the problem of knowledge—that is, divining the relationship between matter and spirit—and as he continues, the meditation
becomes simply astonishing:

> There is the truth speaking pebble itself to affirm to endless ages the thing
> was so. Tell me where is the manufactory of this air so thin, so blue, so
> restless which eddies around you, and which you coin into musical words.
> I am agitated with curiosity to know the secret of Nature. Why cannot
> Geology, why cannot Botany speak & tell me what had been[,] what is, as
> I run along the forest promontory & ask when it rose like a blister on
> heated steel? Then I looked up & saw the Sun shining in the vast Sky &

19. Erwin Panofsky, *Perspective as Symbolic Form,* 41.

heard the wind bellow & the water glistened in the vale. These were the
forces that wrought then & work now. Yes there they grandly speak to all
plainly in proportion as we are quick to comprehend. (*JMN*, 5:423–24)

The secret of Nature, as the first half of this passage shows, is indeed the
relationship between seen and unseen, the pebble now in hand and the
"manufactory" that "eddies around" it through "endless ages," and what is
to Emerson's mind most real. Emerson's cognitive understanding of this
reality is clear enough, to him and to us. Yet he is "agitated," a confession sig-
naling that the reality he apprehends does not yet satisfy the divine imagination—that is, the poet's imagination, which ought to reach outside of the
limits of time and space. The problem arises in that Emerson asks to know
"where" this reality arose. Traditional science, here represented by geology
and botany, cannot provide satisfaction, even though it also seeks to affix a
linear position in time and space to this natural phenomenon, to say
"where" and exactly "when it rose like a blister on heated steel." And yet, as
signaled by the sentences ending the passage, Emerson discovers that his
initial perspective is all wrong: "Then I looked up." Emerson's true meaning
stands out in his use of the word "quick" to refer to vitality as well as speed:
it reveals just what kind of curiosity and imagination he uses to view the
world. What is needed, he argues, is to "look up," to seek answers not as a
matter of spatial position but as a matter of ocular degree, as a matter of
magnitude and declination spreading outward from the living eye. What is
needed is to begin to apprehend, in an image so wonderfully paradoxical,
grandeur "all plainly in proportion." It is the search for this kind of perspective that was to provide the whole substance of Emerson's harping.

And so I direct Panofsky's questions toward Emerson, asking whether he
had perspective and also which perspective he had. The first question has
been frequently asked and, in a positive sense, adequately answered. The second question, much more difficult, has not. The body of criticism on Emerson provides volumes on the first two stones, matter and spirit, yet falls short
in providing in-depth examinations of the third, perspective. Sherman Paul
more than anyone else examines this third stone, arguing that in response to
the "linear logic" of Locke and Hume, Emerson's main task "was that of
erecting the vertical standard of value perpendicular to the horizontal
enslaving of his day." Indeed, Paul argues, Lockean sensationalism and

Humean causation reduce the universe to a single deterministic dimension and negate human agency, free will, and the possibility of miracles, thus separating human beings from the creation. In response, "Emerson felt called on to raise the vertical axis, to give the universe its spiritual dimension, to reinstate the mystery and wonder by giving scope to the mythic, symbolic, and religious components of human experience." Yet Paul's analysis details not so much a response to the linearity of modern thought as an acquiescence to it. He calls the vertical axis "an optical or experiential illusion," arguing that, "as a dimension of the human consciousness, the vertical represents the fact of consciousness known as projection," which arises because "experiencing horizontally, one recognizes the separation of the self and nature, and also one's dependence on the senses for any communion with it."[20] At first, this dynamic of projection may not seem wholly opposed to the claims of active seeing, but the clinical connotations of "projection" (as well as its being a *fact* of consciousness) indicate the intent of Paul's usage. And in Emerson's discussion of the "truth speaking pebble" above—a passage that lends itself so well to Paul's distinction between the vertical and horizontal axes—one is hard-pressed to find clear indications of illusion, projection, separation, or dependence; what little "agitation" Emerson feels arises from curiosity and is fleeting and transient.

Further, Paul sees in his conception of transcendentalist projection something similar to what Buell calls "obsession" and "indecision": "From this essential difference [between self and nature] develops the often irreconcilable tensions that the more sensitive feel in their own conflicting apprehensions of nature: the feeling of dependence on and limitation to the external, and the feeling that projections are somehow justified by something corresponding to them in and/or behind nature, and that this correspondence promises an infinite scope for activity." Paul clearly has an algebraic model in mind: just as the extent of an ordinate is dependent on that of its abscissa, he suggests that the power of the human imagination is dependent on the sensory input of the body. Thus, although the promise of infinite activity along the vertical axis might "extend the meaning of nature," it remains an illusion and a source of irreconcilable tension. The result is that in Paul's own linear, vaguely Cartesian approach, the poet's

20. Paul, *Emerson's Angle,* 21–22.

method is metaphorically interesting but not, it seems, metaphysically true. Paul tries, rather awkwardly, to rescue Emerson from the illusion of vertical projection, claiming that "by raising the vertical [Emerson] intended to assert a multi-dimensional universe of spiritual possibilities rather than to overcome the restraints and trivialities of everyday prudential life" and thus "maintain a living connection between the horizontal-worldly and the vertical-otherworldly, to live on as many of the platforms of experience that intervened as he could." But Emerson's final "technique of vision" remains no more than an experiential illusion, a "prism, which was in itself the product of vision, its promise, and its fulfillment."[21] Ultimately, what gets lost in the abstraction—Emerson's self-acknowledged "curiosity to know the secret of Nature"—seems too great.

The position I take in this study is that Emerson's perspective is, without a doubt, fundamentally nonlinear in character. As a consequence, his metaphysical worldview—his personal perspective on matter and spirit—as it developed in the 1830s, '40s, and '50s resulted from his recognition that modern ways of knowing were increasingly dominated by an emerging worldview that conceived of space by means of a linear perspectival construction, one designed to impart on material objects measurable attributes of location (height, width, and depth) as in the search, cited above, to know "where" "along the forest promontory" the secret of Nature is answered. And such Cartesian linearity leads to a conclusion that anyone familiar with disciplines from modern physics to modern psychology would recognize: the seen becomes presumably more real than the unseen because the unseen cannot be located with linear perspective, whether in the astronomer's star chart or the neurologist's MRI. Further, the knowledge that modern ways of knowing produce, according to Emerson's continued observation, was inconsistent with the fundamental reality of nature, which is not linear but curved. That is to say, natural processes and natural forms are neither modeled on nor composed of straight lines. As both an epistemological and metaphysical device, the straight line is an abstract human construct that has no natural analogue. Admonishing himself "not [to] interrogate life like a college professor," Emerson puts forth two fundamental precepts about Nature: "Every thing in the universe goes by indirection" and "There are no

21. Ibid., 22–23, 25–26.

straight lines" (*JMN*, 9:361). (Again, the assertion is meant literally, not just figuratively. Attempting to recall any straight line in Nature, Emerson lists only two: "the spider swinging down from a twig" and "the hair on a cat's back" [*JMN*, 9:36].) Assertions such as these—found throughout Emerson's work—are meant as a claim to the fundamental nonlinearity of the natural world: *indirection* negates the explanatory power of linear cause and effect, and "no straight lines" establishes the metaphysical primacy of regular and irregular curves. Emerson's statements on Nature cannot be meaningfully read without a firm grounding in these two key ideas.

And they are indeed radical ideas in certain respects. The dominant view in the nineteenth century was that "Euclid's geometry revealed truths about reality," Tom Siegfried notes. "Here's the odd thing, though," he continues. "Euclidean geometry—the geometry that incorporates the lessons from real life—turns out to be the wrong geometry for describing real life."[22] Siegfried points to what most today have come to recognize: the world turns out to be far more complex than what linear Euclidism allows. Although this truth has been slow to spread in the last few centuries, spread it has. In part this change in view has been due to developing understandings of mind and brain. For example, whereas Kant in the *Critique of Pure Reason* (1781) believed that Euclidean geometry so matches the structure of the human intellect that it exists as an example of synthetic a priori knowledge, William James argued in *Psychology* (1905) that since consciousness undergoes constant change from one moment to the next, then "a permanently existing 'Idea' which makes its appearance before the footlights of consciousness at periodical intervals is as mythological an entity as the Jack of Spades."[23] And in part this change has been due to the development of non-Euclidean geometries, beginning early in the nineteenth century, that are more consistent with the complex and dynamic cosmos accepted today. For example, Nikolai Lobachevsky, Janos Bolyai, and Bernhard Riemann each challenged Euclid, and Kant, by constructing geometries in which Euclid's Fifth Postulate on parallel lines does not hold—a physical proof of which did not come until 1919, as part of the confirmation of general relativity; and more recently, string theory has brought forth a possibly limitless number of alternative geometries. But more importantly, this change has been due to the over-

22. Tom Siegfried, *Strange Matters: Undiscovered Ideas at the Frontiers of Space and Time*, 263.
23. William James, *Psychology*, 157.

whelming tendency of nonlinearity to provide demonstrable confirmation of deep structures within chaotic systems, that is, the sort of "insatiable demand of harmony" that so fascinated Emerson and other Romantic naturalists. The rise of nonlinear science in the last several decades has indeed revolutionized our understanding of how the natural world operates.

At issue in the contrast between linear and nonlinear worldviews are two competing, and essentially incompatible, attitudes toward truth. On the one hand, there are those who imagine truth only to correspond directly with observed facts. This view puts forward an underlying linear logic in constructing a universe of modular units (or "building blocks") and proportional cause and effect (for example, Newton's third law of motion or the economic theory of supply and demand). On the other hand, there are those who see truth as existing only within whole systems, as considerations of anything less can only present degrees of truth. In this view, coherence of the whole is key. Today, we can see this much older attitude reemerging, for example, in contemporary fields of climatology, demographics, and epidemiology. That Emerson sees truth as fundamentally systematic is virtually indisputable. The idea saturates his writing: "The philosophy we want is one of fluxions & mobility; not a house, but a ship in these billows we inhabit. Any angular dogmatic theory would be rent to chips & splinters in this storm of many elements" (*JMN*, 9:222). Adopting this holistic viewpoint, Emerson develops a nonlinear perspective on nature. His belief, expressed in "Compensation," that "each new form repeats not only the main character of the type, but part for part all the details, all the aims, furtherances, hindrances, energies, and whole system of every other" (*CollW*, 2:59), opens the door to his insight that "the whirling bubble on the surface of a brook admits us to the secret of the mechanics of the sky" (*JMN*, 7:428): a principle of self-similarity operates throughout nature, at all scales. This same idea motivates modern nonlinear science. James Gleick notes of the pioneers in this diverse field, from mathematicians to meteorologists, that "they had an eye for pattern, especially pattern that appeared on different scales at the same time" and that "they had a taste for randomness and complexity, for jagged edges and sudden leaps." Further, they are "turning back a trend in science toward reductionism" because "they are looking for the whole."[24] Is not Emerson, the Joyous Scientist, of a similar mind-set? It is in

24. James Gleick, *Chaos: Making a New Science*, 5.

this light that this study takes up the proposition that "when we study Architecture everything seems architectural" (*JMN,* 5:215).

I have argued thus far for a reexamination of Emerson's understanding of Nature in light of his views on perspective, geometric form, and nonlinearity. The next chapter provides an overview of Emerson's stance vis-à-vis nineteenth-century science. Primarily, I will review and assess the slowly expanding subject of Emerson and science, but I will also look into Emerson's eventual dissatisfaction with linearity as a model and method of intellectual inquiry. With each passing decade, the influence of science on Emerson's thought, beyond just the early 1830s, gains further credence. As Laura Dassow Walls observes in *Emerson's Life in Science* (2003), Emerson's writing is replete with scientific imagery: "Science permeated his thought and writing at every level, from its deepest structure to his most casual analogies."[25] A handful of other recent books contribute measured amounts to the subject, including Leon Chai's *The Romantic Foundations of the American Renaissance* (1987), Walls's *Seeing New Worlds* (1995), Robert Richardson's *Emerson: The Mind on Fire* (1995), Lee Rust Brown's *The Emerson Museum* (1997), and Eric Wilson's *Emerson's Sublime Science* (1999). More relevant and revolutionary than these, however, are recent studies written out of the emerging field of nonlinear dynamics (or chaos theory) that develop nonlinearity as an analytical tool and treat of a broader connection between modern science and literature. These include James Gleick's *Chaos: Making a New Science* (1987), Katherine Hayles's *Chaos Bound* (1990) and *Chaos and Order* (1991), Philip Kuberski's *Chaosmos* (1994), Harriett Hawkins's *Strange Attractors* (1995), and Gordon Slethaug's *Beautiful Chaos* (2000).

As Katherine Hayles explains, "The importance of chaos theory does not derive . . . solely from the new theories and techniques it offers. Rather, part of its importance comes from its re-visioning of the world as dynamic and nonlinear, yet predictable in its very unpredictability."[26] The surprising fact is that the fundamental ideas that have coalesced in recent decades into

25. Laura Dassow Walls, *Emerson's Life in Science: The Culture of Truth,* 4. Walls also sees in Emerson's immersion in science similar implications on his language as I do: "Few writers were more densely metaphoric than Emerson, yet the paradox is that Emerson himself fought against the metaphoricity of language. What he sought was not linguistic play, but truth, the single reality beyond language" (22).

26. N. Katherine Hayles, *Chaos Bound: Orderly Disorder in Contemporary Literature and Science,* 143.

what is now known as chaos theory have been waxing and waning for centuries. Some, like the cyclical emergence of order from disorder found in Lucretius and Epicurus, hearken back to the very origins of Greco-Roman philosophy. So not only does chaos theory "re-vision" the present world, as Hayles suggests, but also it brings into higher relief its own affinities with the past. As Hayles also notes, "One way to understand the connection between literature and science is to see science as a repository of tropes that can be used to illuminate literary texts"; however, "a bolder and perhaps more interesting move is to posit connections that go beyond metaphor."[27] Emersonian naturalism is but one of the affinities, explored here for the first time, that modern nonlinear science has with the past. But it is not my intention simply to use the tropes of the one to illuminate the texts of the other. The connection is much deeper than metaphor.

"O poet," Emerson writes, "thou shalt serve the god Terminus, the bounding Intellect, & love Boundary or Form: believing that Form is an oracle which never lies" (*JMN*, 8:405). This study, in the largest sense, is an exploration of Emerson's reading of that oracle, not just in the stones of the brook, but throughout nature. Nonlinearity is at the heart of that oracle's message, and geometrizing nature is crucial to helping Emerson read it. My third, fourth, and fifth chapters offer close examinations of the development of Emerson's nonlinear philosophy and the metaphysical insights that flow out of it. In these chapters, my primary goal is not only to suggest the foundational importance of a geometric imagination to his worldview, but also to demonstrate how active it was throughout his writing career, primarily during the middle period. By exploring the development of his nonlinear model of inquiry, these chapters will give the reader a clearer understanding of the unique, radical, and highly original manner in which Emerson envisioned his world. Chapter 3 more closely examines Emerson's understanding of the sense of sight as well as his own visual perspective on the world. As David Jacobson notes, Emerson's gathering eye, which draws the universal into the personal sphere, raises the danger that "the horizon of the eye can . . . become fixed and freeze the fluctuations of natural appearance, imposing a single limit on nature and thereby establishing a static structure of value" that controls "natural presence" and "dominate[s] our lived experience."[28]

27. N. Katherine Hayles, "Introduction: Complex Dynamics in Literature and Science," 20.
28. Jacobson, *Emerson's Pragmatic Vision*, 38.

Linear seeing and linear perspective heighten this danger considerably. Making an entrée into visual perception through the problems of perspective prompted by architecture and painting, I argue that Emerson's active vision—in which he understood the curvature of the eye, as well as that of the visual plane, to create an organic, nonlinear perspective—prevents such fixed points of view and static structures from ever forming.

Chapter 4 explores Emersonian form theory, which is based on the idea of iteration, that follows from his phenomenal and nonlinear way of seeing. Emerson's comments on form provide a way of thinking about process that is a clear contrast to the linear cause-and-effect model favored by conventional nineteenth-century science. What Emerson most opposed was the skepticism inherent to Enlightenment science, a skepticism that filtered out of natural science any questions addressing purpose—the sort of questions Emerson felt most compelled to ask. Further, conventional science was reductive, minimalist, and foundational in its effort to explain all phenomena according to the paradigm offered by Newtonian physics. Emerson, in contrast, looked to form, rather than the atomic particle, as an object's primary feature. And because form is something to be apprehended with the eye, it connects a living observer to his or her natural world. Form provides a means of thinking about nature as a dynamic process because the forms of all things undergo development through time—and this fact becomes the basis of Emerson's thinking about nature in self-similar, or iterative, terms.

Chapter 5 examines Emerson's interest in "nature's primary forms in the secret architecture of bodies" (*JMN*, 4:94)—that is, the structure of the natural world, both how it is organized and how it develops. Because he believed form to be a manifestation of matter and spirit, natural forms were for Emerson the single most important element in a systematic and comprehensive account of Nature. His preference, of course, was not so much for description as for explanation: taking a holistic view, Emerson proclaims, "I wish to write pure mathematics" (*JMN*, 7:88). The best kind of mathematics would present the algorithm of harmony, one that was simple enough to explain both the pebble at his feet and the mechanics of the sky, and one that was powerful enough—to borrow from the passage cited above—to "grandly speak to all plainly in proportion as we are quick to comprehend." Emerson never formulated that all-encompassing algorithm, but his own "pure mathematics" consists of an application of nonlinear thinking that helped him cast doubt on many of the major assumptions of traditional science—namely, that nature does not have a qualitative dimension; that it can be described by analytic functions; that change over time can be predicted from the equations of motion; that nature has a fundamental scale; and that it has no emergent qualities, that is, that it cannot be more than the sum of its parts.

Today, nonlinearity describes ways of seeing the world that represent fundamental departures from traditional Euclidean-Newtonian assumptions, and it offers an alternate perspective on our understanding of the basic elements of Nature, one that sees what we might call "orderly disorder." Katherine Hayles uses this phrase in identifying two general beliefs in nonlinear dynamics, first, that "chaos is . . . order's precursor and partner, rather than its opposite," and second, that "hidden order . . . exists *within* chaotic systems."[29] Both views are very clearly Romantic notions about the nature of Nature. Another clear means of pointing to the difference between linear and nonlinear worldviews is to say that the first claims that Nature can be fully described by ontological models and the analytic functions arising from them and that the second claims it cannot. Analytic functions are regular; that is, they have complex variables but also first derivatives at all points of their given domains. Nonlinearity claims that many of the phenomena we regularly observe (qualitative change, for example) cannot be represented by the regular and continuous functions of mechanics and physics. Qualitative changes, like the phase transitions observed in the change from liquid to gas or in the sudden appearance of turbulence in fluid flow—both common occurrences in the natural world—are notoriously impervious to description via analytic functions, even with the aid of supercomputers. Emerson was a keen observer of the weather, among other things, and perhaps these lines from "The Snow-Storm" are his most readily recognized meteorological observation today:

> Come see the north wind's masonry. . . .
> Speeding, the myriad-handed, his wild work
> So fanciful, so savage, nought cares he
> For number or proportion. . . .

29. Hayles, *Chaos Bound*, 9.

And when his hours are numbered, and the world
Is all his own, retiring, as he were not,
Leaves, when the sun appears, astonished Art
To mimic in slow structures, stone by stone,
Built in an age, the mad wind's night-work,
The frolic architecture of the snow.[30]

Set in sentences that seem to defy grammatical comprehension, Emerson's imperfect blank verse lines mimic the slow structures of linear syntax and make frolic architecture of this imagistic scene. The words and phrases of the poem overhang the implied blank verse structure like snow spilling over the eaves of a building, and the associative patterns of syntax in the poem's final lines render an astonished artfulness. More importantly, the poem makes an argument: the north wind does not care "for number or proportion"—terms suggesting, respectively, amount and quantity, the key elements of linear analysis. The poem communicates Emerson's poetic sense that weather patterns—particularly on the most local level—are beyond linear modes of understanding. What is needed is a sense of what Emerson refers to in the poem as the "tumultuous privacy of storm"—of singularity within the chaos. Of order within the disorder. Of structure emerging from randomness.

What Emerson most sought to know is the language of Nature. "The love of nature," he writes, "what is that but the presentiment of intelligence of it: nature preparing to become a language to us" (*JMN*, 7:412). But this language, he was sure, was unlike any he had ever heard spoken. Further, he was uncertain as to the best way to translate it: the English of his day seemed an inadequate vehicle for the concepts he wished to convey. He writes, "One who looks at the clouds or the aspect of a tree sees how rude & initial our language is, we cannot yet begin to describe these things" (*JMN*, 8:372). Yet the attempt to translate Nature into ready concepts and key principles was one of the highest aims of the Joyous Scientist: "I think that he only is rightly immortal to whom all things are immortal; he who witnesses personally the creation of the world; he who enunciates profoundly the names of [the gods];—knowing full well the need he has of these [names], and [of] a far richer vocabulary; knows well how imperfect & insufficient to his needs lan-

---

30. *Essays and Poems,* 1084.

guage is; requiring music, requiring dancing, as languages; a dance, for
example, that shall sensibly express our astronomy, our solar system, & seasons, in its course" (*JMN*, 9:452). It is my aim here to present the language of
that dance, one that more accurately describes the manner in which Emerson thought and wrote about Nature. By connecting Emerson's understanding of the natural world to some of the premises of nonlinearity, we can
begin to see just how nonlinear Emerson's thinking in fact is.

2

THE PARADE OF SCIENCE

If the labours of Men of science should ever create any material revolution, direct or indirect, in our condition, and in the impressions which we habitually receive, the Poet will sleep then no more than at present; he will be ready to follow the steps of the Man of science, not only in those general indirect effects, but he will be at his side, carrying sensation into the midst of the objects of the science itself.

—WILLIAM WORDSWORTH, "Preface to Lyrical Ballads" (1850)

What a parade we make of our science, and how far off, and at arm's length, it is from its objects!

—RALPH WALDO EMERSON, "Beauty," *The Conduct of Life* (1860)

As David Robinson points out in his 1992 essay "Fields of Investigation: Emerson and Natural History," "Emerson remains valuable to us in part because of his exemplary faith in the congruence of scientific and religious knowledge. Because of the state of science in his age, and because of his own craving to understand nature in every possible sense, his scientific and philosophical quests work in a broad harmony."[1] Emerson's faith in the congruence between differing branches of knowledge was, to him, not just natural but obvious: science and philosophy were alternate sides of the same coin.

---

1. David M. Robinson, "Fields of Investigation: Emerson and Natural History," 94–95.

The kind of interdisciplinary thinking that allowed Emerson to combine the two, however, is in our time quite unusual. Our structures of specialized institutional learning—particularly those of the universities—do not commonly support it, favoring specialization instead. But it is not unknown. Arguing that scientists who study the humanities are more likely to be better scientists, John Polanyi, winner of the Nobel Prize in chemistry, recently stated that "science is a branch of the humanities"—a remarkable comment in that it not only bridges what most have come to accept as a permissible and necessary gap between belles lettres and laboratory work, but also in that it subverts what many would take to be their natural places in the institutional hierarchy. Why should scientists, who have better uses for their time and funding, need to learn how to read literature? Because the humanities, Polanyi argues, is about the study of patterns, about learning a way of reading the intricate design of the world. And so science is one part of the broader humanities because "in science we look for those patterns not in the language of poetry but in such languages as numbers and algebra."[2]

Premised as it is in the belief of a congruence between scientific and religious knowledge, what Robinson calls Emerson's "craving to understand nature in every possible sense" is his abiding receptiveness to nature's creative patterns—patterns that, collectively, point to the organization of the larger whole. As Emerson puts it in his ode to Xenophanes—who himself called on the science of his day to take heed of nature's self-similar patterns[3]—"frugal Nature" shows "her stern necessity" by creating the world according to a single, unifying design, even if that master pattern becomes actuated through a variety of distinct processes:

> It was her stern necessity: all things
> Are of one pattern made; bird, beast, and flower,   ·

2. John Polanyi, quoted in Robert Fulford, "Canadian Science Writing Undernourished, Inferior," n.p.

3. An elegiac and satiric poet of the Eleatic school, Xenophanes is in many ways Emerson's direct precursor. Seeing the divine manifested in and by the world, he argued for the unity and singularity of the godhead by reducing the Greeks' widely divergent polytheism to various meteorological phenomena, especially clouds. He believed God to be a single incorporeal and eternal being, of the same nature as the universe and, like it, spherical in form. In a manner similar to that of Emerson's Poet, Xenophanes' divine being pervades all things and comprehends them within himself.

> Song, picture, form, space, thought, and character,
> Deceive us, seeming to be many things,
> And are but one.

The dissolution of knowledge into myriad spheres of expertise, something that is more familiar today, was to Emerson a sign of cultural weakness and intellectual sedation. True power and vitality are demonstrated by transferring the ways and means of one discipline into another: "To know one element, explore another, / And in the second reappears the first," Emerson advises. "Xenophanes" is but a minor contribution to Emerson's lifelong argument that all natural phenomena share more commonalities than differences. In lines that make a humorous jab at the Linnaean system of speciation, for example, Emerson ends his poem:

> And universal nature, through her vast
> And crowded whole, an infinite paroquet,
> Repeats one note.[4]

We see in the dissimilarity between Emerson's argument here and prevailing attitudes today a fundamental contrast in point of view: the Aristotelian penchant for seeing the particular within the general set against the Baconian preference for evincing the general by regarding the particular.

No matter how arrived at, however, the idea that the universe adheres to one organic design—an admittedly complex but nonaltering set of interrelated biochemical, physical, and causal rules (or, more stringently, statistical probabilities) that help explain everything from the circulation of the blood to the circulation of galactic systems—is revived in the search for patterns that is common to both art and science. Construed as a broadly human endeavor, rather than simply a disciplinary activity, this search clarifies Wordsworth's claim that the Poet "will be ready to follow the steps of the Man of science" and "be at his side, carrying sensation into the midst of the objects of the science itself."[5] Scientist and Poet may each enjoy the partnership of pursuing similar goals. In borrowing this idea as the main thesis of "The Poet," Emerson notes how "the state of science is an index of our self-

---

4. *Essays and Poems*, 1159–60.
5. William Wordsworth, *The Prose Works of William Wordsworth*, 141.

knowledge" (*CollW*, 3:9). It is the particular job of the Poet, he argues, to bring mind (the perception, or "sensation," of meaningfulness) to bear on the discoveries of science. Scientific discovery includes the expansion of our knowledge not only of what is actually there, from galaxies to neutrons, but also of how it all interacts and functions—from causes and effects over time and through space, to implications for the quality of our own lived experience. The interaction of objects in the world creates patterns, and, as I discuss more fully in Chapter 5 in terms of knowledge acquisition, scientific discovery expands the number of these patterns available to our scrutiny. And so whether or not discovery occurs on the macroscopic scale of solar bodies or the microscopic scale of nano-organisms, the patterns are interpreted, or brought toward meaningfulness, on the human scale. Discovery is always self-knowledge.

The Poet "puts . . . a tongue into every dumb and inanimate object" by interpreting the patterns revealed by science—that is, by "show[ing] us all things in their right series and procession" (*CollW*, 3:12). And as Emerson's essay makes clear, the language the Poet uses is itself one of these natural patterns, itself a discovery of the scientific mind. As Emerson earlier argues in *Nature*, "words are signs of natural facts" (*CollW*, 1:17), and so they are a product of the natural world. Thus language is not intercessory: because we understand the patterns of nature through the natural pattern of language, Emerson argues, "we are symbols, and inhabit symbols"—each one a nexus of meaning in a world "put under the mind for verb and noun" (*CollW*, 3:12). In this regard, "a rhyme in one of our sonnets should not be less pleasing than the iterated nodes of a sea-shell" (3:15) because the two are contiguous with one another. Emerson's words here are descriptive, not prescriptive: rhyme and node are both segments of a much larger structure of patterns, a series and procession of things existing across all scales through which we become aware of the world.

Patterns are important to Emerson because they are signs of repetition, reflection, reversal, iteration, and cyclical progression—often because they are visible tropes for reflexive knowledge. But patterns are each one highly unique, structured according to their own rules of rhythmic expression. This is why patterns—as outward signs of inner truths—lead Emerson to interdisciplinary thinking: patterns, by their very nature, require multivalent approaches if they are to be properly comprehended. They require understanding throughout many planes of knowledge if we are to follow the directions in which they lead. The scientific mind, as Emerson understood it, is that which embraces the world in just such a way.

In this chapter, I examine the meaning *science* had for Emerson, and the various roles critics have given it in the development of his natural philosophy. As with so many things, Emerson's approach to science is two-sided, both embracing and highly critical. Well-versed in the latest and most significant scientific advances of his day, he recognized the ability of science to open new frontiers of knowledge. Yet he was also highly suspicious of what he called "this arid departmental *post mortem* science" (*CollW,* 6:152), the kind of mechanistic, linear school of thinking that for him tended to examine its subjects at arm's length rather than bring them closer through heightened awareness and understanding. Emerson's graded response to classification, as both a precise scientific tool and a broad intellectual methodology, opens up the contrast in Emerson's regard for science most fully and is a key point of discussion here. Additionally, Emerson's critical reception in the twentieth century with regard to science is also wide-ranging, varying between those, on the one hand, who regard his scientific interests as little more than a passing whim, and those, on the other, who recognize the seriousness and insight with which he regarded scientific subjects. More recently, critics have begun to realize that science underscores virtually all of Emerson's thought and provides a deep and enriching point of contact for our understanding of the man and his worldview. In preparation for following chapters, I introduce some of the ways in which this is so.

During the Enlightenment, scientific discourse started on its way toward becoming the most authoritative discourse in the Western world, and already by the middle of the nineteenth century, it began to gain recognition as a system of inquiry and learning complete unto itself. Even so, science in Emerson's time was different in many ways from science today. The most obvious difference is that now we live in an age in which the physics of relativity and quantum mechanics hold sway, having supplanted the old Newtonian way of thinking. To most nineteenth-century scientists, however, the universe was mechanical, much like a machine running in one direction through time according to mathematically defined rules and physically deterministic laws. Space and time were both generally taken to be uniform and absolute, such that bodies and events existed in precise locations that could be known empirically. Furthermore, interactions between physical bodies were explained by means of identifying strictly linear causal chains, especially since forces like heat and gravitation were understood to be kinetic in nature. Most now see the universe as being much more complex than what the prevailing nineteenth-century view implies, but some (though not all) of the habits of mental action by means of which it ordered the world—take, for example, Mendeleyev's periodic table or Linnaeus's biological taxonomy—still survive today.

Another way of noting the difference is to observe how we use scientific discourse—signified by the umbrella shorthand "science"—in order to denote a certain type of knowledge (delivered most often from the natural sciences and physics in particular) that is observable, demonstrable, and predictable. In short, *science* today means an assemblage of *data*, a vast body of information taken as the product of a very specific kind of procedural logic or experimentation. The chief characteristic of scientific data is that it is governed by a hard determinism, thus allowing it to be seen as self-evident. This way of thinking about what constitutes science results from its ever-tightening matrix bond with an increasingly sophisticated array of technology and is further illustrated by the fact that "bad" data sets—ones that do not accord with the accepted patterns established by "good" data sets—are often thought to indicate bad science. Further, data that cannot potentially be applied toward some end is useless, and is thus not "real" science.

So the greatest difference between modern science and nineteenth-century science lies not in the proliferation of data between then and now—that is, in the contrast between the breadth and specificity of the patterns we recognize versus the patterns our predecessors did. Rather, the difference lies in the views of mental action, the processes of thought that constitute an acceptable scientific response to the world. In the early decades of the nineteenth century, what was thought of as science was not yet the limited discourse of specialized fields. It was instead very much a part of the wider culture and a key aspect of the larger intellectual life. Scientific work was still performed by self-taught individuals in addition to medical doctors and other specialists. Scientific papers appeared in the same journals as poetry, belles lettres, criticism, and political editorials. Artists, politicians, and natural philosophers discussed the same books and attended the same lectures. A great many movements, social theories, and academic and artistic trends attempted to replicate, with varying degrees of success, the cognitive model presented by physics, astronomy, and mathematics. Set within this context, the word *science* still had much wider application. Science referred less to a certain type of knowledge (that is, discrete facts derived from standardized procedures) and more to a certain way of construing the world.

Emerson has this very assumption in mind when he notes in the "Worship" chapter from *The Conduct of Life* how scientific thinking can be applied to many areas of inquiry:

> Our recent culture has been in natural science. We have learned the manners of the sun and of the moon, of the rivers and the rains, of the mineral and elemental kingdoms, of plants and animals. Man has learned to weigh the sun, and its weight neither loses nor gains. The path of a star, the moment of an eclipse, can be determined to the fraction of a second. Well, to him the book of history, the book of love, the lures of passion, and the commandments of duty are opened: and the next lesson taught, is, the continuation of the inflexible law of matter into the subtile kingdom of will, and of thought; that, if, in sidereal ages, gravity and projection keep their craft, and the ball never loses its way in its wild path through space,—a secreter gravitation, a secreter projection, rule not less tyrannically in human history, and keep the balance of power from age to age unbroken. For, though the new element of freedom and an individual has been admitted, yet the primordial atoms are prefigured and predetermined to moral issues, are in search of justice, and ultimate right is done. (*CollW*, 6:116)

Emerson thinks of the chief contributions of science in terms of mental action. Before its split from classical philosophy (with its questions relating to metaphysics) and, before that, religion (with its questions relating to agency and causation), *science* meant inquiry via the use of logical principles and skeptical indifference toward the truth—insofar as *that* meant preparing oneself for any truth, religious or secular. Science taught its adherents to look for and appreciate what the world was *really like,* and that sort of stance, in and of itself, was what scientific thinking was all about.

The important point to remember is that such an approach was not necessarily experimental, and so a scientific methodology could be applied to any subject ready for investigation. In this regard, Henry David Thoreau's search at Walden Pond for "only the essential facts of life" is of a piece with the same aggressive intellectual spirit at midcentury that spawned the new social sciences of history, psychology, medicine, economics, and the like, all of which aimed to transfer the principles and methods of natural science into the personal, social, and political realms in order to systemize and evaluate human behaviors. Thoreau articulates his concerns with a cool matter-of-factness that helps characterize this wider nineteenth-century transition into what was seen as an increasingly scientific understanding of the world:

> Let us settle ourselves, and work and wedge our feet downward through the mud and slush of opinion, and prejudice, and tradition, and delusion, and appearance, that alluvion which covers the globe, through Paris and London, through New York and Boston and Concord, through church and state, through poetry and philosophy and religion, till we come to a hard bottom and rocks in place, which we can call *reality*, and say, This is, and no mistake.

Outlining here his goals for *Walden*, Thoreau performs the sort of foundationalist maneuver indicative of Francis Bacon and the scientific tradition grounded in his method. Noting that "the intellect is a cleaver" as it "discerns and rifts its way into the secret of things," he, like a surgeon, wields Ockham's razor, his most important intellectual scalpel, and proposes to wend his way through the historical accretion of ideas to the presumably hard bottom of reality, through which he can then proceed forward with a presumably assumptionless (and thus unpolluted) insight. And even though he "wanted to live deep and suck out all the marrow of life," Thoreau proposes to find that marrow by "reduc[ing] it to its lowest terms" according to the dictates of mechanistic natural science.[6]

As a catalog of Thoreau's observations of nature, *Walden* contains a great deal of valuable ecological data. But today the sort of truths he discovered about living deliberately are often taken as not much more than culturally determined conjectures: at best only quasi-scientific and certainly not as "real" as the data generated by hard science. Indeed, Thoreau's experiment at Walden Pond fails the test of reproducibility, to say nothing of predictability. But it is one thing to allow that figures like Emerson and Thoreau

6. Henry David Thoreau, *Walden*, 90, 97–98, 91.

are frequently indebted to science, and quite another to allow that their thinking was frequently scientific—that, like nineteenth-century science generally, they engaged in a rational investigation of the world as it really is. The case for Emerson is even more difficult because Emerson never goes so far as Thoreau in imitating the Baconian method; in fact, he generally goes in the opposite direction by challenging many of the fundamental precepts of Bacon's non-Aristotelian thought. Nonetheless, Emerson's thinking engages science in a number of ways.

Emerson has traditionally been seen as one who, like the Transcendentalists generally, stands outside the bounds of scientific thought. His concerns with the world are taken to focus mainly on the personal, and so personality has become the dominant window through which to view his life. In *The Life of Ralph Waldo Emerson* (1949), Ralph Rusk outlines Emerson's career in terms of a progression from skepticism in the early years to optimism in midlife to disillusionment and acquiescence in the years approaching the Civil War and after. In *Freedom and Fate* (1953), Stephen Whicher reads Emerson's transcendentalism as "steadily giving way to a basic empiricism" such that "with time Emerson became sharply aware of the contrast between the transcendental Self and the actual insignificant individual adrift on the stream of time and circumstance."[7] And so one received notion of Emerson's career describes a trajectory rising up through self-doubt and confusion in the 1820s, peaking at an apex of unbounded optimism and confidence in the self during the 1830s, descending into a disillusionment brought on by the tragedies and losses of the 1840s, and then dropping rapidly into a resigned acceptance of the limits of the human will in the 1850s and '60s. Thus Emerson remains for many only a soft-minded idealist, best understood mainly through the lenses of Goethe and Coleridge, and too self-absorbed to face up to the scientific objectivism a true tough-mindedness—as exhibited, for example, by Emerson's Germanic descendants Nietzsche and Freud—would require.

But this career arc, as Leonard Neufeldt notes in *The House of Emerson* (1983), presents an "efficient assumption . . . that conveniently throws Emerson into familiar relief and abbreviates both the reading and the critical analysis of his works. Well-timed and energetically stated critical inter-

---

7. Stephen Whicher, *Freedom and Fate: An Inner Life of Ralph Waldo Emerson*, 97, 171.

pretations have, in the absence of forceful counterstatements, become lords of the critical life." One of these persistent lords is the notion that Emerson, as Whicher puts it, "was hardly scientific": more interested in Coleridge's notion of the potential "humanity of science" than in science as a professional pursuit or as an intellectual tool for examining the world, Emerson shows himself to be, Whicher writes, "on the whole unsympathetic with the patient experimentation on which scientific achievement is based." Carl Strauch's 1958 essay "Emerson's Sacred Science" attempts to provide a silver lining by advising, "We should not deplore Emerson's 'feeble' grasp on nineteenth-century science because he lumped it so uncritically with outmoded forms of thought like Platonism and Neoplatonism; for . . . it is probably *because* Emerson 'believed in' emanation that he 'believed in' evolution." For Strauch, Emerson's beliefs about science and nature may exhibit their "extravagance," but they also have their "charm," for they arise from "the gnomic and occult art that was the only kind Emerson, by his special talents and peculiar limitations, could practice." In short, we can respect Emerson for some of his very high-minded ideals and "beliefs"—at least they allow him to affirm certain respectable scientific theories, like evolution—but surely they are not of the sort one could today reasonably call objectively rational. Thus, what Whicher calls "the desultory years" of the early 1830s have Emerson only dabbling in scientific subjects, perusing the "ordinary fare available to the general reader," and lecturing to other "amateur students of science like himself."[8]

A survey of the major essays shows that the influence of science on Emerson's thinking was often more than casual, yet critical studies have focused mainly on the early 1830s. Harry Hayden Clark, in the 1931 essay "Emerson

8. Leonard N. Neufeldt, *The House of Emerson,* 12–13; Whicher, *Freedom and Fate,* 90; Carl Strauch, "Emerson's Sacred Science," 238; Whicher, *Freedom and Fate,* 89–90. Whicher's beliefs are likely encouraged by Emerson's remarks at the beginning of "The Naturalist," a lecture delivered to the Boston Natural History Society: "I shall say what my opinion is to excuse such persons as myself who without any hope of becoming masters of any department of natural science so as to attain the rank of original observers, do yet find a gratification in coming here to school, and in reading the general results of Naturalists and learning so much of the classifications of the sciences as shall enable us to understand their discoveries" (*EL,* 1:70). But Emerson's self-deprecation here is a deliberate rhetorical tactic meant to create a feeling of connection between speaker and audience, and by no means diminishes his perceptive observations, here and elsewhere, on the role and meaning of scientific inquiry for the general culture.

and Science," was among the first to recognize that "Emerson's interest in science helped to motivate . . . his turn against ecclesiasticism and an antiquar-
ian devotion to the past," an observation that has influentially characterized
Emerson's interest in science as being almost exclusively a subset of his theology, and has (unintentionally) helped to limit subsequent inquiry on the
subject mostly to his early career. For example, Clark points to Emerson's
reading in astronomy shortly before the time of his resignation from the Old
North Church, in particular Mary Somerville's *The Mechanism of the Heav-
ens* (1831) and J. F. W. Herschel's *A Preliminary Discourse on the Study of Natural Philosophy* (1830) and *A Treatise on Astronomy* (1833). In addition to
these, Emerson was also familiar with Copernicus, Galileo, Kepler, Laplace,
Newton, and Kant—all of whom "impressed him with . . . the concept of *law*"
in the cosmos. Clark also discusses Emerson's first trip to Europe, and the
Paris Muséum d'Histoire Naturelle in particular, as an important tour of
Europe's leading scientific institutions, one that fueled his lasting interest in
biology, natural philosophy, and evolution. The trip helped spark in subse-
quent years a deepened understanding of the conceptual theories of Leibnitz,
Kant, Goethe, and Coleridge as well as the scientific theories of Linnaeus,
Buffon, Cuvier, Lamark, Lyell, Agassiz, Darwin, and others.[9]

Clark's outline of Emerson's scientific interests in his early career is valuable for the questions and possibilities it raises. Certainly, as Clark notes,
Emerson is not "an inductive scientist"; rather, "Emerson approaches natural history with a method essentially *a priori,* ethical, and deductive, like that
of Plato, Schelling, Goethe, Kant, and Coleridge." But Clark also argues that
science served to provide Emerson only "novel *reinforcement* for views which
were primarily . . . native, Christian, classical, Oriental, romantic, or transcendental"—that is, views that might otherwise be considered mostly outside the sphere of the chief scientific debates of the day. In short, Clark's
tentative assessment regards Emerson's thinking as somewhat unscientific
and dilettantish, even though Clark identifies certain avenues of inquiry that
would suggest otherwise. Consider, for example, "To what extent did scientific analogies and illustrations give pattern to his thought and aid him in his
endeavor 'to give moral nature an aspect of mathematical science'?" and "If
'Time and Space relations vanish as laws are known,' to what extent was this

9. Harry Hayden Clark, "Emerson and Science," 225–26, 230; see also 250–58.

doctrine derived not only from Kant but also from science?" Answers to questions such as these, Clark writes, "would modify, in part at least, the present conventional tendency to regard Emerson as a mystical and irresponsible traveler in realms of Whim."[10]

Robert Richardson suggests as much when he argues in his 1995 biography, *Emerson: The Mind on Fire,* that "his reaction to the Jardin des Plantes was not that of a scientist." Richardson's assessment is true only if a scientific reaction is something that takes place in a laboratory. Gay Wilson Allen's 1975 follow-up on Clark's essay, "A New Look at Emerson and Science," examines the ample evidence of Emerson's scientific reaction, more broadly construed, to the Paris institution. Allen is the first to accept, and not defend, implicitly or explicitly, Emerson's scientific interests, and he focuses on four early lectures on science delivered in 1834, just after Emerson's European trip. The first of these, "The Uses of Natural History," recounts Emerson's experience of the Jardin des Plantes and Cabinet of Natural History; along with "On the Relation of Man to the Globe," it is a prolegomenous sketch for *Nature.* A third lecture, "Water," focuses on that substance, and "The Naturalist" argues for science in education. Allen's analysis of these lectures stresses the important influence of geology on Emerson's thinking in the early 1830s, in contrast and in addition to the astronomy Clark connects directly to Emerson's resignation from the ministry. Importantly, Allen argues that Emerson's "theory of language" in his early career "might have developed in either of two directions: phenomenologically or mystically (in a Neoplatonic sense)," and he gives the phenomenological direction greater weight. Commenting on Emerson's later lecture "The Humanity of Science," for example, Allen notes that Emerson "came even nearer to spelling out phenomenology" in a formal sense, but "the extent of Emerson's anticipation of twentieth-century phenomenology is his conviction that thought (consciousness) cannot exist without the world's body; thought and nature are co-related."[11]

However, the natural sciences had a significant influence on Emerson's reading of nature, Allen observes, such that the four early lectures on science "reveal his reading and thinking about science before he had fused his

10. Ibid., 228, 229, 258, 260.
11. Robert D. Richardson Jr., *Emerson: The Mind on Fire,* 142; Gay Wilson Allen, "A New Look at Emerson and Science," 437.

ideas thus derived with the Neoplatonic and 'transcendental' ideas of Plotinus, Swedenborg, Wordsworth, Coleridge, Carlyle, and seventeenth-century English Platonists." Thus, two of the most basic and influential concepts of Emerson's philosophy can clearly be seen to have their roots in the laws of mechanistic science: compensation is essentially a reformulation of Newton's third law of motion, and polarity takes as its analogy the positive and negative charge in electrodynamics. To which Allen lists a third: "To these might also be added 'circularity,' which translated in poetic metaphors the principle of 'conservation of energy.'"[12]

David Robinson, in his 1980 essay "Emerson's Natural Theology and the Paris Naturalists," develops and expands the Clark thesis that Emerson's early interest in science helped motivate his eventual break with revealed religion. Focusing on Paris, and the botanical classifications of Antoine-Laurent de Jussieu as presented at the Muséum in particular, Robinson points out that the experience of visiting the Jardin des Plantes gave Emerson a "first hand exposure to classification rather than an exposure through books." Actually seeing plants and animals arranged in a system of classification impressed Emerson not with the idea of classification itself, but with "the physical evidence of [science's] power to reflect the truth, that truth being the unity and dynamism of nature." As Emerson was to put it later, "Not only man puts things in a row, but things belong in a row. The immense variety of objects is really composed of a few elements. The world is the fulfillment of a few laws. Hence the possibility of Science" (*EL*, 2:25). If, as Clark argues, Emerson's approach to science is essentially a priori, ethical, and deductive, then "the fact should not obscure the impact of science on his thought," writes Robinson: "If Goethe and Coleridge were finally more influential (as they were), and if Emerson more nearly resembles them in his pursuits than the actual scientists of his day, there is still much to be said about the contribution of pure science to the pattern of his development. . . . In short, Emerson was not entirely ready to abandon revealed theology until his experience at Paris, and he had no clear vision of how nature might support the moral sense until he had worked through this experience." The contours of Robinson's read on the importance of Jussieu's garden for the most part follow the pattern given by Jonathan Bishop, in *Emerson on the Soul* (1964). As Bishop notes, the

12. Allen, "New Look," 441, 445.

Jardin des Plantes presented "an order discovered to be intrinsically natural, though just as evidently imposed by the mind"—in other words, "it was a living metaphor that was literally true." Like Clark, Bishop makes note of the influence of astronomy on Emerson, especially its peculiar power to "exhibit sharply the epistemic gulfs between eye and object, instrument and conclusion, model and reality."[13]

Clark, Allen, and Robinson offer the best studies of Emerson's early career, but the truth is that science had lasting influence on Emerson throughout his life. Leonard Neufeldt's 1977 essay "The Science of Power: Emerson's Views on Science and Technology in America" is perhaps the first to demonstrate Emerson's attention toward American science beyond the 1830s, particularly in the technology of the industrial revolution that began to radically redefine American culture during the 1850s. At this time, there was virtually no distinction between applied and pure research, so science was closely associated with technological invention. As Emerson notes in "The Uses of Natural History": "The history of modern times has repeatedly shown that a single man devoted to science may carry forward the mechanic arts and multiply the products of commerce more than the united population of a single country can accomplish in ages wherein no particular devotion to scientific pursuits exists" (*EL*, 1:12). Indeed, notes Neufeldt, "among literary figures Emerson was virtually alone in his endorsement of the possibilities of technology and science for the individual and the culture"; for Emerson, technology generally and machines particularly were products of the mind and hence part of Nature.[14]

Thus technology's value lay in its potential to help expand, in a scientific sense, our knowledge of and contact with nature. In fact, Neufeldt continues, "as his ambivalence toward America increased in the 1850's and 60's, [Emerson] turned even more to technological and scientific progress for

13. David M. Robinson, "Emerson's Natural Theology and the Paris Naturalists: Toward a Theory of Animated Nature," 76, 79, 70, 71; Bishop, *Emerson on the Soul*, 54, 53.

14. Leonard N. Neufeldt, "The Science of Power: Emerson's Views on Science and Technology in America," 330. Consider, for example, this passage from "Art": "Is not the selfish, and even cruel aspect which belongs to our great mechanical works,—to mills, railways, and machinery,—the effect of the mercenary impulses which these works obey? When its errands are noble and adequate, a steamboat bridging the Atlantic between Old and New England, and arriving at its ports with the punctuality of a planet, is a step of man into harmony with nature" (*CollW*, 2:218).

signs of intellectual, moral, and imaginative growth in his generation and the next." In the early 1870s, for example, Emerson cataloged many of the technological advances he had witnessed through the years: "The splendors of this age outshine all other recorded ages. In my lifetime, have been wrought five miracles, namely, 1. the Steamboat, 2. the railroad; 3. the Electric telegraph; 4. the application of the Spectroscope to astronomy; 5. the photograph; five miracles which have altered the relations of nations to each other" (*JMN*, 16:242). But as Neufeldt demonstrates through his reading of "Works and Days" (first delivered in 1857 but not published until 1870), Emerson clearly understood the perils of industrialization during and after the Civil War. This address is in many ways a paean to the astonishing number of technological advancements Emerson saw taking place around him. But it also expresses his concern that an industrial society could easily become mindless, skeptical, and fatalistic without "the right sort of men, and the right sort of women" (*CW*, 7:164) to keep it sufficiently balanced—those who understood, as Neufeldt puts it, that "man's work needed to be humanized" and that "the moral needed to keep pace with technological and scientific advances rapidly outstripping it."[15] The "five miracles" Emerson lists in his journal may have indeed altered the relations of nations to each other, but for good or ill was not always clear.

Importantly, Neufeldt argues that Emerson's remarks on technology and the machine show how he understood science to be "any vital intellectual discipline—not a faculty or delimited area of investigation but a quality of mental action." Like the Scholar or the Poet, the true Scientist continually exhibits a broad engagement with the natural world. So "although his visit to the Jardin des Plantes of Paris did not transform Emerson into a scientist of the new school," or one who prefers the craft of the laboratory, "as a scholar who celebrated man perceiving, guessing, symbolizing, theorizing, in short 'man thinking,' he welcomed a new age of science in America even as he praised the Keplers, Lamarcks, Newtons, and Daltons" of an earlier age.[16]

Throughout his life, Emerson shows how, as a pattern-seeker, the Poet is at home in the world of science. In addition to finding beauty in "the galvanic battery, the electric jar, the prism, and the chemist's retort" (*CollW*,

15. Neufeldt, "Science of Power," 330, 342.
16. Ibid., 333, 334.

2:218), the Poet makes use of what Neufeldt calls the "quality of mental action" science helps to promote. Laura Dassow Walls also notes how Emerson was clearly at home with scientific thought—more so perhaps than today's readers appreciate:

> Emerson, like most intellectuals of his day, was perfectly at ease folding scientific truth into moral truth, reading literature and science together as part of a common intellectual culture. He took scientific literacy so much for granted that his scientific metaphors sink out of sight; worse, from his time to ours, the divorce between "the two cultures" of literature and science has made his deep debt to science virtually invisible. The result is that later generations have allowed this characteristic and crucial aspect of Emerson's thought to go largely unnoticed and unremarked. Moreover, the very goals and assumptions that once yoked poetry and science as allies in a common cultural enterprise are no longer accepted as part of science. Hence the whole Emersonian complex has been swept into "literature," with little recognition of the loss this entails to an understanding of the common roots of literary and scientific thought in America.

Walls's book *Emerson's Life in Science* (2003) is the first on that subject—the first to consider scientific inquiry as one of Emerson's lifelong aspirations, and the first to consider "the place of Emerson in the development of modern science."[17] In addition to a reevaluation of the view that Emerson's was a casual interest, understanding Emerson's deep immersion in scientific subjects and thought requires, as Walls suggests, renewed appreciation, in our time, of what "science," as an intellectual exercise, can mean.

Classification provides an illustrative example of the influence of scientific thought on Emerson, particularly as his response to scientific classification reveals the importance of noting the difference between means and ends. Even before he started taking metaphors and images from natural science to illustrate important concepts in his early essays, Emerson's mind was, by the time he arrived in Paris, already immersed in astronomy and the natural theology of Joseph Butler and William Paley, both of whom, as Clark details, had a great influence on him. Butler and Paley each respond to the eighteenth-century debate over the widening gap between revelation and scientific materialism. Butler's *The Analogy of Religion, Natural and*

---

17. Walls, *Emerson's Life in Science*, 3.

Revealed, to the Constitution and Course of Nature (1736) defends revelation as providing guiding principles for the interpretation of nature, which, Butler argued, itself points toward mankind's immortality. Paley's better-known apology, *Natural Theology* (1802), presents the famous watchmaker metaphor, which argues that nature's complex design implies a designer, and challenges Kant and Hume in its claim that the adaptability of organisms to their environments suggests mankind's ability to discover and know the fundamental principles of nature.

Thus Emerson was prepared in 1833 to understand the model of classification he found on display in the Paris Muséum's collection as being a function of both Nature's self-organization and the mind's tendency to order the world. Emerson clearly understood in a tangible way while walking through the Muséum the power of science to uncover metaphysical truths, as his journal account of the experience shows, because "science for Emerson was not a rarified method or specialized field of study but the highest form of mental action."[18] But interpretations of his response have varied widely. Robinson notes that "the impact of the experience lay in its forceful presentations of the implications of botanical and zoological classification to Emerson's mind, emphasizing both the appeal of scientific procedure itself, and its potential philosophical uses," a key point of the four science lectures delivered after Emerson's return from Europe. Following Clark, Robinson segregates Emerson's interest in science to the early 1830s. But what leads Emerson, as Robinson argues, to "abandon the pursuit of [natural] science yet maintain his commitment to natural philosophy" is the fact that "when natural science becomes mere naming, or dead classification, it loses its vital connection to larger philosophical truths. . . . Emerson realizes the danger of the means, classification, becoming an end in itself." Thus, "an Orphic poet, and not a natural scientist, is the hero of *Nature*."[19]

---

18. Ibid., 4.

19. Robinson, "Emerson's Natural Theology," 70–71, 86, 85, 88. Additionally, Robinson elsewhere argues, "By the early 1840s Emerson's initial enthusiasm for science was overshadowed by two other aspects of his intellectual life. He felt a gradual, worrying diminishment of the religious or ecstatic experience that had been a significant part of his vision. That such experiences had often been connected with the natural world helped to render scientific thought secondary. He also felt a rising pressure for political commitment, as the antislavery cause and other reform movements increasingly controlled the discourse of New England's intellectuals" ("Fields of Investigation," 102).

For Elizabeth Dant, however, classification becomes the end because of the means. Her 1989 essay "Composing the World: Emerson and the Cabinet of Natural History" provides a succinct overview of the lyceum movement of the 1830s and '40s, but in aiming "to uncover certain tendencies in his thinking," as it relates to natural science, Dant offers no evidence for the generalized anxiety she sees motivating Emerson's use of the cabinet model "to provide a means of shrinking and reducing an often threatening and recalcitrant physical world." For Dant, the cabinet provides a metonymic "object lesson" in systematizing diffuse knowledge while at the same time erasing the personal and aesthetic concerns driving the nineteenth century's desire to catalog the natural world, and Dant is correct in pointing out the effect of the cabinet to create a dubious objectivity. However, it does not follow that "it is generally the aim of Emerson's art of metonymy to shrink what threatens to overwhelm—a reality too vast to be otherwise comprehended," nor that this aim "is matched by a habit of substituting the private fragment for the universal law, of making the fragment speak from the depths of an unfathomable wholeness." The indisputable fact is that Emerson's writing is full of statements reflecting his abiding belief that reality is comprehendible. The notion that Emerson finds the physical world threatening, and in response substitutes the private for the universal, reverses what is generally taken to be the case: that Emerson reads the world analogically and searches the particular for evidence of the general, a moral law that might free individuals from the constraints of history, on the one hand, and social expectation, on the other. Indeed, Emerson gives no indication that others should fear the world any more than he does; if anything, the opposite is true. Lectures such as "The American Scholar" are characterized by their call for original action, both intellectual and social, and not, as Dant concludes, by their asking listeners simply to change the way they "choose to perceive and *arrange*," as in a cabinet, the "deplorable realities of the present."[20] Even though it argues unconvincingly that Emerson was

20. Elizabeth Dant, "Composing the World: Emerson and the Cabinet of Natural History," 18, 31, 32, 42–43. Dant is not alone in reading the meaning of Emerson's Paris experience in a state of unease. In his 1994 essay "Emerson, Paris, and the Opening of the Scientific Eye," Lee Rust Brown interprets the garden as telescoping spheres of reflexive subjectivity: "The museum . . . was the best available model for the innermost speculative self, a self unknowable by others and accountable for all otherness, a self Emerson would methodically lay out on common ground in America. This was the place where visibles were rendered invisible

engulfed by the explanatory power of the Muséum's displays, Dant's essay nonetheless illustrates how a particular model of thinking can overwhelm one's perception of the world, a concern Robinson correctly identifies as central to Emerson's science lectures.

At issue here is a contrast between subjective and objective understandings of experience and the various ways in which scientific knowledge is culturally encoded. In the nineteenth century, whole realms of knowledge, like vast regions of the globe, remained unmapped and unknown to the Western mind, and so the contrast between ignorance and awareness of the world stood out in high relief on much more personal scales than today, a time when the unknown mostly refers to the microscopically small and the infinitely large. William Rossi points out in his 2000 essay "Emerson, Nature, and Natural Science" that—in marked contrast to today's standards for scientific discovery—in the early nineteenth century, "in an era when post-Enlightenment science was rapidly becoming the principal interpretive authority of nature, a solitary experiential encounter with nature's 'truth' also carried overtones of scientific discovery." In Emerson's time, science was still mostly an exploratory discipline, exploratory because it was so individualistic and individualistic because it was so exploratory. Thus it was possible in Emerson's view that the poet could adopt a scientific frame of mind, just as the scientist could adopt a poetic one: the two would lend themselves well to one another in the establishment and categorization of so much new knowledge. But, as Rossi also points out, "like the representations and explanations it produces, science, too, is necessarily embedded in history and culture. Consequently, just as the disciplinary definitions of natural knowledge changed from 'natural history' to 'natural science' in accord with the increasing professionalization and sophistication of science, so the meaning of 'nature' as mediated by science also changed dramatically in the five decades of Emerson's career."[21] During that time the overall direction of science

---

and invisibles rendered visible, the place that resolved everything exotic into interior terms by exposing the exotic as a masked projection of that very interior. Beyond the colorful distractions of subject matter, the spectator beheld himself, in his clearest possible reflection, as still another instance of the museum" (343). Both the museum's design and the model of classification it offers for interpreting the natural world, Brown argues, simultaneously appropriate and project the self—without regard to "the colorful distractions of subject matter," a condition that exposes the circularity of Brown's argument.

21. William Rossi, "Emerson, Nature, and Natural Science," 103.

changed tack—becoming a team-oriented, laboratory endeavor dependent on technology and geared toward the production of data—because the "uses" of nature changed. Described in *Nature* as something to be apprehended, nature became in contrast something to be objectified through systems of classification emphasizing practicality and control. Described by Emerson as something to be subsumed within the experience of oneself, it became something to be managed through the isolation and manipulation of discrete units and particles.

Classification leads to greater and greater degrees of specialization, not so much because an understanding of the natural world requires it but because the proliferation of data—that is, the development of science into a mainly empirical enterprise—does. The idea of unity between mind and nature in Romantic science developed, therefore, in response to specialization, a trend in empirical science that tends to cut human beings off from personal experience of the natural world. In this context, Stuart Levine argues in his 1982 essay "Emerson and Modern Social Concepts" that "Emerson's vision of unity, then, is in part a way of talking back to fragmentation"—as is the analogical method of many Transcendentalist thinkers. One way of reading Transcendentalism, then, has been to see it as a sort of cultural backlash, a response to scientific empiricism that might not have developed so vigorously without it. However, such a backlash can also be seen as the reassertion of much older, much more influential ideas. Transcendentalism may have promoted a vision of holistic unity that seems peculiar, but as Levine notes, "similar world views have been the opinion of most of the human inhabitants of the globe for most of human history." We must recall "that it is not merely small tribal societies, which perhaps strike us as 'primitive,' that see the world in this unified way, but also several high civilizations."[22]

Additionally, Emerson's response to classification may have changed relatively quickly—at the Muséum, it was a kind of revelation, whereas the lecture "The Naturalist" presents a much more qualified view—but his response demonstrates how one need not become a Baconian laboratorian to engage and incorporate a scientific view of the world. As Levine points out, the truth is that, intellectually speaking, "modern science paradoxically provided not only part of the threat to the artist, but also access to what seemed a model of artistic survival, worth, and power." Walls notes how the

22. Stuart Levine, "Emerson and Modern Social Concepts," 177, 170–71.

new science certainly provided a model for Emerson: "the creative method of science, by showing how to incorporate mind and nature into a new whole, gave Emerson the key to the universe."[23] But of course he altered this model to fit the needs and uses of his own response to the world.

There are obvious contrasts, but also significant similarities. Emerson radically departs from his empiricist contemporaries, of course, in his preference for the vague, abstract, and holistic aspects of reality.[24] In *Nature*, Emerson argues that such elements lead to "the manly contemplation of the whole." (*CollW*, 1:39). He suggests that the holistic vision indicated by abstract intuitions might render more useful insight into the order of nature than discrete discriminations. Part of this approach stems from a matter of definition: what is most real in nature, Emerson believes, is the principle by which it is organized, not nature itself—for it matters not so much that nature exists as that it exists for a purpose.

In *Splintered Worlds* (1993), Robert Greenberg suggests that Emerson's reading of Hume, in addition to Montaigne, "gave Emerson what he needed to pursue his project of Unity while remaining true to the psychological realism that science required—the Humean courage to explore the variety of the self and the stability of Montaigne to occupy the middle ground where faith in unity could wait for propitious moments."[25] Emerson stresses the unity of man and nature, mind and world. In a metaphysic of this kind, subject and object are unified; inner self and outer reality flow on shared "currents" of "circulation." For Emerson, this relationship was the most fundamental, the most meaningful, to any human being's existence in the world because it allows for the individual to exercise "practical power," the conversion of thought into action and thus the ability for the individual to have a direct impact on the environment—perhaps the chief, if not always the most beneficial, end of scientific investigation.

Emerson also shares certain underlying beliefs about reality that accord with the psychological realism in Enlightenment thinking giving rise to

23. Levine, "Emerson and Modern Social Concepts," 171; Walls, *Emerson's Life in Science*, 2.

24. For example, in *Sporting with the Gods: The Rhetoric of Play and Game in American Culture* (1991), Michael Oriard explores Emerson's use of "play" in essays such as "The Poet" or the "Divinity School Address" as a "symbol for freedom: spontaneous, instinctual, indulged for its own sake; denying regulation and limits, existing in a timeless present" (371).

25. Robert M. Greenberg, *Splintered Worlds: Fragmentation and the Ideal of Diversity in the Work of Emerson, Melville, Whitman, and Dickinson*, 58.

mechanism in science. He assumed, for example, a deep and pervading order behind natural events. In *Nature* he notes that "whatever curiosity the order of things has awakened in our minds, the order of things can satisfy" (*CollW,* 1:7). Supporting such a view is the assumption that human inquiry can raise no questions to which answers cannot eventually be found. In addition, Emerson affirmed the significance of the human perspective, and with it the assumption that conscious humans have a metaphysically reliable point of view on the world. This assumption is one of the themes at the heart of "Self-Reliance" and its advice to "trust thyself: every heart vibrates to that iron string" (*CollW,* 2:28). And perhaps most importantly, Emerson believed that a life of the mind can, and should, accord with how one lives. Like Hume, Emerson felt that one's *way* of living and one's *attitudes* toward life should justify or account for one another. "If we live truly, we shall see truly" with the result that "when we have a new perception, we shall gladly disburden the memory of its hoarded treasures as old rubbish" (2:39). By disburdening the memory, Emerson suggests, one leaves behind naive assumptions about the world that are incongruent with newfound and more fundamental truths. Naturally, a change in thought brings a change in action, for "nothing can bring you peace but the triumph of principles" (2:51). Indeed, Emerson passes stern judgment on those who do not seek out a congruence between how and why they live: "I, at least, hate to see persons of that lumpish class who are here they not know why, & ask not whereto. . . . If mankind should pass a vote on the subject, I think they would throw them in sacks into the sea" (*JMN,* 5:284). Simply put, a life of the mind was not to be of the mind alone.

Despite such congruencies, Emerson differs perhaps most importantly with the isolating function of the scientific mind, a proclivity that can be traced back to Francis Bacon and earlier. By reformulating scientific inquiry as a two-pronged approach—first, clear the mind of various biases, or "idols"; and second, when examining any phenomenon, carefully discern between where it is present, where it is absent, and where it exists in degree—Francis Bacon's *Novum Organum* (1620) compartmentalizes knowledge of the world into discrete data sets. Emerson was very familiar with Bacon's work and also deeply suspicious of it because it separates (on false premises he believed) the poetic from the rational faculties of the mind. Though he praises Bacon as another "universal mind" in addition to Shakespeare (*EL,*

1:321), Emerson also notes: "His works have not that highest perfection of literary works, an intrinsic Unity, a method derived from the Mind. . . . All his work lies along the ground, a vast unfinished city. He did not arrange but unceasingly collect facts. His own Intellect often acts little on what he collects. Very much stands as he found it—mere lists of facts material or spiritual. All his work is therefore somewhat fragmentary" (335). Because he did not arrange, but only collected, facts, Emerson argues, Bacon's science is incomplete: by failing to seek patterns within his data, he presents only fragmentary, and therefore meaningless, lists. Further, Bacon's materialism, by focusing only on experiences as they are offered to our senses, can indicate what the course of nature was and what it still is, but it cannot prove the necessity or universality of any law. This is perhaps the chief reason Emerson believes strict empiricism to be limiting. In direct response to *Novum Organum,* he lays out his own view, in *Nature,* that the best sort of science is at heart a pattern-seeking endeavor that draws on the creative and imaginative faculties of the mind: "The best read naturalist who lends an entire and devout attention to truth, will see that there remains much to learn of his relation to the world, and that it is not to be learned by any addition or subtraction or other comparison of known quantities, but is arrived at by untaught sallies of the spirit, by a continual self-recovery, and by entire humility. He will perceive that there are far more excellent qualities in the student than preciseness and infallibility; that a guess is often more fruitful than an indisputable affirmation, and that a dream may let us deeper into the secret of nature than a hundred concerted experiments" (*CollW,* 1:39). Emerson calls for a science in which possibilities have as much importance as probabilities. By limiting the mind to a closed set of actions and focusing the attention on a particular kind of data collection, empiricism minimalizes not only our knowledge but our experience as well.[26]

Emerson's belief about the superiority of a guess or a dream may indicate his impatience with empiricism, but it does not indicate a complaint

26. Walls argues somewhat against the contrast I am developing here, claiming that Emerson valued Bacon because "any reader who wishes to take Bacon at his word must become himself the organizing center of Bacon's words. . . . Thus to read Bacon well is perforce to *become* Baconian, to become one's own inventor of knowledge—to invent oneself. Emerson found, in the self-deconstructing authority of Bacon, the authority for the American Scholar's primary principle, self-trust" (*Emerson's Life in Science,* 36).

against science generally. In articulating his position on natural philosophy in *Nature,* Emerson records his concern that science has a tendency to separate the individual from his environment, especially when "the natural" is not always something one can precisely measure. This theme makes a regular appearance throughout his work. He writes in *The Conduct of Life:* "The motive of science was the extension of man, on all sides, into Nature, till his hands should touch the stars, his eyes see through the earth, his ears understand the language of beast and bird, and the sense of the wind. . . . But that is not our science. These geologies, chemistries, astronomies, seem to make wise, but they leave us where they found us" (*CollW,* 6:151). Additionally, Emerson notes how epistemological biases and preconceptions tend to frame one's view of nature. The tendency toward Baconian measurement and categorization has its consequences: "The invention is of use to the inventor, of questionable help to any other. The formulas of science are like the papers in your pocket-book, of no value to any but the owner. Science in England, in America, is jealous of theory, hates the name of love and moral purpose. There's a revenge for this inhumanity. What manner of man does science make? . . . He has got all snakes and lizards in his phials, but science has done for him also, and has put the man into a bottle" (151). If technological invention is of use only to the inventor, then this condition results from the fact that the Baconian materialism of science has no demonstrable universality or necessity. It is, in short, inhuman, lacking in the sort of intentionality—what Emerson calls "love and moral purpose"—that gives all things their value to us in the first place.[27]

Even if it had a tendency to hold its objects at arm's length, Emerson believed that natural science still had a great deal to recommend it, particularly as regards its advancement of human knowledge. In an 1867 address from *Letters and Social Aims* (1875), he notes that "one of the distinctions of our century has been the devotion of cultivated men to natural science. The benefits thence derived to the arts and to civilization are signal and

27. See also Charles Schweighauser's 1995 essay, "'Know Thyself, Study Nature': The Contemporary Scientist's Dilemma," which examines the ways in which modern science departs significantly from the model of scientific inquiry offered by "The American Scholar." Chief among these differences are a dependence on technology, specialization and the "proliferation of trivia," and digitization, each of which tends to preclude the phenomenal discovery and self-discovery championed by Emerson.

immense. . . . But over all their utilities, I must hold their chief value to be metaphysical. The chief value is not the useful powers he obtained, but the test it has been of the scholar. He has accosted this immeasurable Nature, and got clear answers" (*CW*, 8:220–21). As a model of intellectual inquiry, he praised "the great analogical value of most of our natural science" (*JMN*, 5:384), or the way in which advances in one discipline can potentially lead to advances in others. Emerson's ultimate criticism of science is to be expected, however, given that the tradition of Ockham's razor generally cleaves in a direction opposite to that of Emersonian naturalism. Unlike the scientific empiricists, Emerson affirmed that teleological explanations of natural phenomena are valid and normative. He notes in *Nature*, for example, that "the moral law lies at the center of nature and radiates to the circumference. It is the pith and marrow of every substance, every relation, and every process" (*CollW*, 1:26). Even Emerson's use of the terms *substance, relation,* and *process* is significant. The Scholastic's philosophical idea of substance was left by the wayside in the eighteenth century as not having any "material" meaningfulness, and conceptions of relation and process were modified to conform to the materialist worldview. Emerson resuscitates these terms with their original teleological signification.

Many of these ideas are expressed in the lecture series on science, which Emerson delivered upon his return from his first European tour. They are the first of his long and accomplished career on the lecture circuit, and they record Emerson's response to having visited many of Europe's most important scientists and scientific institutions. The intellectual height of the trip came in Paris with Emerson's now famous decision to be a naturalist, and so collectively, these four lectures indicate what kind of naturalist Emerson wanted to be. But they also express his reaction to the state of science in his time. The lectures present Emerson's new understanding of a unified and dynamic nature, emphasizing process over product, but also the danger of substituting means for ends.

Emerson's confidence in scientific inquiry was certainly high—"To the powers of science no limit can be assigned," he writes (*EL*, 1:13)—and his first lecture lists the same sort of uses for natural science he would expand on in *Nature*, namely, health, service (or commodity), delight in truth, the improvement of mind and character, and keys to self-knowledge. Science's greatest use lies in the potential of its systematic approach. As Emerson remarks in "The Uses of Natural History," "Nothing is indifferent to the wise. If a man should study the economy of a spire of grass . . . it would show him a design in the form, in the color, in the smell, in the very posture of the blade as it bends before the wind" (17), and so demonstrate the integration of each part within the whole. But classification and the systematic organization of knowledge, Emerson argues, ought not be taken to signify mastery. Science, if anything, should teach as much about what one does not know as about what one knows. The lecture "The Relation of Man to the Globe" expands on this idea in its observations "that man is made just strong enough to keep his place in the world; that he is not any stronger than he need to be; that the adjustment of his forces to the forces of nature from which he would be in danger, is very nice, and if it had been a little less, would have been insufficient" (35). The lecture "Water" makes this point as well, with its acknowledgment of water's seemingly extraordinary power to transform the natural world and its remarkable catalog of what is known and not known about this most primal of chemical compounds. "Water" is certainly the most technical, in a generic sense, of Emerson's four lectures, and it evidences his own appreciation for a scientific accumulation of facts. But the final lecture, "The Naturalist," addresses more particularly the broader theme I have pursued thus far: the respective roles of Poet and Scientist.

Emerson's emphasis in "The Naturalist" is that Nature is more than what either poets or scientists, individually, can say about it. The natural world preserves unto itself a sophistication even at what seem to be rudimentary levels of life: "The slender violet hath preserved in the face of the sun and moon the humility of his line and the oldest work of man is an upstart by the side of the shells of the sea" (*EL*, 1:71). And unlike "whatever theology or philosophy we rest in, or labor after," the violet and shell are never "false or unsuccessful" because each preserves in its shape a key to the design of the universe, a kind of "open secret" (78) that science promises to make clear.

And so it is best to see Nature not so much as a cache of secrets and hidden causes but more as a vast cyclorama on display. We must recall, Emerson argues, that "the whole force of the Creation is concentrated upon every point. What agencies of electricity, gravity, light, affinity, combine to make every plant what it is, and in a manner so quiet that the presence of these tremendous powers is not ordinarily suspected" (*EL*, 1:72). The forces creating the simple curve of the violet or the ridges on the surface of the shell are indeed tremendous. What is missing in our response to this "open secret" is that very few, poets and scientists alike, have learned how to observe it, namely because the human response to Nature is conditioned by the systems we use to observe and interpret it. "A willow or an apple is a perfect being; so is a bee or a thrush," but "the best poem or statue or picture is not" (72). Comparatively, all art is little more than artifice.

In other words, we must not mistake epistemology for metaphysics, or means for ends. Both the poet and scientist can be guilty of this fault. They do not always grasp Nature's elegance and simplicity, Emerson argues, because each can in time become self-reflexive and unmindful of what the true object ought to be: "The poet loses himself in imaginations and for want of accuracy is a mere fabulist; his instincts unmake themselves and are tedious words. The savant on the other hand losing sight of the end of his inquiries in the perfection of his manipulations becomes an apothecary, pedant" (*EL*, 1:79). Because of the rising dominance of science and the rapid expansion of its domain, however, it is particularly important for the savant, or the scientist, to keep an open perspective. Science is indeed of great value to our understanding of the world, and its observational norms and experimental methods are of course the primary reason for its power to expand our knowledge of the world: "The necessity of nomenclature, of minute physiological research, or the retort, the scalpel, and the scales, is incontestable. But there is no danger of its being underestimated. We only wish to insist upon their being considered as *Means*" toward "the elemental law, the *causa causans,* the supernatural force" (80). For example, "to this end of furnishing us with hints, intimations of the inward Law of Nature, a cabinet is useful" (81), but it by no means should be taken to provide a comprehensive demonstration of its specimens, let alone the wider context of natural relations in which they exist.

These passages from "The Naturalist" provide an early example of what became Emerson's criticism of the isolating and reductive influence of the laboratory.[28] But "The Naturalist" argues that because empirical science

---

28. On the use of microscopes, for example, Emerson writes: "Yes our microscopes are not necessary[.] They are a mechanical advantage for chamber philosophers[;] she [Nature] has magnified every thing somewhere. Each process, each function, each organ is disproportionately developed in some one individual. Go study it there, instead of wearing your eyes out in your 6 million magnifier" (*JMN,* 4:268).

places all phenomena into primarily physical categories and taxonomies—
of which the Muséum in Paris is a vivid example—other essential relationships can become lost. As is the case with Hume, things such as agency and
causation come to be presumed not to exist, or, in the case of causation, only
to exist in the most mechanistic of terms. As Emerson writes in "The Poet,"
"Our science is sensual, and therefore superficial" (*CollW,* 3:9). What concerns Emerson, then, is the extent to which the means of scientific investigation can severely limit the wider framework of understanding. In the *Novum
Organum,* for example, the only important data is that which comes from
the observation of matter and the movement of matter, and so the laws reg-
ulating phenomena are physical facts lacking metaphysical support.

But this sort of problem continues to this day. Perhaps the clearest example can be seen in science's ability to observe the effects of gravity, but not
to explain gravity itself. The problem of the origin of consciousness provides a similar example. In each case, we are presented with an undeniably
physical phenomenon that remains inscrutable to empirical science, and we
cannot turn to science alone for a complete understanding of what, exactly,
each is. In *Nature* Emerson highlights this issue by repeating the claim that
"empirical science is apt to cloud the sight, and, by the very knowledge of
functions and processes, to bereave the student of the manly contemplation
of the whole." Without some sort of wider metaphysical framework in
which to understand these functions and processes, "the savant becomes
unpoetic" (*CollW,* 1:39).

Nonetheless, empirical science produces a great deal of data that must be
classified and categorized in some way if it is to contribute to an expanding
knowledge of the world. In commenting on the necessary intellectual work
of classifying so much emerging knowledge, Emerson articulates in "The
American Scholar" an idea of Mind that emphasizes direct contact, comprehensive reach, and streamlined interfacing among subdomains:

> Classification begins. To the young mind, every thing is individual, stands
> by itself. By and by, it finds how to join two things, and see in them one
> nature; then three, then three thousand; and so, tyrannized over by its own
> unifying instinct, it goes on tying things together, diminishing anomalies,
> discovering roots running under ground, whereby contrary and remote
> things cohere, and flower out from one stem. It presently learns, that, since

the dawn of history, there has been a constant accumulation and classifying of facts. But what is classification but the perceiving that these objects are not chaotic, and are not foreign, but have a law which is also a law of the human mind? The astronomer discovers that geometry, a pure abstraction of the human mind, is the measure of planetary motion. The chemist finds proportions and intelligible method throughout matter; and science is nothing but the finding of analogy, identity, in the most remote parts. The ambitious soul sits down before each refractory fact; one after another, reduces all strange constitutions, all new powers, to their class and their law, and goes on for ever to animate the last fibre of organization, the outskirts of nature, by insight. (*CollW*, 1:54)

The description of the intellect Emerson offers emphasizes movement upward from one scale to the next, from particles to systems, from single units to structural wholes. Mind works to absorb all things within itself, like a catch-all web. This is the way in which Emerson believed the scientist-savant would remain poetic.

Thus it is that Emerson comes to criticize empirical science not so much for what it does, but more for the explanatory options it rules out. For example, by ignoring causation, a concept without which Emerson found it impossible to meaningfully discuss parts within wholes, "We dwell on the surface of nature. We dwell amidst surfaces; and surface laps so closely on surface, that we cannot easily pierce to see the interior organism. Then the subtlety of things! Under every cause, another cause. Truth soars too high or dives too deep, for the most resolute inquirer. See of how much we know nothing. See the strange position of man. Our science neither comprehends him as a whole, nor any one of its particulars."[29] As this passage from "The Senses and the Soul" argues, strictly mechanical explanations cannot pierce interiors, meaning that they cannot reveal organic development through time. Additionally, mechanistic science de-emphasizes lived experience by treating knowledge as something to be institutionalized. The tendency is to record the results of scientific experimentation in journals and books, which is only a first step toward isolating scientific research in laboratories and institutes and codifying scientific data into a stream of facts, figures, and tables for textbooks, professional papers, and technical manuals. Against this

29. *Essays and Lectures*, 1190.

trend, Emerson argues in "New England Reformer": "The lessons of science should be experimental also. The sight of the planet through a telescope, is worth all the course on astronomy: the shock of the electric spark in the elbow, outvalues all the theories; the taste of the nitrous oxide, the firing of an artificial volcano, are better than volumes of chemistry" (*CollW*, 3:152–53). The development of a specialized method and discourse for science means that fewer and fewer people will have access to its lessons. Scientific discourse might say something about how we can more richly experience the everyday, rather than provide a compendium of facts about the world to be taken from books. If not for its esoteric vocabulary and peculiar critical apparatus—its emphasis on the production and interpretation of data—a volume of chemistry might otherwise be able to do just that.

Quoting *Nature*, Clark argues that "one must not be led astray by [Emerson's] recurrent theme that 'empirical science is apt to cloud the sight,' that 'all the facts in natural history taken by themselves, have no value,' for he prizes science not so much for its mere description of phenomena or for its advancement of our physical well-being as for its ethical symbolism."[30] However, these "themes" recur in Emerson's work for the very reason that they are central premises in his long-term critique of Enlightenment science. That strict empiricism clouds the sight and that scientific facts, as such, are valueless are both, as I have argued above, only two of the limitations Emerson identifies in Enlightenment thinking. For Emerson, knowledge is active, not static. It is to be found in apprehension, a much more active process than mere recognition. Knowledge unfolds algorithmically according to the same formulae activating nature: the processes that create order and harmony in the natural world are the same processes that create consciousness and insight in the human mind. Emerson's argument points to the idea that knowledge is an activity because Nature itself is not an object but an activity: Nature cannot be comprehended in a body of facts or an all-embracing methodology, as empirical science tries to do. Knowledge must be adaptive and not static. Thus, the science that produces knowledge must rest securely in the idea that mind is not a product but a process.

In a broad sense, then, the definition of nature determines the definition of science. If nature is dynamic, then science must also be dynamic. But if

30. Clark, "Emerson and Science," 226.

nature, after the Newtonian model, is seen as being composed of fundamentally inert particles participating in random interactions, then science will also be similarly static and inert. This is why Emerson is so critical of traditional mechanistic science and its associated modes of linear thought. The larger point here is that our appreciation of Emerson's engagement with science depends on our definition of *science*. As I have shown, one response to this problem is to draw a contrast between so-called true science—mathematically abstract and laboratorial—and everything else, such as occult beliefs or primitive pseudoscience. In this conception, Romantic intellectuals such as Emerson get lumped with the latter and become "hardly scientific"— a viewpoint that ignores both the scientific contexts of the philosophical and poetic ideas that emerge in Romantic thought as well as the great number of references to scientific information to be found in their work.

Another response is to draw a contrast between traditional science and "Romantic" science, so as to illustrate the ways in which these differing world-views prioritize human experience. Leon Chai, for example, in his 1987 study *The Romantic Foundations of the American Renaissance,* has defined Romantic science to include general characteristics such as theoretical simplicity, a "belief in the presence of a thought element" in Nature, and an understanding of thought as "an activity . . . of the material substance itself rather than of the rational intelligence seeking to establish relations between things." Thus in this conception, Nature participates in a kind of sentience much broader than the self-awareness and rules of logic used to define consciousness in human beings. "By a process not unlike that of chemical or elective affinities, Nature and mind are thus brought together. Their interaction is possible insofar as they represent in essence two forms of a single all-pervading energy," through which "knowledge assumes the form of recognition: in external Nature, mind comes to recognize its own nature."[31] For this reason, Romantic science affords a much greater role than does classical science to the individual experience of Nature, which explains the near universal Romantic wish to understand Nature by engaging it out-of-doors and in its natural setting rather than in the controlled environment of the laboratory.

Segregating Romantic science into a separate category is only moderately useful, however, because traditional science and Romantic science

31. Leon Chai, *The Romantic Foundations of the American Renaissance,* 154, 149.

need not be seen as opposed. Walls points out that Romantic science did not as a whole "deny the accomplishments of 'mechanistic' science"; rather, Romantic thinkers believed that "mechanistic science had to be renovated and incorporated into a new, reconceived, 'higher' science in which the lost unity of self and nature would be restored." By insisting that true science was, or at least ought to be, moral, synthetic, dynamic, progressive, and interdisciplinary, Emerson "should not be conceived as aligning himself with a special cadre of specialists or as a participant in some Romantic fringe movement sealed off from the genuine article. He was placing himself in the center of intellectual ferment in his time."[32] Nor was Emerson alone in this endeavor. Writers of the Victorian era frequently made use of scientific ideas, metaphors, and images in poetry and fiction, as many recent studies have begun to demonstrate.[33]

Walls discusses Emerson's reading in science—in natural theology, natural history, and natural philosophy—over a forty-year period, from the more intensely focused years of the early 1830s right into the 1870s: "Emerson pursued his reading of science at a time when science was expanding and changing rapidly, too rapidly for anyone to keep up. Fields were emerging and separating and mutating in a wild stew of energy." Within this historical context, the influence of science on Emerson was not simply deep, but profound—contributing to the construction of a whole life: "His entire project depends on elevating science to a creative art—not just marrying science and poetry, but merging the two in a new, prophetic power." Indeed, argues Walls: "In his long career Emerson worked to modernize America, and nowhere more so than when he adjured his readers to identify the truth

---

32. Walls, *Emerson's Life in Science*, 8, 10.

33. See, for example, not only Laura Dassow Walls on Thoreau and science (*Seeing New Worlds: Henry David Thoreau and Nineteenth-Century Natural Science* [Madison: University of Wisconsin Press, 1995]), Lee Rust Brown on Emerson and the French naturalists (*The Emerson Museum: Practical Romanticism and the Pursuit of the Whole*), and Eric Wilson on Emerson and electromagnetic force *(Emerson's Sublime Science),* but also Gillian Beer on George Elliot (*Darwin's Plots: Evolutionary Narrative in Darwin, George Elliot, and Nineteenth-Century Fiction* [London: Routledge, 1983]), Marilyn Gaull on Coleridge ("Coleridge and the Kingdoms of the Worlds," *Wordsworth Circle* 22, no. 1 [1991]: 47–52) and on the English Romantics (*English Romanticism: The Human Context* [New York: Norton, 1988]), John Wyatt on Wordsworth (*Wordsworth and the Geologists* [Cambridge: Cambridge University Press, 1995]), and George Levine on Victorian fiction (*Darwin and the Novelists: Patterns of Science in Victorian Fiction* [Cambridge: Harvard University Press, 1988]).

of the heart with the 'self-evident' law of nature, producing America as the generative heart of empire, and nature as simultaneously transcendent over and subservient to humanity. Emerson thus helped to reify science as the carrier of absolute truth, for he imagined that science alone escaped the human."[34] If mechanistic science was not always up to par with the Romantic ideal, that was only because such concentrated rationalism had yet to be merged with poetry's analogizing insights to produce a new way of seeing the world with creative power.

Emerson fills this gap with a vision of what Walls calls "gnomic science," a "marriage" of Romantic ideas and traditional science that brings together their differing methods and conceives of the world according to a few very specific ideas. The principles of gnomic thinking, as Walls outlines them, are simple and straightforward, and they are at heart geometrical. First, like mathematical axioms, gnomic truths are clear and direct, to the point of being self-evident. Second, gnomic figures are self-similar, constructed according to the proportions' geometric and organic growth. Third, gnomic objects are self-determining, existing unto themselves and for no other purpose than to be exactly as they are. Thus, "the gnomic impulse is characterized by the urge to signify infinitely, to collapse the greatest into the smallest," and "the goal of gnomic science is to grasp the infinitely large by revelation of its principle of production." But perhaps the most important characteristic of gnomic science is its tendency to envision nature as a systematic whole that "literally embodies in matter the divine idea or formula of its genesis, revealing nothing less than the harmonic proportions that create and govern the universe." Organicism similarly marries Romantic ideas with traditional science in its systemic view of nature, but not in the same way. The organic metaphor (born of rationalistic, linear mechanism, but going "by a sweeter name") "relates various components as constituents of a whole, constituted by some outside force, will, or intelligence," in the manner of Bacon or Coleridge. However, "the gnomic metaphor collapses all parts into self-similar versions of the whole, and it suspends all movement in time as well: it creates its object as a motionless container for all potential motion." So, whereas organicism sees "timeless cyclic stages in the natural process of birth, growth, senescence, death, rebirth," gnomicism

34. Walls, *Emerson's Life in Science*, 62, 50, 88.

collapses these into a single whole: "All its stages are the same stage."[35] I expand on similar ideas more fully in my discussion of Emerson and non-linearity in Chapter 5, after first exploring the geometric aspects of Emersonian perspective and form theory in Chapters 3 and 4, respectively.

More immediately, I would like to use this introduction to Walls's discussion of gnomic science to suggest that another way of thinking about and measuring Emerson's placing himself in the center of intellectual developments in science is to recognize the extent to which Emerson's ideas foreshadow certain tenets of nonlinear thinking. In Chapter 1, I argue that a particular style of visually centered geometric thinking characterizes Emerson's contact with the natural world. As I argue in subsequent chapters, the fact is that many of Emerson's views regarding nature have also emerged as key concepts in contemporary nonlinear science. It is neither unusual nor surprising that this should be so.

As Katherine Hayles explains, the conservative view that science has been more rigorous, more inquiring, and therefore more broadly influential than literature, presupposes a largely false dichotomy between the "two cultures":

> Frequently the [literary] critic assumes that the scientific theory has discovered the way reality actually is, and that the writer is adapting or interpreting this truth for her own ends. . . . From this standpoint it seems clear why the lines of influence between literature and science are one-way streets. If science is the source of truth to which literature responds, then of course it will influence literature much more than literature will influence it, for it is in direct contact with reality, whereas for literature reality is mediated by science. This kind of approach ignores at its peril the growing body of work demonstrating that scientific theories are themselves social constructions.[36]

Science is as much a human "art" as literature, so it is always better to recognize, as Emerson does, the broad continuities between the arts and sciences rather than their differences, if we are to have a more comprehensive view of each.

---

35. Ibid., 113 (see also 112–13), 118, 111, 119.
36. N. Katherine Hayles, "Turbulence in Literature and Science: Questions on Influence," 229.

Indeed, it is often an open question as to whether writers or labora-torists first nurtured certain scientific ideas. In *Strange Matters* (2002), Tom Siegfried outlines what he calls "prediscovery": the theoretical anticipation, or description lacking empirical evidence, of ideas that emerge in future scientific work. Prediscovery occurs for a variety of reasons, not least important of which is that intellectual development, in the sciences in par-ticular, does not occur in a vacuum; each novel "discovery" is anticipated, to varying degrees, by any number of ideas preceding it. As Siegfried points out, mathematics is often an important element in prediscovery: "Most of the prediscoveries of the past have exploited the power of mathematics to represent reality, even parts of reality that have until then never been seen." The prevailing view since Hobbes, however, is that mathematics is entirely a human invention—that is, that it offers no insights, in the Pythagorean sense, into the metaphysical aspects of reality unless and until we direct it toward that end. In other words, Hobbes believed that mathematics is always descriptive, never predictive. Siegfried writes, "The idea of math as merely a human invention may explain much of its success. But I do not see how it explains the way that math reveals unseen, even unimagined, fea-tures of reality. It's one thing to fit equations to aspects of reality that are already known; it's something else for that math to tell of phenomena never previously suspected"—as in, for example, the discovery of antimat-ter following its prediction in the equations of Paul Dirac. Prediscoveries occur most often, then, when mathematical thinking is brought to bear on what is known in order to imagine what is unknown, but this mental action can take place in a writer's notebook as easily as on a physicist's chalkboard. Some examples include Edwin Abbott's theorizing multiple dimensions in *Flatland* (1884) and Edgar Allan Poe's remarkable cosmic speculations in *Eureka* (1848). Poe offers the solution to Olbers's paradox (on why the sky is dark at night), a description of black holes, and the first, somewhat rudimentary articulation of Big Bang theory. "It was just literary imagery mixed with physical philosophy," Siegfried notes, but it was important nonetheless: Poe was a favorite author of Alexander Friedmann, who presented in 1922 the first mathematical description of the expanding universe Poe predicted.[37]

---

37. Siegfried, *Strange Matters,* 7, 9, 117 (see also 116–18).

In subsequent chapters, I focus on a very narrow subset of Emerson's philosophy, his metaphysical and experiential considerations of the natural world. However, a consideration of prediscovery in Emerson could cast a much wider net. Certainly, the idea that we can find prediscoveries in Emerson's writing is a minority view. A more common assumption has been that science provided the (lucky) corrective that kept Emerson's thinking from becoming purely ethereal—and by implication, insubstantial. Robert Richardson, for example, argues that, "though he was no scientist, he was extremely interested in the mind of the scientist and in the meaning of science for modern life" such that "science kept his thought ballasted with fact and observation and his writing anchored solidly in the real world."[38] In other words, an interest in science kept Emerson from becoming, to borrow Clark's phrase, "a mystical and irresponsible traveler in realms of Whim."

In his 1981 biography, however, Gay Wilson Allen notes that Emerson "anticipated some twentieth-century discoveries in atomic physics and revolutionary theories on the nature of matter." Allen also notes how Emerson anticipated certain key ideas in his own time as well. Discussing evolution in "Poetry and Imagination," for example, Emerson, in 1854, coined the phrase "arrested and progressive development" five years before Charles Darwin published his theory of natural selection. But evolutionary ideas, as it were, were in the air: Emerson's knowledge of evolution came by way of reading John Hunter and Robert Chambers, important precursors to Darwin's achievement. However, as Allen writes, "more surprising today is Emerson's statement about the impermanence and fluidity of matter": "First innuendos, then broad hints, then smart taps are given, suggesting that nothing stands still in Nature but death; that the creation is on wheels, in transit, always passing into something else, streaming into something higher; that matter is not what it appears;—that chemistry can blow it all into gas. Faraday, the most exact of natural philosophers, taught that when we should arrive at the monads, or primordial elements (the supposed little cubes or prisms of which all matter was built up), we should not find cubes, or prisms, or atoms, at all, but

38. Richardson, *Mind on Fire*, 153. More particularly, Richardson writes, "Emerson's interest in science and his interest in the natural world reinforce each other. He read books of science and scientific biography. He became particularly fascinated with the working of the scientific mind, with the nature of scientific knowledge, and with the strange union of precision and wonder in scientific inquiry" (142).

spherules of force" (*CW*, 8:4). Allen observes that eventually "some physicists, such and Niels Bohr and Robert Oppenheimer, began to perceive that this world of physical reality strongly resembles the 'reality' taught for centuries by Hindu, Buddhist, Taoist, and Zen mystics. By contemplating the inner world of the mind, or consciousness, the mystics arrived at concepts startlingly parallel to those of the modern physicists when they explored the external world with sophisticated instruments."[39] Today, physics asserts that matter consists not of primordial elements, the cubes and prisms of stable and inert atoms, but "spherules of force"—subatomic energy fields traversed at terrific speeds by electrons, quarks, and leptons, the behaviors of which are chaotic and capricious. In the centuries-long gap between Eastern mysticism and Western physics, Emersonian natural philosophy provides a bridge between the two. In yoking together phenomenological ideas about consciousness and speculations about the dynamic and stochastic qualities of particle physics, Emerson anticipated an expanded way of thinking about the world that is only recently being appreciated.

Additionally, Emerson's insights were more than just lucky hunches. Jonathan Bishop's brief consideration of Emerson and science, in *Emerson on the Soul* (1964), responds to Clark's questions about scientific analogies and raises some very important points. Bishop notes that Emerson "does not champion science naively." Bishop understands that if Emerson's interest in science is to be considered, in Whicher's view, "amateur," or his own scientific habits of mind, in Strauch's, "feeble," then nineteenth-century science must also be considered a very amateurish and feeble enterprise. Indeed, Bishop notes, "considering the innocently materialist and inductive habits of mind one usually associates with nineteenth-century science, Emerson's sensitivity to the subjective element in the scientific imagination is strikingly prescient." Compared to twentieth-century standards, nineteenth-century science was profoundly disorganized and unfocused.[40] Even so, Emerson still "was somehow able to single out just those aspects of the scientific quest

39. Gay Wilson Allen, *Waldo Emerson: A Biography*, 575–76.

40. As Emerson points out in the "Works and Days" chapter of *Society and Solitude*, "The savant is often an amateur. His performance is a memoir to the Academy on fish-worms, tadpoles, or spiders' legs; he observes as other academicians observe; he is on stilts at a microscope, and his memoir finished and read and printed, he retreats into his routinary existence, which is quite separate from his scientific" (*CW*, 7:183).

on which recent philosophers of science have put the most stress." In focusing on "the intellectual note of discovery" in science and in using images from science to make "images of natural mental action," Emerson anticipates some of the most important ideas of the later twentieth century.[41]

Prediscovery and *anticipation,* however, are the wrong words in this context, insofar as they are taken to indicate direct influence. Influence imputes a simplistic cause-and-effect relationship where, in this case, none is presumed to exist. Nor need it exist. The numerous correspondences between Emersonian naturalism and late-twentieth-century nonlinear science (chaos theory) are lucky coincidences in that perhaps we may be more receptive to just how radical certain of Emerson's ideas truly were, but his ideas about nonlinearity would still be there whether readers recognize them or not. Our appreciation after the fact, via Clark, Bishop, or Allen, should not obscure the necessary observation that Emerson's understanding of the world, as original as it surely is, was not worked out in a vacuum. As Eric Wilson observes in *Emerson's Sublime Science* (1999), "Indeed, the Romantic period, with its craving for an amalgamation of disciplines, particularly of poetry and science, is particularly fertile ground for an archaeological excavation of forgotten scientific nuances. Romantic uses of 'spirit,' 'energy,' 'force,' [and] 'attraction,' may have specific scientific subtexts buried underneath, undercurrents that do not reduce the meaning of the words, but give them more density, more scope, literary power."[42] The undercurrents of Emerson's science are in fact overcurrents: overt arguments about certain fundamental, nonlinear characteristics of Nature. When we consider the roles of the Poet and the Scientist in the Romantic milieu, we see that in Wordsworth's formulation of their partnership, the Poet plays the junior role. Insofar as their drawing headlong into the future is concerned, the Poet follows in the Scientist's footsteps, interpreting the Scientist's discoveries, but never leads the way. For Emerson, they stand on equal footing most of the time because, ideally, they can be one and the same figure. Both are on the leading edge of intellectual advancement, and the Poet can be the trailblazer who defines the Scientist's role as often as the Scientist can define the Poet's.

41. Bishop, *Emerson on the Soul,* 50.
42. Wilson, *Emerson's Sublime Science,* 10.

Harriett Hawkins argues in *Strange Attractors* (1995) that "as citations from artists and scientists alike may serve to demonstrate, by suggesting that comparable laws are operative both in art and in nature, chaos theory currently provides the most fruitful of all conceptual bridges between 'the two cultures.'"[43] As a first step toward exploring that idea further as it relates to Emersonian naturalism, in the next chapter I delve more deeply into the role of the Emersonian Poet/Scientist, focusing on the intersection of the actively seeing eye (as discussed in Chapter 1) and geometry (via architecture and perspective theory), in order to expand on the notion introduced in the last chapter that seeing like Emerson, and adopting his perspective in a literal way, is a necessary step toward reading Emerson and understanding his natural philosophy. By drawing connections between the functioning of the eye, the contrasts between linear and nonlinear perspective, and the conceptual problems posed by contemplations of space and infinity, I hope to begin to demonstrate in a more nuts-and-bolts manner the sort of interdisciplinary approach, discussed in this chapter, that is indicative of Emersonian science in its nineteenth-century milieu.

43. Harriett Hawkins, *Strange Attractors: Literature, Culture, and Chaos Theory,* xi.

3

THE LINES OF NATURE

The lines of nature are alike in all her works; simpler or richer in combination, but the same in character; and when they are taken out of their combinations it is impossible to say from which of her works they have been borrowed, their universal property being that of ever-varying curvature in the most subtle and subdued transitions, with peculiar expressions of motion, elasticity, or dependence.

—JOHN RUSKIN, *The Stones of Venice* (1853)

Who taught Raffaelle & Corregio how to draw? Was it Signor Quadro, the perspective-master, with his rule & dividers? No, it was the weather-stains on the wall; the cloud over the house-roof yonder, with that shoulder of Hercules, & brow of Jove; it was marbled paper; it was a lucky scratch with a bit of charcoal, which taught the secret of possibility, & confounded & annihilated Signor Quadro, & themselves also.

—RALPH WALDO EMERSON, journal entry circa April 1850

Requiring that architecture "act well," "speak well," and "look well," John Ruskin believed that the principal virtue of the Gothic mind was that it was "capable of perpetual novelty." Taking their examples from organic forms, Gothic builders sought variety rather than similarity and creativity over order, and thus they were able to create an architecture that excelled in conduct, manners, and appearance—an architecture, in other words, that reflected a mind-set fully steeped in a decorous, but unrefined, natural world. The principal defect of the Renaissance mind, on the other hand, was the extent to which it stood against the inherent disorder of the natural in its "unwholesome demand for *perfection,* at any cost," a demand seen in its architecture of similitude, equipoise, and control. The cost, it seems, was an unrealistic vision of space: Renaissance architecture makes a demand for evenness that Gothic architecture finds unworkable, "and it is one of the chief virtues of the Gothic builders, that they never suffered ideas of outside symmetries and consistencies to interfere with the real use and value of what they did."[1] For all their imbalance, dissymmetry, and grotesquery, Gothic buildings are eminently functional. They define space with an eye toward how it will be used, how it will be lived in, and what activities it is meant to support. Renaissance architecture on the other hand, building on classical aesthetic roots, defines space with an eye toward how it will appear. Consistency and symmetry dominate the aesthetic: a feature on the left calls forth a counterpart on the right; what is above must be balanced by what is below; what appears in the front must find counterexpression in the rear.

One of Ruskin's principal points is that Gothic architecture makes use of what he calls the lines of nature, and thus is integrated into its environment in a way Renaissance architecture is not. To be sure, Ruskin defends his judgment primarily on his own aesthetic grounds: Gothic architecture is better because of its affective impression on the human subject. It acts, speaks, and looks well. But Ruskin's larger point is worth noting: Renaissance architecture evidences an emerging preference among its builders for "outside" symmetries and "outside" consistencies. Rather than bounding space by means of "ever-varying curvature," thus suggesting "motion, elasticity, or dependence," neoclassical architecture is eminently linear, suggesting stasis, rigidity, and control. That is, its ideas about space are not intrinsically related to the materials at hand nor to the ultimate uses of the structure being made. Rather, they are abstract and artificially imposed by the builder. Renaissance architecture is—to make use of a well-worn phrase—not art but artifice.

The manner in which Gothic architecture acts, speaks, and looks made an impression on Emerson's mind as well.[2] Like Ruskin, Emerson valued

---

1. Ruskin, *Stones of Venice,* 29, 167, 228, 168.
2. The nineteenth-century debate over neoclassicism and the Gothic was mostly an English and Continental one, but a few Americans participated. In *English Traits,* Emerson writes, "At Florence, chief among artists I found Horatio Greenough, the American sculptor. . . . He was

internal symmetries and consistencies over external ones—"Greek architecture is geometry. Its temples are diagrams in marble, & not appeals to the
imagination like the Gothic powers of the square & cube" (*JMN*, 11:40)—
something that seems lost in post-Gothic structures. While the neoclassical
aesthetic betrayed remarkable control and simplicity of design, the Gothic
builder, he notes in "History," seems tapped into something more uniquely
human: "A Gothic cathedral affirms that it was done by us, and not done by
us. Surely it was by man, but we find it not in our man. . . . We remember
the forest dwellers, the first temples, the adherence to the first type, and the
decoration of it as the wealth of the nation increased; the value which is
given to wood by carving led to the carving over the whole mountain of
stone of a cathedral" (*CollW*, 2:7). Further, the Gothic builder was closer in
understanding to the ancient worldview of forest dwellers, one that seems
nearly lost in a post-Renaissance world. Thus, "when we have gone through
this process" of remembering and of imagining how the Gothic builders
envisioned their world, "we have, as it were, been the man that made the
minster; we have seen how it could and must be" (8).

Expanding on the same idea, Emerson points out in his lecture "Intellect
and Natural Science" that "in the designer of Gothic piles, is a reduction of
nature's great aspects in caverns and forests, to a scale of human convenience. And there is a conviction in the mind, that some such impulse is
constant; that, if the solar system is good art and architecture, the same
achievement is in our brain also, if only we can be kept in height of health,
and hindered from any interference with our great instincts" (*LL*, 1:162). To
see how architecture could and must be, then, is to understand that the best
architecture is modeled on the lines of nature—that is, on organic forms
that, once replicated in stone, reconcile man to nature and join human
imagination to nature's art. Indeed, no "lover of nature enter[s] the old
piles of Oxford and the English cathedrals, without feeling that the forest
overpowered the mind of the builder, and that his chisel, his saw, and plane
still reproduced its ferns, its spikes of flowers, its locust, elm, oak, pine, fir,
and spruce" (*CollW*, 2:12). One of Emerson's—and Ruskin's—main points

---

a votary of the Greeks, and impatient of Gothic art. His paper on Architecture, published in
1843, announced in advance the leading thoughts of Mr. Ruskin on the *morality* in architecture, notwithstanding the antagonism in their views of the history of art" (*CollW*, 5:2–3).

is that such understanding is disappearing, as the lover of Nature does not feel the forest in modern structures. In his essay "Beauty," Emerson repeats Ruskin's point that the Gothic sensibility, whether expressed in stone or other media, eschews artifice: "The lesson taught by the study . . . of Gothic art, of antique and of Preraphaelite painting, was worth all the research,— namely, that all beauty must be organic; that outside embellishment is deformity" (*CollW*, 6:154–55).[3]

Ruskin believed the preference for "outside symmetries and consistencies" to be a deficiency of the Renaissance mind, but he did not fully explore his implied preference for *inside* symmetries and consistencies. For Emerson, exploring these inside elements is the most important task, and his careful observations about architecture serve as a proper starting point: "The doctrine we preach in life is taught in architecture" (*JMN*, 12:278). Emerson suggests that outside embellishment, or artifice, does not in itself account for the deficiencies of modern architecture. Ruskin, by basing his judgment on decorum—and on the values held by the builder—emphasizes impression, or how an object is received aesthetically by the observer. In directly connecting Gothic architecture to the mind of the builder, however, Emerson emphasizes perception, or the manner in which an object is apprehended by both maker and observer. By referring to the "feeling that the forest overpowered the mind of the builder," Emerson introduces a problem of observation and insight—a matter of perspective concerned not so much with sensibility as with point of view. What Emerson stresses here is that the very act of seeing puts one in a particular relationship to what is seen, a relationship both physical and mental. Thus, the eye is an organ of the body as well as the mind, distinctive not so much for what it sees as for how it sees. To be sure, "point of view is of more importance than the sharpness of sight" (*JMN*, 3:269).

Emerson's interest in point of view is highly significant, and it indicates a wider interest in the theory of perspective. If "to be aware of perspective is

---

3. Interestingly, Emerson's opinion on "outside embellishment" seems to go against the popular notion that Gothic architecture is highly embellished and adorned, in contrast to the functional austerity of unadorned neoclassicism, but this notion is inherited from classicism itself and, to a certain extent, from the modernist aversion to Victorian ornament. Emerson's emphasis falls here on the word *outside:* embellishment itself is not a problem, but embellishment not grounded in the structural and spatial integrity of the whole certainly is.

to be aware not only of what is seen, but also of the way our particular point of view lets the seen appear as it does—to be aware of the conditions that rule our seeing," then Emerson's understanding of perspective stops not with simply an architectural or artistic problem. Perspective poses a perceptual problem deeply embedded in his entire encounter with the world, with architecture and beyond—not just in what he sees but also in how he comes to see it. "In this sense the theory of perspective is phenomenology. So understood, phenomenology lets us understand why things present themselves to us as they do."[4] But it also presents a particularly human quandary: what kind of perspective is best?

On a cosmic scale, the earth itself provides a good vantage point, a lesson almost daily taught by the discoveries of astronomy. Commenting on perspective in "The Relation of Man to the Globe," the second in Emerson's series of lectures on science, he notes that, "as if this planet were a living eye sailing through space," "the earth is to the astronomer a *moveable observatory*, enabling him to change his place in the universe, and get a base of two hundred millions of miles, as a surveyor would take new stations in a field to form triangles" (*EL*, 1:46–47). By changing one's place in the universe, and thus gaining multiple points of view, one can obtain a more comprehensive view of the whole. On other scales, however, moving from place to place is not necessarily a practical solution for the living eye. For example, Emerson's consideration of his own perspective on the world prompts him to think about what can be seen but also what cannot be seen: "A person gets a better knowledge of the fortune & results of a battle from an eminence which commands the whole tho' he see it thro' much smoke and at a far distance than the soldier can get who fights hand to hand in some corner of the field. The eye too near turns the fairest proportions of architecture or of sculpture into deformity. . . . God who is infinite may contemplate any point or atom & it will orderly reveal the whole as it *is* to him. But man who is finite must be set in the right place to see or the order will become confusion to his microscopic optics" (*JMN*, 3:269). That Emerson stresses point of view—that for him issues of insight involve issues of physical perspective—is important because understanding his way of thinking about the world means examining the literal way in which he sees it, a challenge implied throughout most

4. Karsten Harries, *Infinity and Perspective*, 42, 69.

of his writing on nature. As Robert Richardson notes, "For Emerson it is always the instructed eye, not the object seen, that gives the highest delight, that connects us with the world. Partly for that reason his favorite symbol for inquiry and knowledge and wisdom was the image of the active eye."[5]

The "image of the active eye" to which Richardson refers is that of a real, living eye. Implicit in the journal passage cited above is an acute attention to the physical placement of the observer, making clear that in referring to an act of seeing, Emerson suggests not simply a preset mental view, or a particular way of thinking about the world. At stake is the perspectival arrangement through which the living eye looks at the world, the "right place to see." The principal problem is this: vantage point, what Emerson here calls "eminence," plays a determining role not just in the act of seeing but also in the act of interpretation, of obtaining "better knowledge." The threat of "confusion" always looms. Importantly, the "right place to see" is the place that as much as possible "commands the whole." God, who in fact commands infinity, does not see with the eye but "contemplates" with the mind; the architecture and sculpture of the creation appear as they are meant to. Human beings, on the other hand, gain their "better knowledge" through the eye such that interpretive thought and vision go hand in hand. There is little difference between the mind and the eye, Emerson suggests, and they both possess similar limitations. Not only must one "see" to avoid "confusion," but also one must contend with the fact that physical sight leads directly to the possibility, even the impossibility, of insight. Thus, what cannot be seen is just as significant. While corporeality ensures a particular angle of vision through which to view the world, eyesight, and thus insight, sometimes proves to be somewhat myopic: "The human mind seems a lens formed to concentrate the rays of the Divine laws to a focus which shall presently be the personality of God. But that focus falls so far into the infinite that the form or person of God is not within the ken of the mind" (*JMN*, 5:84). In "Spiritual Laws," "Our eyes are holden that we cannot see things that stare us in the face, until the hour arrives when the mind is ripened" (*CollW*, 2:85) and the eye is instructed by its own point of view.

Questions of perspective and infinity necessarily address concerns about the nature of the divine, and vice versa. In what might serve as one control-

5. Richardson, *Mind on Fire*, 155.

ling presupposition of this chapter, Karsten Harries writes: "A passionate interest in perspective and point of view . . . offers a key to the shape of modernity. That interest in perspective is in turn bound up with theological speculations centering on the infinity of God. Only when we learn to understand these presuppositions of the destruction of the house-like cosmos of the medievals do we begin to understand its justification (or lack of justification); only then can we begin to inquire into the legitimacy of the modern world."[6] If, as Emerson writes, "The human mind seems a lens formed to concentrate the rays of the Divine laws," the focus of which "falls so far into the infinite that the form or person of God is not within the ken of the mind," then the destruction of the house-like cosmos of the medievals—insofar as it was possible in such a house to make reliable speculations about the form or person of God—becomes a very serious matter. Man, who is finite, stands in a problematic relationship to the divine infinite: How is it possible for human beings—bound by time and space—to attain the "right place to see" something not so bound, something so otherworldly as to be beyond the ken of the mind? And if infinity is part of the physical world, as indeed it is, then where can one stand, where can one obtain the correct point of view, to see it? The traditional solution to such a problem is to say that God's presence is made known through revelations of various sorts, whether historical, sacramental, inspirational, or creative. To Emerson—a man who resigned his pulpit over an issue concerning divine revelation—such a solution is suspicious in its simplicity, to say nothing of its doctrinal demands. The better, more reliable solution seems to lie within the self: in the eye, in the manner in which it sees, and in the modes of thought resulting from the act of seeing. An examination of human perspective will inevitably lead to clues regarding divine perspective; human beings, who are finite, might thus find the right place to see something of the infinite.

Perspective theory is most readily understood if grounded in its painterly contexts, yet its implications are quickly seen to have much wider reach. For Emerson, the artist's eye, that is, the artist's particular way of seeing, could in itself potentially attain knowledge of the metaphysical or the hyperrealistic. He writes in "History," for example: "A painter told me that nobody could draw a tree without in some sort becoming a tree. . . . I knew a

6. Harries, *Infinity and Perspective*, 19.

draughtsman employed in a public survey, who found that he could not sketch the rocks until their geological structure was first explained to him" (*CollW*, 2:10). Perspective brings another dimension to the question of artistic sight and representation in art because it reveals not just something about the subject of a painting as a finished product, but also something about the means by which it was imagined before brush ever touched canvas. Extrapolating to a grand scale, then, perspective can be theorized as a means by which to investigate acts of creation in the world at large. Emerson writes:

> Thus this morning I read in a Treatise on Perspective that "the end of a Picture was to give exclusive prominence to the object represented and to keep out of sight the means whereby it was done." And change the terms & of what art is not this true? It is an attribute of the Supreme Being so to do & therefore will be met throughout Creation. Every primal Truth is alone an expression of all Nature. It is the absolute Ens seen from one side, and any other truths shall only seem altered expression of this. A leaf is a compend of Nature, and Nature a colossal leaf. An animal is a compend of the World, and the World is an enlargement of an animal. There is more family likeness than individuality. (*JMN*, 5:137–38)

Emerson here quotes a passage that reveals a key insight, that is, that the picture hides the means whereby it was done insofar as the artist's intent is to guide the eye without the viewer being conscious of the fact. Presuming the artist to be successful, that is, presuming the artist is able to give *exclusive* prominence to the object represented, then the artist's method will not call attention to itself—another way of saying that the objects represented by the picture are in proper relationship to one another and that they achieve a convincing degree of verisimilitude. Making use of the metaphor, the same case applies to the picture presented by Nature, the grand canvas on which God depicts primal truths—not just the material phenomena of the natural world but also their relationship to one another. The means whereby it was done remain obscured. Yet, just as one can reconstruct the perspectival system used by the drawing master, Emerson argues, one can also, by careful use of the eye, reconstruct the perspectival system used by God in making the world. Approached the right way, divine perspective can be experienced with the whole body: "We penetrate bodily this incredible beauty: we dip our hands in this painted element: our eyes are bathed in these lights and forms" (*CollW*, 3:101). Such direct experience shows how Nature gives exclusive prominence to the real, the "absolute Ens." Each thing has its place and is evidenced by the direct experience of it: "Things are so strictly related, that according to the skill of the eye, from any one object the parts and properties of any other may be predicted" (106). Such being the case, the promise of discovering the means whereby it was done seems close at hand.[7]

As already noted, human eyesight is limited in that it cannot see all things at once. Likewise, Emerson argues, because he is finite, man can see the canvas—the painted element and the absolute Ens it presents—only from one side. Discovering the method, then, becomes in one sense a matter of seeing in reverse. Rather than look into the picture, one must look outwardly from it and thus recreate, as it were, the artist's point of view. In this way, one begins to see as the artist sees. From *Nature:*

> The first effort of thought tends to relax this despotism of the senses, which binds us to nature as if we were a part of it, and shows us nature aloof, and, as it were, afloat. Until this higher agency intervened, the animal eye sees, with wonderful accuracy, sharp outlines and colored surfaces. When the

---

7. Emerson's comments on painting, and the arts generally, emphasize process over finished product: "Beautiful details we must have, or no artist, but they must be the means, and never other. A purpose, a purpose" (*LL*, 2:217). His expectations of what art should be and do are very narrowly defined, and thus there is much in his public and private writing that seems to lend weight to Henry James's oft-quoted view that, regarding the arts, "there were certain chords in Emerson that did not vibrate at all." Commenting on their 1872 visit to the Louvre, James writes, "I was struck with the anomaly of a man so refined and intelligent being so little spoken to by works of art. It would be more exact to say that certain chords were wholly absent; the tune was played, the tune of life and literature, altogether on those that remained. They had every wish to be equal to their office, but one feels that the number was short—that some notes could not be given" (*Partial Portraits*, 30). However memorable James's opinion, it is nonetheless incorrect. What Emerson frequently objected to was the artificial exaggeration and, to his mind, lack of genius in many works of art. Above all, he valued simplicity and realism: "We ask authentic proof that an artist has been there also" (*JMN*, 7:223). Commenting on his well-documented 1832–1833 trip, Emerson writes:

> When I went to Europe, I fancied the great pictures were great strangers; some new unexperienced pomp & show; a foreign wonder; . . . When I came at last to Rome & saw with eyes the pictures, I was suddenly taught better. I saw that the picture was the reverse of all this; that it left for little people the gay & fantastic & ostentatious, & itself pierced directly to the simple & true; that it was familiar & sincere; that it was the old eternal fact I had met already in so many forms . . . I now require this of all pictures[,] that they domesticate me not that they dazzle me. (*JMN*, 7:222–23)

eye of Reason opens, to outline and surface are at once added, grace and expression. These proceed from imagination and affection, and abate somewhat of the angular distinctness of objects. If the Reason be stimulated to more earnest vision, outlines and surfaces become transparent, and are no longer seen; causes and spirits are seen through them. (*CollW*, 1:30)

As both the eye and the mind begin to see with "more earnest vision," the superficial indicators of perspectival alignment—outlines, surfaces, angular distinctions—give way to transparency, and the artist's point of view—the causes and spirits underpinning his methodology—becomes known. Earnest vision is possible because perspective necessarily unifies the artist's point of view. It dictates the elements of the picture insofar as it determines the proportional relationship of objects represented. In other words, one area of Nature's canvas cannot suggest an alternate set of relationships and thus an alternate point of view: God sees the world the same way in all times and all places because divine vision is not dependent on a fixed vantage point.[8] "The moral law lies at the centre of nature and radiates to the circumference. It is the pith and marrow of every substance, every relation, and every process" (*CollW*, 1:26). Thus it is possible, let alone true, that "a leaf, a drop, a crystal, a moment of time, is related to the whole, and partakes of the perfection of the whole. Each particle is a microcosm, and faithfully renders the likeness of the world" (27). Emerson's argument here implies a metaphysics of the grandest kind: reveal the means whereby the leaf was done, and one shall in turn reveal the method of the whole of creation. Such, in Emersonian terms, is the awesome promise of perspective.

In a familiar passage, Emerson writes, "let us not longer omit our homage to the Efficient Nature, *natura naturans,* the quick cause, before which all forms flee as the driven snows, itself secret, its works driven before it in flocks and multitudes, (as the ancient represented nature by Proteus, a shepherd,) and in undescribable variety" (*CollW*, 3:104). The quick cause, the living motivation as it were, of natural phenomena surrounds humankind and

---

8. One sees here the theological implications of postperspectival movements such as Expressionism, Impressionism, and, in particular, Cubism, all of which Emerson would certainly have regarded with suspicion. On the other hand, certain of the Impressionists—Cézanne and Matisse, for example—may very well have delighted him with their emphases on the primacy of form and color.

yet remains elusive. Why has this knowledge, or "homage," of the world seemed fleeting, as distant as "the ancient" and his gods? Why do we not already see that Nature "publishes itself in creatures, reaching from particles and spicula, through transformation on transformation to the highest symmetries, arriving at consummate results without a shock or a leap"? Because "we knew nothing rightly, for want of perspective" (*CollW*, 3:105). But if, as Emerson writes in his journal, "man who is finite must be set in the right place to see or the order will become confusion to his microscopic optics" (*JMN*, 3:269), then in this context a "want of perspective" becomes an injunction to adopt a position quite different from a system of central projection implied by the metaphor of the painted picture I have explored thus far. Divine perspective seems to be something else entirely, and, in fact, the method of central projection dictated by linear perspective serves as a very useful counterexample of the divine perspective Emerson seeks.

The search for proper perspective opens our eyes to a deeper problem, that of how to define space, the three-dimensional area any given object is presumed to occupy. The epistemology of vision reveals a metaphysics of space, but just how the two are linked is not always immediately clear, as Emerson suggests when he touches on this subject in his lecture "Moral Sense." Emerson begins by asking his listeners to "look" and "see": "Look at the house of nature, in which [man] is lodged. . . .—See the mysterious foundations of the house. Set your thought upon the space itself. Is it boundless? How can it not be? And yet again, is it? Bring home the miracle to your mind of that space, upon whose area the worlds of God are a mere dot, and the far-computing thought of man can only enter on its margin. All that exists is lost in the bosom of its great night" (*LL*, 2:145–46). Space exists, but what is it? The mystery or "miracle" of that problem presents a potentially disabling intellectual conundrum. Even though Emerson presents to his audience the comforting image of a house to frame the unfathomable expanse of the universe, the paradox verges on irreconcilable contradiction, and perhaps even absurdity: no "house" can contain an infinite space. All that exists is potentially lost in the bosom of its great night because the far-computing thought of man, though it can theorize a boundless space, cannot conceptualize or experience it in any direct way. In a similar passage from his lecture "Progress of Culture," Emerson asks his listeners again to look and consider the incalculable and "dizzy vastitudes" of the cosmos: "Look out into the July night and see the broad belt of silver flame which flashes up the half of heaven, fresh and delicate as the bonfires of the meadowflies. Yet the powers of numbers cannot compute its enormous age, lasting as space and time, embosomed in time and space. And time and space,—what are they? Our first problems, which we ponder all our lives through, and leave where we found them; whose outrunning immensity, the old Greeks believed, astonished the gods themselves; of whose dizzy vastitudes all the worlds of God are a mere dot on the margin; impossible to deny, impossible to believe" (*CW*, 8:225). As Emerson suggests in "Moral Sense," humans are stuck looking on the margin, looking but stuck nonetheless. Thus, the attempt to look, see, and think about a boundless house of nature drives us toward either psychological contradiction or a reconsideration of what it means to "see." Emerson clearly prefers the latter, and so we have, then, three problems that shall be the subject of the remainder of this chapter: the nature of space and its relationship to the eye's field of vision; the mystery of infinity as a conceptual phenomenon; and, of course, perspective and the challenging relationship of vision to thought, the very issue that leads Emerson to reflect on space and infinity in the first place.

The idea of cosmic space is a relatively modern concept. Despite our use of the same word to indicate intergalactic expanses, the Greeks' understanding of *kósmos* (a Pythagorean and Homeric term meaning "order") was very limited, as was their knowledge of the stars. Even so, Greek forays into the concept of space, in terms of definable regions, did not go much beyond the physical realm. Euclid did not theorize a background space for his geometry, and neither Archimedes nor Ptolemy conceived of the mathematical objects of their analyses as existing anywhere in particular. Early modern scientists, such as Galileo and Copernicus, followed largely in their steps, believing space to be a matter of speculation. Thus they also lacked an analytical space. Indeed, a background space for geometry, mathematics, and astrophysics did not find formal articulation until the development of Cartesian algebra, Newtonian physics, and nineteenth-century descriptive and projective geometry. Yet creating some idea of a formalized background space, different though it may be from cosmic space, was important because without it, the kind of analysis offered by Enlightenment science would have little bearing on observed phenomena, and vice versa. To speak meaningfully of not just forms and structures but also forces, vectors, and gravitation, one needs a background space in which these phenomena can take place and be observed. Thus, though the background space of mathematics, the operational space of the laboratory, and cosmic space are distinct, they must in some sense remain analogous to each other.

Certain early understandings of space reached beyond the limited range of mathematics and physical science. Early Pythagoreans, as much mystics as they were mathematicians, theorized a *kenon,* or void—a concept rejected by Aristotle. Plato distinguished between developing space, or *chora,* and *topos,* or finished space—what we think of as "place." Aristotle extended the idea of *topos* to include operational space, but limited it to the inner boundary of any given system. Newton's "absolute" space, which he defined as "always similar and immoveable,"[9] had no such limitation, and, like his mathematical theories of motion, it was fundamentally Euclidean in character. And Kant, reacting against the empiricist suggestion that all knowledge is at its core developed solely from human experience, also relied on the presumably indisputable self-evidence of Euclidean geometry to argue that space and time are not derived directly from experience but are preconditions to the possibility of knowledge, and thus absolute.

However, the arrival of non-Euclidean geometry in the nineteenth century made absolutist claims suspect, and since then many logically self-consistent geometries, each with its own spatial conditions, have developed. In the twentieth century, Newtonian physics was largely superseded, and mathematics has come to recognize that all measures of space are finally contingent upon the methods and instruments of measurement and the peculiarities of the phenomena under consideration. Thus, questions about the "real" nature of space have yielded to considerations of utility and expedience: what kind of measurement does the best job of presenting experimental information in formats capable of achieving particular ends? Thus it is that we distinguish, for example, between the classical, absolute space of *Elements* and the *Principia,* the many abstract mathematical and statistical spaces used by various disciplines ranging from geography to quantum mechanics, the cosmic space-time defined by Einstein as part of his theory of general relativity, and more popular notions, such as the newly emerging cyberspace, the properties of which are still being tested and defined.

9. Isaac Newton, *Principia Mathematica,* 8.

Of these varied conceptions of space, ancient and modern, architectural space—and from it, the space of linear perspective—is closest in character to Newtonian or Euclidean space, one element of a larger paradigm that dominated nineteenth-century understandings of space. The idea of Euclidean space, however, is not without its cautions. The points, lines, and regular shapes of Euclidean geometry lend a certain implication to the visual cues given by structures assembled after the Greco-Roman model. Even so, *Elements* does not explore the relationship of the implied space of Euclid's geometry to physical reality, an arena in which points, lines, planes, and solids do not exist with anything like the same exact and absolute properties. Further, while the properties of geometric objects are proposed, they are never asserted as necessary, and Euclid never describes or interprets the nature of space or spatiality, leaving it as only a consequence of his geometrical propositions. Two of the postulates at the start of *Elements*, however, do much in particular to indirectly define the general character of Euclidean space. Postulate Two proposes that it is possible to produce a finite straight line indefinitely. Postulate Five proposes that if a straight line is drawn to intersect two given straight lines, such that on one side of the intersecting line the sum of the interior angles is less than two right angles, then the two given straight lines, if extended indefinitely, will meet on that side (alternately, it says that two parallel lines, if extended indefinitely, will not meet). Taken together, these two postulates imply a space that is homogeneous, isotropic, and isomorphic. Which is to say, neither of the postulates will hold true unless space is the same everywhere, unless forms in space remain the same no matter where they are located, and unless forms of equal identity in two different positions in space are equal. These are the same absolutist claims taken up by Newton in the *Principia*. But as these postulates are only given, never proven, the relationship between Euclidean space and actual space remains undefined.[10]

Despite its shaky Euclidean founding, architectural space is necessarily a phenomenological construct, intimately bound up with not only the rou-

10. On the other hand, in February 2003, Euclidism found renewed cosmic relevance in the results of the Wilkinson Microwave Anisotropy Probe, which, in addition to providing the best data to date in confirmation of Big Bang theory, predict a geometrically flat universe, meaning that despite the claims of general relativity, at the largest universal scales parallel lines will not meet.

tine actions but also the very meanings of daily life. Paying particular attention to the dwelling houses of one's life reveals that architectural space is more than a mere Cartesian "extension," more than a simple area having properties of height, length, and breadth, and more than a singular expression of the homogeneous, isotropic, and isomorphic character of Euclidean space. As Brian Massumi points out, "Stable forms can be designed to interact dynamically, as bodies move past or through them singly or in crowds, or as sounds mute or reverberate, or as relations of surface and volume change with the time of day or season, or as materials change state with levels of moisture or temperature, or as the connection between inside and outside varies as an overall effect of these variations in concert with the rhythms of activity pulsing the city or countryside as a whole."[11] In other words, a building inside and out is more than the draftsman's blueprint reified. In the interplay between form and function, function claims a greater role: architectural space is neither static nor unresponsive to the world in which it exists. Form is one element in a greater context of time and movement. Thus, architectural space is potentially a living space, providing not just shelter and structural containment but a model of sentience as well. The structures one inhabits are an indication of one's thought: found in the interaction of light, form, and space is mind.

As the "house of nature" passage cited above suggests, Emerson felt most comfortable discussing cosmic space in architectural terms. But he also understood architectural space to be a metaphor, a model, and even an analogue of the entirety of one's thought. For example, just as he believes architectural space must flow from the human body, in the same manner ideas inhabit and determine the architecture of his "Scheme": "The philosophy we want . . . must be tight & fit to the form of man, to live at all; as a shell is the architecture of a house founded on the sea. The form of man, the soul of man must be the type of our Scheme, just as the body of man is the type after which a dwelling house is built" (*JMN*, 9:222–23). In a similar way, the thought/space pairing frequently extends to geographic and even cosmic structures. In praising Plato, Emerson writes, "One would say, that his forerunners had mapped out each a farm, or a district of land, or an island, in intellectual geography, but that Plato first drew the sphere" like an

11. Brian Massumi, "Sensing the Virtual, Building the Insensible," 22.

"all-knowing Greek geometer" or a "Euclid of holiness" who "marries the two parts of nature." And further: "He kindled a fire so truly in the centre, that we see the sphere illuminated, and can distinguish poles, equator, and lines of latitude, every arc and node" (*CollW,* 4:48–49).

Thus, just as point of view qualifies the act of seeing, so too do models of space reflect the conditions that govern the act of thinking. Rectilinear *perspectiva,* on which so many of the early ideas on architectural space depend, is a clear case in point. It developed in multiple variations, but the first written account occurs in Leon Battista Alberti's *De Pictura* (1435), a widely disseminated work, that was the most commonly known in the period. Modern terms for the method—vanishing point, horizon line, and the like—were first used by Brook Taylor, in his *Linear Perspective* (1715). The development of rectilinear perspective arose from an increasing emphasis on scientific naturalism over theological realism in Renaissance art. In its use of imaginary lines converging toward vanishing points located on a horizontal horizon line, the linear perspective developed during the Renaissance period offers a powerful system of representing objects drawn on a flat canvas in relative proportion. Indeed, "the most obvious function of [linear] perspective was to rationalize the representation of space: With the advent of perspective, it became much easier to stage, as it were, elaborate group scenes organized in a spatially complex fashion." Following from this advance were two other key benefits for the artist, "the means to produce a compelling illusion of depth" and "the means for drawing the spectator's eye to the key figure or action in the painting."[12] Indeed, artists who mastered perspective were adept at using it to create illusion, narrative focus, structural focus, and symbolism. In other words, linear perspective provides the means not just to rationalize space but to psychologize it, to control not only what is seen but also what meaning can be taken from it.

The significant breakthrough of linear perspective, the method initially described by Alberti, is that it breaks the picture plane into interrelated regions—the long-familiar foreground, midground, and background—in such a manner that the sizes of objects depicted in these regions retain a precise proportional relationship, no matter how far they might appear to recede into the background. Thus, linear perspective creates the illusion of

12. Michael Kubovy, *The Psychology of Perspective and Renaissance Art,* 1–2; see also 3–7.

depth and distance, an impression of three-dimensionality on a flat surface, presented as though, in the case of a painting hung vertically, one were merely looking out a window into the landscape or even, in the case of a ceiling fresco, into the sky overhead. In this manner, perspective purports to give a verisimilar impression of reality, and not until the advent of photography would this feat be outdone. However, "it is essential to keep in mind that the scheme of central projection is a convenient geometric fiction" because "it can be misleading to link it too closely with vision."[13] The simple fact is that linear perspectival representation deviates widely from the mechanics of actual sight. "For the sake of achieving his mastery of appearances the painter reduces experience to momentary, monocular vision and places us on a flat earth"—a conception of vision that is patently untrue. In this way, "the perspectival art of Alberti subjects what it presents to a human measure that has itself been subjected to the demand for ease of representation."[14]

Despite its advantages in representation, linear perspective offers up a false impression of reality; that is, it does not represent space as it is actually perceived by the observer. The first critic to point out this problem with more than a passing degree of ingenuity was Erwin Panofsky in his monograph essay *Perspective as Symbolic Form*, published in 1927. Receiving widespread attention because it offered critics a new means of analyzing the historical emergence of abstraction in modern art, *Perspective as Symbolic Form* argues that linear perspective could be seen as "a particular constructional approach for representing pictorial space . . . which happened to be peculiar to the culture of the Italian Renaissance." Thus, Panofsky "seemed to be saying that linear perspective was not the last word in pictorial truth, that it, too, could pass away as had all earlier artistic conventions." What is important in Panofsky's argument is that it suggests how "each historical period in Western civilization had its own special 'perspective,' a particular symbolic form reflecting a particular *Weltanschauung*."[15] The fact of the matter is, though, that Renaissance conceptions of space, tied as they are to the rise of modern science, spread far wider than the time and place in which they originated. Indeed, the effort to mathematize and psychologize

13. Ibid., 20–21.
14. Harries, *Infinity and Perspective*, 77.
15. Samuel Y. Edgerton, *The Heritage of Giotto's Geometry: Art and Science on the Eve of the Scientific Revolution*, 153, 157.

nature along linear perspectival foundations had its impact well into the twentieth century.

In his evaluation of modern linear perspective, Panofsky observes that "this 'central perspective' makes two tacit but essential assumptions: first, that we see with a single and immobile eye, and second, that the planar cross section of the visual pyramid can pass for an adequate reproduction of our optical image." In truth, Panofsky argues, we see with two moving eyes whose visual field is spherical, an observation similar to one Emerson makes in *The Conduct of Life:* "The senses interfere everywhere, and mix their own structure with all they report of. Once, we fancied the earth a plane, and stationary. In admiring the sunset, we do not yet deduct the rounding, coordinating, pictorial powers of the eye" (*CollW,* 6:166). Such is the power of the circular eye that it exposes any false abstractions held in the mind of the viewer. Because of its rounding power, we eventually see, Panofsky writes, that "exact perspectival construction is a systematic abstraction from the structure of . . . psychophysiological space," that is, space as one actually experiences it.[16] The contrast between psychophysiological space and the space constructed by rectilinear perspective is worth noting carefully. The picture rendered with linear perspective offers a kind of window on the world, but, as Panofsky points out, the "world" as rendered by linear perspective is a very abstract one. For example, it assumes a planar ground surface, neglecting the fact that, assuming a round planet, a true ground surface is curved. Further, a true horizon is created when the curved ground surface drops below our line of sight, and it wraps around the visual field to the left and right. Linear perspective, on the other hand, offers a straight horizon of presumably infinite length extending beyond the picture frame, neither created nor constituted according to the limitations of actual vision. It also offers a planar visual field, a construct most frequently reinforced by a flat canvas.[17]

16. Panofsky, *Perspective,* 29, 30.

17. Emerson writes, "The rainbow & the horizon seen at sea are good curves" (*JMN,* 9:36). The perceptual abstraction posed by the infinite horizontal horizon line is perhaps more easily perceived if one imagines not a horizontal but a vertical, parallel to the viewer's own body. Such a line would, in real life, appear to wrap behind the viewer both overhead and underfoot, an effect readily noticed when one stands next to the objectively flat wall of a very tall building. A similar and greatly exaggerated effect can be created in a photograph by means of a wide-angle lens.

Panofsky's argument is grounded in certain observations on the nature of perception made by the formalist Swiss art critic Heinrich Wölfflin, who argued that just as one cannot experience an infinite space, one also cannot experience a homogeneous space—that is, one that is fundamentally the same at all points and in all directions. However, in simply assuming that one can, linear perspective "transforms psychological space into mathematical space."[18] Panofsky's point in this analysis is that such a transformation leads to the ascendancy of an abstract mode of perceiving the world that is cut off from direct experience. Indeed, "by the early seventeenth century ... perspective theory had arrived at such a position of abstraction from the effects of nature, that it became a deductive science"[19]—so much so that, by ignoring the effects of natural perception, linear perspective effectively removes the natural human observer from the picture, even as it confines the observer by concentrating the visual image toward a fixed and immobile point of view.

Panofsky adhered to two controversial positions, namely that ancients such as Euclid and Vitruvius conceived of the visual world as curved, and that the concave surface of the retina makes for a curved visual plane. Both of these beliefs were soon challenged. But the ancients did have a somewhat more holistic approach toward perspective: "The medieval science of *perspectiva* [or optics] was a complete science of vision. It dealt not only with the nature and behaviour of light but also with such matters as the anatomy and functioning of the human eye. On the whole, in the Middle Ages, as in ancient times, philosophers were agreed that seeing was an active process." In this light, Panofsky's argument—simply that the presumably infinite and homogeneous spaces arising from linear perspective do not accord with our perception and experience of actual space—is not without merit. At stake for Panofsky is a contrast between an ancient worldview and a modern one, in which the perceiving human subject is removed. In Albertian perspective, such attentiveness to the biology of sight disappears. Further, these two worldviews contrast most pointedly in the way they perceive objects in the world. In the ancient and medieval view, "if two magnitudes are of equal size then the one which is nearer the eye will appear larger—in the sense

18. Panofsky, *Perspective*, 31; see also 30–31.
19. Martin Kemp, *Geometrical Perspective from Brunelleschi to Desargues: A Pictorial Means or an Intellectual End?* 91.

that it subtends a larger angle at the eye." Thus "antique optics maintained, always and without exception, that apparent magnitudes (that is, projections of objects onto a spheroidal field of vision) are determined not by the distances of the objects from the eye"—as in Renaissance perspective—"but rather exclusively by the width of the angles of vision." Antique optics necessarily limits outward space according to the structures of psychophysiological space. In short, it imagines the world based on the way the eye sees it. Renaissance perspective does no such thing. "That this rationalized artificial perspective does violence to the natural perspective that rules our visual experience is a fact of which a Leonardo or a Kepler was well aware. But such violence was a price gladly paid for greater mathematical control."[20]

Linear perspective represents space as homogeneous and boundless, and it seems no accident that this is so. The presumption of an infinite, homogeneous space containing the greater structures of the universe was of primary importance to the development of the early modern sciences (particularly astronomy) in their various attempts to replace an Aristotelian, church-sanctioned cosmology with a Galilean, and eventually Newtonian, account of the universe. After all, if the newly developing laws of physics were to apply everywhere, space had to be of such a nature as to allow for this possibility. At the heart of the new scientific endeavor, however, was an attempt not merely to understand and not merely to predict, and thus control, the natural world. Rather, the goal was to account for the development of the natural world in extrahuman terms, in an ideal language whose universal applicability would pertain without check. The endeavor widened to embrace several aspects of human life as well, as "painting was just one activity to draw mathematics into its service: merchants and bankers, masons and goldsmiths had come to insist on a certain mastery of mathematics"—a certain mastery that only mathematical analysis could provide. Indeed, the development of linear perspective and the emergence of other early modern sciences—from navigation to economics—go hand in hand. In a large sense, the modern age is marked by a "replacement of the teleological and organismic pattern of thinking and explanation by the mechanical and causal pattern." More specifically, it is marked by the emergence of "the belief that the universe is ordered and rationally explicable in terms of [Euclidean] geome-

20. J. V. Field, *The Invention of Infinity: Mathematics and Art in the Renaissance*, 6–7; Panofsky, *Perspective*, 35; Harries, *Infinity and Perspective*, 78.

try" and "a deterministic world-picture which viewed nature as stable and unchanging, and considered that mastery of it could be achieved by universal mathematical principles." Linear perspective both arises from and contributes to such assumptions in that "the spatial illusionism of one-point perspective reflected a world which was permanent and fixed in its ways, modeled on an absolute space and time unrelated to any outward circumstance."[21] Though certain meteorological phenomena might evidence the most obvious counterargument, this prevailing belief would not meet serious challenge until the early twentieth century.

We see in Emerson that, rather than being an attempt to rationalize space, the examination of perspective is a process of self-discovery: "There is no cheaper way of giving great pleasure than when we simply describe from our center the disk, & direction of the ray of the surrounding orbs"; and its result runs much deeper than intellect alone: "The drawing of the line is for the time & person a perfect solution of the formidable problem & gives great pleasure when Iphigenia & Faust do not" (*JMN*, 7:92). Emerson's most important meditation on perspective is to be found in the essay "Circles," which, as its very title suggests, explores a perspectival system more in line with ancient and medieval understanding (*CollW*, 2:177–90).[22] Fashioning what has been called "a paean to nonlinearity,"[23] the argument of this essay flows directly from Emerson's interest in perspective, and it demonstrates the powerful impact ideas about perspective had on his thinking.

The epigraph poem from "Circles" explicitly addresses the perceptual problem posed by perspective, the link between point of view and intellectual insight:

> Nature centres into balls,
> And her proud ephemerals,
> Fast to surface and outside,
> Scan the profile of the sphere;
> Knew they what that signified,
> A new genesis were here.

21. Harries, *Infinity and Perspective,* 16; Alexandre Koyré, *From the Closed World to the Infinite Universe,* 31; S. Gablik, *Progress in Art,* 70.

22. In the following discussion of "Circles," all quotations from the essay may be found in these pages.

23. Rossi, "Emerson, Nature, and Natural Science," 127.

The opening paragraph of the essay summarizes the epigraph poem, beginning with the image of the sphere of Nature scanned by seeing human beings, "her proud ephemerals": "The eye is the first circle; the horizon which it forms is the second." Emerson was a keen scanner of the earth's natural horizon. He lists "the horizon seen at sea" as one of nature's "good curves" (*JMN*, 9:36), and his 1833 crossing to Europe gave him ample opportunity to learn the method of the navigator—"I am learning the use of the quadrant. Another voyage would make an astronomer of me"—and ponder its implications: "The experiment of the philosopher is but a separation to bring within his optics the comprehension of a fact which is done masterly & in harmony in God's laboratory of the world" (*JMN*, 4:107). But by referring in this essay to the circular horizon *formed* by the circular eye, Emerson refers to the visual plane, not to the natural horizon of the earth. Importantly, the visual plane is not flat, as a rectilinear canvas would have it, but spherical, as though the viewer were standing inside the sphere formed by the surrounding natural world. In this sense, then, the "horizon" also refers to the boundary between seen and unseen, pointing to the crucial difference between human sight and divine sight. He continues: "Throughout nature this primary figure"—that is, the circle—"is repeated without end. It is the highest emblem in the cipher of the world." This statement in itself argues that the unity of subjective experience and material reality is derived from phenomenal curves—the key to understanding divine sight—yet, Emerson argues, mankind has not yet begun to understand this cipher: "We are all our lifetime reading the copious sense of this first of forms" and its consequent effects, that "every action admits of being outdone" and that "every end is a beginning." These phrases interpret, respectively, the phrases "what that signified" and "a new genesis" from the last lines of the epigraph poem. What Emerson suggests here is that Nature's circularity is not simply static: the structural pattern undergirding material phenomena admits of process and development. Nature's sphere is not simply geometric, but algorithmic as well. It must be understood as a design folding and unfolding in a continuous series.

Emerson's claim at the beginning of "Circles" about the essential circularity of Nature, and the centrality of human perception, is only a starting point for his larger claims about the fundamental character of the natural world. The main argument of the essay begins with the beliefs that Nature is dynamic and spatially expansive but also that it is neither infinite nor homogeneous as a linear conception of space demands. In linear space, objects are fixed, located and locatable along a regularized grid work of lines and their points of intersection. In dynamic, or nonlinear, space, such regularity disappears. "There are no fixtures in nature. The universe is fluid and volatile. Permanence is but a word of degrees." This is the key supposition of the whole essay. To an eye scanning the whole sphere of Nature, not just the second circle formed by the visual horizon but everything it contains, permanence is quite literally a matter of degrees. The world changes according to one's point of view, one's angle of vision. It cannot be rendered simply as a "mass of facts" arranged in a linear series. Emerson's main point here is that, for all of its mystery, the "cipher of the world" is deceptively simple. Process takes precedence over stasis, and evolutionary action over inert materiality. Thus nature presents a dynamic system, not a static construct. "Every ultimate fact is only the first of a new series," he writes. "Every general law only a particular fact of some more general law presently to disclose itself." Thus, there is an infinitude, a kind of permanence, to be found in iteration, or the method of continuous replication suggested by the image of the primary figure of the circle repeated without end. The material phenomena one encounters through the senses are not merely discrete entities, objects explained by a "mass of facts" such as linear quantification would allow. No, "the principle that seemed to explain nature will itself be included as one example of a bolder generalization." Indeed, although at first "Nature looks provokingly stable and secular," "it has a cause like all the rest," a "secret" that can be brought into view. "Once I comprehend that, will these fields stretch so immovably wide," Emerson writes. "Every thing is medial. Moons are no more bounds to spiritual power than bat-balls."

If the logical consequence of Nature's circularity is that it has no "fixtures," then "the key to every man is his thought," and the key to his thought is his vision. In other words, man is inevitably part of the cipher he sees because the "second circle" formed by the eye is in fact two circles, both an outward horizon and an inner one. Emerson's point is that subjective experience is the key toward understanding material reality, and not vice versa. "The life of man is a self-evolving circle, which, from a ring imperceptibly small, rushes on all sides outwards to new and larger circles, and that without end." As such, the individual soul, and not just the eye, is the perceiving element in man. Perspective, because it dictates subjective experience, contains a spiritual element, and "the extent to which this generation of circles ... will go, depends on the force or truth of the individual soul."

If "step by step we scale this mysterious ladder" of new principles being constantly discovered among the old, we only do so when, as suggested by the epigraph poem, we know what the encounter with Nature's circles signifies. "The eye is the first circle" one encounters, and the "horizon it forms," or the visual plane it perceives, is the second. In this manner, "the eye" and "this mysterious ladder"—the series of circles one continues to encounter as the primary figure of Nature—"are effects of one cause." Here Emerson announces the bold phenomenological proposition of the essay: the curved eye forms the bridge between Nature (that is, tactical space) and Mind (that is, psychological space). What he suggests is that the cipher of Nature is a circle *because* the eye is round, and this primary fact informs the first stage of his whole contact with Nature. For example, a clearer articulation of this idea appears in "Fate," from *Conduct of Life:* "I do not wonder at a snow-flake, a shell, a summer landscape, or the glory of the stars; but at the necessity of beauty under which the universe lies; that all is and must be pictorial; that the rainbow, and the curve of the horizon, and the arch of the blue vault are only results from the organism of the eye" (*CollW,* 6:26). Before he contemplates beauty as an effect, Emerson recognizes the "necessity" of beauty, or its inevitable cause: the innate curves of a fundamentally "pictorial"—that is, perspectival—natural world resulting from the action of the seeing eye. As a result, the secret of Nature must be read in the eye's circular shape and the organic perspective it produces. Similarly, in "Circles," just as the permanence of Nature (the presumption that it can be understood as a "mass of facts") is but a word of degrees (or relative to one's line of sight), so too must it be true that "there are no fixtures to men, if we appeal to consciousness." In this conception, then, tactical space and psychological space, through the action and structure of the eye, *must* coincide. Any distinction between objective and subjective collapses; the Me and the Not-Me become one. As in Nature, so in man; as in man, so in Nature. Potentially, he can occupy both positions at one time: "I am God in nature; I am a weed by the wall."

The only true constant in this configuration is the endless iteration of the primary figure. As Emerson writes in "History": "Nature is an endless combination and repetition of a very few laws. She hums the old well known air through innumerable variations" (*CollW,* 2:9). And in "Compensation": "each new form repeats not only the main character of the type, but part for part all the details, all the aims, furtherances, hindrances, energies, and whole system of every other" (*CollW,* 2:59). For this reason, Emerson writes in "Circles," if "man who is finite must be set in the right place to see," then the proper attitude for him to take is like that of the eye: stable, yet sensitive to Nature's steady motion, "so that a man cannot have his flank turned, cannot be out-generalled, but put him where you will, he stands. This can only be by his preferring truth to his past apprehension of truth; and his alert acceptance of it, from whatever quarter." Insight then becomes a "flash of the eye" that "burns up the veil which shrouded all things, and the meaning of the very furniture, of cup and saucer, of chair and clock and tester, is manifest.... All that we reckoned settled shakes and rattles; and literatures, cities, climates, religions, leave their foundations, and dance before our eyes." Seeing is an act of creating, akin to the medieval view that the eye, rather than gathering rays of light, sends out beams of its own.[24]

From this point, Emerson again makes the claim that meaning, in its fullest sense, is determined by how one sees, and that thought is intimately linked to perspective: "Much more obviously is history and the state of the world at any one time directly dependent on the intellectual classification then existing in the minds of men. The things which are dear to men at this hour are so on account of the ideas which have emerged on their mental horizon, and which cause the present order of things as a tree bears its apples." Emerson's argument is similar to Panofsky's: he states that each age has its own understanding, its own perspective through which it views the world. To take hold, the insight of a new age—the "flash of the eye"—must render a new perspective, such that all things, "property, climate, breeding, personal beauty, and the like, have strangely changed their proportions." True insight produces a new way of seeing, and "here again [we] see the swift circumspection" of the eye scanning a horizon. By way of example, Emerson explores the role literature—"a point outside of our hodiernal circle, through which a new one may be described"—plays at different times for different groups. Like architecture, "we see literature best from the midst

24. Emerson refers directly to eyebeams, for example, in *Conduct of Life,* and notes that "the organ of sight is such a vehicle of power" (*CollW,* 6:96).

of wild nature, or from the din of affairs, or from a high religion" because it, too, is subject to the perspective of the eye. "The field cannot be well seen from within the field. The astronomer must have his diameter of the earth's orbit as a base to find the parallax of any star." Indeed, parallax, the apparent displacement of celestial bodies caused by changes in the position of an observer due to the earth's rotation and orbit, becomes a dominant theme in this essay. As previously mentioned, the first circle of the eye and the second circle of the horizon are not fixed and stable: "The natural world may be conceived of as a system of concentric circles, and we now and then detect in nature slight dislocations, which apprize us that this surface on which we now stand is not fixed, but sliding." These dislocations, which result in the effects of parallax, highlight the extent to which one must be continually aware of perspective, but they apprize us also of the dynamic systems underlying natural phenomena. Our understanding is determined by the act of perception conducted by the eye, but we are, as it were, "sliding" and always in motion. Perception itself is subject to a kind of movement, and parallax a consequence of any attempt to see things as they really are.

Such being the case, Emerson addresses the main question that arises from his analysis: what then, if anything, can be considered objective in a strict sense? Summarizing his critics' response, he writes, "O circular philosopher, I hear some reader exclaim, you have arrived . . . at an equivalence and indifference of all actions, and would fain teach us that, *if we are true*, forsooth, our crimes may be lively stones out of which we shall construct the temple of the true God!" His response is to remind readers that the divine imagination of the individual soul, and the all-encompassing act of perception, remains at the center of all circles. "This incessant movement and progression which all things partake could never become sensible to us but by contrast to some principle of fixture or stability in the soul." In other words, movement is only perceptible when one's perspective, if not one's perception, is stable. In this, Emerson imagines individual perspective as being somewhat akin to temperament: "That central life is somewhat superior to creation, superior to knowledge and thought, and contains all its circles." Thus, the proper role of human beings—the key to their happiness—is something of a paradox as it consists in assuming an attitude of creative discovery: "Whilst we converse with what is above us, we do not grow old, but grow young. Infancy, youth, receptive, aspiring, with religious eye looking upward, counts itself nothing, and abandons itself to the instruction flowing from all sides. . . . People wish to be settled; only as far as they are unsettled is there any hope for them." Creative discovery reveals a kind of infinitude, a kind of eternity. It is to embrace not just the primary figure, but the repetition. "The one thing we seek with insatiable desire is to forget ourselves, to be surprised out of our propriety, to lose our sempiternal memory, and to do something without knowing how or why; in short, to draw a new circle." The only caveat is that we must be prepared to draw such circles without end. To Emerson's mind, the "religious eye looking upward" symbolizes the attempt to find and assume a divine perspective, and what it sees will be an iterated series touching all things, flowing onward without beginning or end.

Like the ancients in Panofsky's analysis, Emerson considered the mechanics of sight to be of major significance. Though he held that "point of view is of more importance than the sharpness of sight," Emerson understood that the mind's ability to compose a visual image was in part dependent on the structure of the eye, and perhaps more. "Such is the constitution of all things," he writes in *Nature*, "or such the plastic power of the human eye, that the primary forms, as the sky, the mountain, the tree, the animal, give us a delight *in and for themselves;* a pleasure arising from outline, color, motion, and grouping. This seems partly owing to the eye itself." Emerson gives the eye's "plastic power" just as much importance as the natural arrangement of the objects one sees. He continues: "The eye is the best of artists. By the mutual action of its structure and of the laws of light, perspective is produced, which integrates every mass of objects, of what character soever, into a well colored and shaded globe, so that where the particular objects are mean and unaffecting, the landscape which they compose, is round and symmetrical" (*CollW,* 1:12). The key word in this passage, aside from language suggesting curvature, is "integrates." It signals the fact that perspective, as Emerson here conceives of it, is phenomenological. The active eye is a "well colored and shaped globe," and it creates, in turn, a "round and symmetrical" visual image as a result. The curvature of the eye directly impacts the manner in which one sees, creating an organic perspective that is clearly not rectilinear. In what might serve as an explanatory gloss to this passage from *Nature,* Kepler, in *Ad Vitellionem Paralipomena,* writes: "This world is indeed visible and is itself concave and round, and whatever in the hemisphere we perceive as greater than it in a single glance, this is equal in its rotundity. It therefore follows that the proportion of individual things to the entire hemisphere is estimated by vision in proportion to the image entering in upon the hemisphere of the eye. And this is commonly called the angle of vision."[25] The eye is the best of artists. Seeing is a creative act, setting otherwise "mean and unaffecting" objects into harmonious relationships, set in proportion according to the manner in which they are seen. In so doing, it brings to light the angle of vision, the point of view, the perspective through which one sees the world. It makes the eye an organ of the mind. Indeed, "What is life but the angle of vision?" Emerson asks. "A man is measured by the angle at which he looks at objects" (*CW*, 12:10).

Emerson begins his essay on circles with a clear understanding of universality; his is not just a meditation on human ethics but on cosmic structures as well. The circle stands as the "first of forms," emblematic of the fact "that there is no end in nature, but every end is a beginning; that there is always another dawn risen on mid-noon, and under every deep a lower deep opens." As a cipher, the circle symbolizes the fact that "our globe seen by God is a transparent law, not a mass of facts," a law that "dissolves the fact and holds it fluid." By embracing the circle, "around which the hands of man can never meet," Emerson hopes to gain something of the perspective of the divine artist of the world. He hopes to attain, as it were, a vision of all-encompassing space and infinitude. Further, in referring elsewhere to the "globe" of the eye and the "round" landscape of the visual image, Emerson's words suggest something other than a linear conception of perspective: if by the "mutual action of its structure and of the laws of light" the eye produces a perspective, it does not naturally produce a rectilinear perspective.

The problems of perception arising from the mechanics of the eye and the organic perspective it produces prompt deeper problems, namely those of how one conceives of infinitude. Infinity is traditionally understood to be that which is eternal, unlimited, immeasurable, without beginning or end, or without frontier. It naturally prompts theological questions regarding the

---

25. Johannes Kepler, *Joannis Kepleri Astronomi Opera Omnia,* 2:167. On this point, Kepler elsewhere cites Wilhelm Schickhardt of Tübingen: "Our vision does not in fact have a plane surface like a tablet, on which it contemplates the painting of a half-sphere, but rather that image of the sky, against which it sees comets, it produces in itself as spherical by natural instinct of vision; and if the image of objects is projected into a concave sphere with straight lines of extension, the representations of those lines will be not straight, but in fact curved, just as in the circle, no doubt, of the greatest sphere, if it is seen from its center, as we teach about projection in circular astrolabes" (*Appendix Hyperaspistis* 19, in *Opera Omnia,* 7:292).

absolute and the perfect. Infinity has not been seen as simply a religious question, but its relationship to the human sciences, and to mathematics in particular, has nonetheless been strained. Mathematics, even in its simplest arithmetic form, presupposes the infinite, yet many have considered infinity to be beyond useful study, and empiricists such as Berkeley and Hume regarded it as a concept one could, and should, do without. Not until the advent of transitive arithmetic in the nineteenth century did it become an object of formal study.

The central mystery of infinity is that no matter how one defines it, it always seems to remain just beyond one's grasp: though human beings can theorize infinity, they cannot directly experience it. Two ancient examples illustrate the problem. The paradoxes of Zeno—for example, the stadium paradox, which argues that a runner will not reach the finish line of a racetrack because he must first reach the halfway point of the decreasing distance to the line, ad infinitum—argue for the infinite divisibility of time and matter (a real property), yet they seem to have no practical application to reality. And the square root of two, discovered by the Pythagoreans (likely by Pythagoras himself), has very useful practical applications, but its infinite fractionality destroys any notion of a universe constituted by and intelligible through positive integers. In both instances, mind and matter are at odds over a problem created by infinity. To resolve it, Aristotle proposed two ways of thinking about infinity by distinguishing in the *Physics* between the actual infinite and the potential infinite. The actual infinite exists in its entirety at some defined point in time. The potential infinite exists over time and not at any single given moment. Having developed this distinction, Aristotle questioned whether or not the actual infinite even exists, but he believed the potential infinite to be a fundamental feature of reality. Following on Aristotle's distinction, Kant, though skeptical of infinity, held that time and space (both part of an *a priori* nonphysical reality) are infinite in the sense that both are unbounded and endlessly divisible. The contents of space and time, however, present another matter, and as physical beings, Kant argued, we have no way of knowing, nor ever using, such infinitudes in any practical way.[26]

---

26. Of course, in proposing his conception of the sublime—the apprehension of certain phenomena that go beyond the ability of the mind to fully "contain" them by means of its perception or comprehension—Kant argued that such disturbing experiences do indeed serve as an indirect way for the human subject to sense the power of the moral law within.

By positing a conception of space as boundless and homogeneous, linear perspective takes infinity for granted. As Panofsky points out, linear perspective makes certain assumptions about space that do not pass the test of visual perception, namely that space is infinite and homogeneous. As such, space becomes decentered and entropic, and linear perspective becomes merely a means of asserting analysis and control over this kind of abstract space. By ignoring the parameters and conditions imposed by direct experience and the act of seeing, linear perspective in effect lifts consciousness out of the mind, insofar as it presents as true-to-life a visual image that clearly is not so. However, direct experience, as mediated by the biological act of seeing, suggests a different conception of space. One sees with moving eyes in a spheroidal field of vision, framed by a circular periphery. Space appears both bounded and heterogeneous: consciousness necessarily forms a center, and the brain's arrangement and framing of a coherent visual image suggest cohesion. In addition, the fact that the relationships through which one perceives spatial dimension (such as near/far, up/down, left/right, and the like) are not absolute further suggests the shifting characteristics of space.[27] More than this, however, rectilinear perspective presents only the option of the actual infinite, of an ever-expansive space presented in a single moment in its entirety. Alternately, nonlinear perspective, the biological perspective produced by the eye, presents a potential infinity. In this conception, space is not infinitely expansive and homogeneous. Rather, it "flows" and "slides":

27. Reflections, mirages, illusions, and other *trompes l'oeil* frequently reorder one's perceptual construction of space and further suggest its heterogeneity. While some would dismiss such phenomena as being no more than amusing psychological and/or physiological *errors* (presuming such exist), to do so calls into question the mind's ability to perceive "real" space at all, as well as its intimate connection to consciousness and perception. The essay "Experience" clarifies the fact that Emerson considers the whole cosmos—and by extension, space—to be a product of the eye. In this essay, optical perception serves as a running metaphor for teleological considerations of nature and human life. "Of what use is genius," Emerson primarily asks, "if the organ [that is, the eye, a common analogue for the mind in Emerson's writing] is too convex or too concave, and cannot find a focal distance within the actual horizon of human life?" (*CollW,* 3:30). In such situations, "our life is not so much threatened as our perception" (27). Emerson's response, of course, is to point to temperament—which causes one to see things slightly out of focus. But even so, he suggests, our optics might not be perfected: "There is no end to illusion. Life is a train of moods . . . [that] prove to be many-colored lenses which paint the world their own hue, and each shows only what lies in its focus." Thus, finally, Nature "belong[s] to the eyes that see [it]" (30) and "thus inevitably does the universe wear our color" for "as I am, so I see" (45, 46).

the bounded circle is its primary form made evident by the structure of the eye and the curve of the visual field.

These different conceptions of infinity, and the conflicts to which they give rise, struck Emerson deeply and personally. Perhaps some of the most familiar passages in Emerson's writing (for example, from *Nature*, "Standing on the bare ground,—my head bathed by the blithe air, and uplifted into infinite space . . . I see all; the currents of the Universal Being circulate through me; I am part or particle of God") and his most familiar themes (such as the "infinitude of the private man") convey a sense that conceptions of infinity posed little problem for Emerson. This assumption is furthered by certain memorable passages from his private writing, as for example when he claims, "Through the running sea of forms I am truth & love & I transcend form & time & space" (*JMN*, 7:429). However, referring only to passages such as these is apt to convey an incomplete picture; the spectrum of Emerson's vision is much more variegated. There is an inherent inconsistency in his search for a divine perspective (capable of seeing an actual infinity) that will replace the human perspective (capable of seeing only potential infinities) to which all persons are inevitably bound. By recognizing the limits of one's capacity for insight, how can one hope to see beyond a human point of view? Noting this problem, Emerson writes: "My geometry cannot span the extreme points which I see. . . . I affirm the divinity of man; but, as I know well how much is my debt to bread, & coffee, & flannel, & heated room,—I . . . do affirm also with emphasis the value of these fomentations. But I cannot reconcile that absolute with this conditional" (*JMN*, 11:210). The contrast he sees between absolute and conditional highlights a relatively straightforward complaint, that divinity and mortality stand in opposition. But a recognition of the fact that his geometry cannot, in cause-and-effect fashion, span the extremes also directly influences what Emerson believes may be accomplished by one's experience of the infinite: one's movement through space and time is limited. As mapped out by "Circles," "The life of man is a self-evolving circle, which, from a ring imperceptibly small, rushes on all sides outwards to new and larger circles, and that without end" (*CollW*, 2:180). Here, Emerson's space expands outward from the individual. It is, in a sense, infinitely expansive, but that is not all. Its circularity betrays a certain measure of reflection. That which rushes outward on all sides is marked by continuous return; endpoints are presumably never achieved: "The great mind finds ample spaces, vast plains, yea populous continents, & active worlds moving freely within these elastic limits & indeed never approaches the terminus on either side" (*JMN*, 5:89). Elsewhere he writes, more simply, "Extremes meet: there is no straight line" (*JMN*, 8:396). So, while a great degree of movement is possible, all-encompassing movement is not. While "God's ways are parabolic projections that do not return into themselves" (*JMN*, 9:172), man's ways are circles, concentrically aligned around the self, extending outward, yet always falling within "elastic limits." Confirming this view, Emerson later writes that rather than be part or particle of God, "I am part of the solar system. Let the brain alone & it will keep time with that as the shell with the sea-tide" (*JMN*, 9:218). In this comparison, the self is, like the solar system, described by a series of concentric circles but, like the ocean's tides, blanketed by a series of rhythmic emanations. Elsewhere, he writes to similar effect, "It seems to me that in the procession of the soul from within outward it enlarges its circles ever like the pebble thrown into the pond or the light proceeding from an orb" (*JMN*, 7:86). The constant mixing of metaphors may seem like only a peculiar—sometimes irritating, sometimes quaint—habit of Emerson's Romantic mind, but in actuality it displays a very personal attempt to grapple with and articulate the problem of infinity.

If Emerson's geometry cannot span the extreme points, where, then, is divine perspective to be found? Where can the human mind find greater insight into the infinite? The answer is that space and infinitude must be reconfigured as something internal, something inward-looking. As such, the important structures—structures that illuminate cosmic architecture— must also be found internally—not necessarily within the self, but always within the various objects of nature. For example: "If such slight & transient things often produce in us deepest results . . . what may we not expect from a familiar & full comprehension of the amazing discoveries that the Naturalists of this day have made: from the wonderful application of polarized light to the discovery of periodical colors in refrangible substances & so to the uncovering of nature's primary forms in the secret architecture of bodies" (*JMN*, 4:94). Behind this passage lie fundamental assumptions about space and infinitude. Within nature's primary forms (that is, organic forms), both inside bodies and inside the mind, the scientist's presumed linearity does not exist, for certainly "there is more beauty in the morning cloud than the prism can render account of" (*JMN*, 4:95). If an examination of perspective shows that linearity does not describe the world as one actually experiences it, then linearity cannot describe the entirety of the world as it really is. Looking inward, or rather looking into, to find internal structures ought reasonably to reveal what sort of nonlinearity will apply.

Certainly discovering the secret architecture of Nature is not an easy task, as the sheer breadth of the material world presents itself to the mind as being beyond total comprehension. And even if space is best understood as something internal, the universe, like infinity, may by definition be too vast to be comprehensible. On several occasions, Emerson confirms this view: "Quite analogous to the deceits in life, there is, as might be expected, a similar effect on the eye from the face of external nature. . . . Her mighty orbit vaults like the fresh rainbow into the deep, but no archangel's wing was yet strong enough to follow it, and report the return of the curve" (*CollW*, 3:111–12). Still, even though *external* nature's mighty orbit seems too vast for practical use, there is a great deal of spatial awareness informing Emerson's thought. What does he mean, then, when he refers to space? "Emerson's description of the oversoul or his expanding 'circle' of experience," writes Taimi Olsen, "suggests spatial and temporal dimensions. Emerson created an entire spatial map for his philosophy, one that includes a field of depth (through a three-dimensional concept of the oversoul) and of expansion (the circle). He used his spatial imagination to free his thought."[28] Olsen's comments highlight the fact that Emerson did indeed make use of a spatial map—but one must recognize it as a mental map more than anything. To Emerson, ideas of space and infinity appeal to the inner self; he generally does not use these words to refer to something objective and "out there." Rather, space is the product of a psycho-temporal map; it is a psychological construct that serves visual perception as well as the mind: "The relations of parts and the end of the whole remaining the same, what is the difference, whether land and sea interact, and worlds revolve and intermingle without number or end,—deep yawning under deep, and galaxy balancing galaxy, throughout absolute space, or, whether, without relations of time and space, the same appearances are inscribed in the constant faith of

28. Taimi Olsen, *Transcending Space: Architectural Places in the Works of Henry David Thoreau, E. E. Cummings, and John Barth*, 32.

man? Whether nature enjoy a substantial existence without, or is only in the apocalypse of the mind, it is alike useful and alike venerable to me. Be it what it may, it is ideal to me, so long as I cannot try the accuracy of my senses" (*CollW*, 1:29). What Emerson suggests here is that space is not a thing to him; it is not objective (that is, "absolute") in the Newtonian/Humean sense. Rather, space is the habitude of the soul, that animating force of life which is made manifest in form—what Emerson calls "the visibility of spirit" (*JMN*, 9:117). While perception is sometimes antithetical to the action of the soul, as when it makes the "mighty orbit" of nature seem too vast to comprehend—or when, in "The Over-Soul," "the influence of the senses has, in most men, overpowered the mind to that degree, that the walls of time and space have come to look real and insurmountable"—"yet time and space are but inverse measures of the force of the soul" (*CollW*, 2:162). The soul, not the eye or the mind, "circumscribes all things" and "abolishes space and time" (162), rendering both unnecessary.

Hence the reliance in Emerson's philosophy on form, and the ability of form to lay open the secret lines of nature's architecture. Thus, space must be reconfigured as being not that which gives, in a Cartesian sense, extension to objects in the world—suggesting that an inherent property of material objects is their ability to impinge on other material objects—but that which gives them their form. In this conception, space is not a void to be filled but rather like a mold that determines structure, pattern, and shape—a force, as it were, that bestows containment and cohesion. While in "Intellect" "Nature shows all things formed and bound" (*CollW*, 2:194), also in "History" "Nature is a mutable cloud, which is always and never the same. She casts the same thought into troops of forms" (*CollW*, 2:8). The cosmos, like a cloud, is uniformly heterogeneous—always and never the same. The same force of containment creates the unending variety of nature—"The adamant streams into soft but precise form before it, and, whilst I look at it, its outline and texture are changed again. Nothing is so fleeting as form; yet never does it quite deny itself" (8)—such that delineating the secret lines of nature becomes only a problem of perception.[29] "Painting teaches me the splendor of colour, & the expression of form. . . .—And then is my eye educated to see

29. Note that his use of the noun *adamant* (meaning "hard substance" or discrete matter) underscores that *form* in Emerson's usage is not Platonic.

the eternal picture which Nature paints" (*JMN*, 7:177). Not only that, though. The eye is educated to see beauty, order, cohesion, flow, and congruity—the relationships of space, nature, and form as they truly are:

> The pleasure a palace or temple gives the eye, is, that an order and method has been communicated to stones, so that they speak and geometrize, become tender or sublime with expression. Beauty is the moment of transition, as if the form were just ready to flow into other forms. . . . Beautiful as is the symmetry of any form, if the form can move, we seek a more excellent symmetry. The interruption of equilibrium stimulates the eye to desire the restoration of symmetry, and to watch the steps through which it is attained. This is the charm of running water, sea-waves, the flight of birds, and the locomotion of animals. This is the theory of dancing, to recover continually in changes the lost equilibrium, not by abrupt and angular, but by gradual and curving movements. (*CollW*, 6:155–56)

The opening sentence of this passage from "Beauty" reiterates the lessons taught in the same essay by Gothic architecture, "that all beauty must be organic; that outside embellishment is deformity" (155). More importantly, though, two general points here signal an explicit account of the nonlinear character of space, nature, and form. "If [forms] can move," Emerson writes, they will "flow into other forms" thereby producing "a more excellent symmetry"—a result unavailable to static, absolute, linear accounts of space and perception. Further, such natural symmetry "stimulates the eye" and causes it to "watch the steps" by means of which symmetry is produced. "Not by abrupt and angular" steps, "but by gradual and curving movements" is this balance attained: no single object exists discrete and alone, and all things partake of the harmony of the whole system. Hence Nature, its vast array of "troops of forms," engages the eye in a kind of dance, an unfolding series of "gradual and curving movements," the next movement always growing out of the previous one. "The new mode is always only a step onward in the same direction as the last mode; and a cultivated eye is prepared for and predicts the new fashion" (156). It is in this sense that endpoints are never achieved, that location cannot be rendered explicit in absolute terms, that infinity is never absolute, and that all phenomena partake of the curvature of the eye.

The "cultivated eye" sees that form is the visibility of spirit, that it lays open the contours of space and, as a result, the lines of nature. Reading these lines for the secrets they contain is always a matter for the eye, when properly trained in organic and nonlinear modes of perspective. Only then, Emerson believes, does one truly become an artist. And more than anything else, Emerson sees himself as an artist, painting in hues of spectacular vibrancy:

> Instead of lectures on Architecture I will make a lecture on God's architecture, one of his beautiful works, a Day. I will draw a sketch of a Winter's day. I will trace as I can a rude outline of the foundation & far assembled influences[,] the contribution of the Universe whereon this magical structure rises like an exhalation, the wonder & charm of the immeasurable Deep. The bed of a day is eternity, the groundplan is Space. The account of its growth is Astronomy. Its nearer phenomena are Chemistry, Optics, Agriculture, Hydrostatics, Animated Nature. It ends again in Astronomy when it has carried forward by its few rounded hours the immense Beneficence. (*JMN*, 4:60)

Like the master of a new school, Emerson proposes to paint in words a canvas in which architecture, infinity, space, and science (most notably astronomy) come together, revealing the "magical structure" of the whole. In the next chapter, I explore Emersonian form theory in terms of both natural geometry and organizing principles. This "flowing law," as Emerson called it, is at the heart of his natural philosophy and reveals what he believes to be deep insufficiencies in the methods of traditional Newtonian science. As well, it introduces the ways in which Emerson theorized nonlinearity in the natural world.

4

FLOWING LAW

The Universe is like an infinite series of planes, each of which is a false bottom, and when we think our feet are planted now at last on the Adamant, the slide is drawn out from under us. Value of the skeptic is the resistance to premature conclusions. If he prematurely conclude, his conclusion will be shattered, & he will become malignant. But he must limit himself with the anticipation of law in the mutations,—flowing law.

—Ralph Waldo Emerson,
journal entry dated Autumn, 1845

As the eyes of Lyncaeus were said to see through the earth, so the poet turns the world to glass, and shows us all things in their right series and procession. For through that better perception he stands one step nearer to things, and sees the flowing or metamorphosis.... This insight, which expresses itself by what is called Imagination, is a very high sort of seeing, which does not come by study, but by the intellect being where and what it sees; by sharing the path or circuit of things through forms, and so making them translucid to others.

—Ralph Waldo Emerson,
"The Poet," *Essays: Second Series* (1844)

In Chapter 3, I argued that the primary role of Emerson's Poet is to provide a model for a certain kind of visual perception. More particularly, I argued that the theory of perspective Emerson develops is phenomenal—that is, Emersonian perspective is grounded in the curved and living eye, leaving virtually no room for abstract and unnatural linear models of seeing. One major consequence of this Emersonian perspective, however, is that the infinity suggested by unbounded and endlessly divisible space becomes a product of the mind, experienced inwardly: space becomes in Emerson's account a psychotemporal event, not simply an outward and independent reality. What Emerson's active seeing and nonlinear perspective also show is that our human point of view on the world can indeed reveal much about "flowing law," or the interrelatedness of natural forms as revealed by "muta-tion." If the Poet's insight occurs, as has often been noted, "by the intellect being where and what it sees," it also occurs when vision allows the Poet to "shar[e] the path or circuit of things through forms." Thus, if the Poet "turns the world to glass" by employing a particular kind of active seeing— "a very high sort of seeing"—then the kind of psychophysiological perspec-tive such seeing engages in teaches us that all things participate in a kind of "flowing or metamorphosis" expressed by the image of iterating circles, from the curvature of the eye to the spheroidal shape of the visual plane to the incidence of primary shapes repeating themselves without end. In addi-tion, the algorithm guiding the development of living organic bodies—the sort of "programming" that today is commonly attributed almost exclu-sively to genomic encoding—also describes a process of iteration. This chapter addresses the theory of form, grounded in a model of iteration, that follows from Emerson's phenomenal and nonlinear way of seeing and high-lights certain points of contrast with the cause-and-effect model favored by conventional nineteenth-century science.

Emerson looked primarily to the arts for a description of what he fre-quently calls the "true science" of nature, but even there he did not always find what he sought. In "Nominalist and Realist," he writes: "Art, in the artist, is proportion, or, a habitual respect to the whole by an eye loving beauty in details. . . . Proportion is almost impossible to human beings. . . . In modern sculpture, picture, and poetry, the beauty is miscellaneous; the artist works here and there, and at all points, adding and adding, instead of unfolding the unit of his thought. Beautiful details we must have, or no artist: but they must be means and never the other. The eye must not lose sight for a moment of the purpose" (*CollW*, 3:138).[1] Emerson regularly connects flowing law and metamorphosis directly to the beautiful. *Beauty*, however, is admittedly a vague term in Emerson's writing—as he himself knew: "I am warned by the ill fate of many philosophers," he notes, "not to attempt a definition of Beauty" (*CollW*, 6:154). Most often, however, Emerson refers alternately to some ineffable quality inherent to natural objects or to a proclivity of the mind for organization. In an early work such as *Nature*, for example, "the plastic power of the human eye" reveals beauty, such that "the primary forms, as the sky, the mountain, the tree, the animal, give us a delight *in and for themselves;* a pleasure arising from outline, color, motion, and grouping" (*CollW*, 1:12). In a later work such as *The Conduct of Life*, "Beauty is the form under which the intellect prefers to study the world. All privilege is that of beauty; for there are many beauties; as, of general nature, of the human face and form, of manners, of Brain, or method, moral beauty, or beauty of the soul" (*CollW*, 6:153). However it may be defined, a common point of emphasis in Emerson's discussions of beauty is that it occurs when the details—in art as well as nature—display "a habitual respect to the whole." Beauty, in other words, emerges harmonically, when even the very small and the very large resemble each other across their respective scales. Emerson's Nature is telescopic: true proportion, even if "almost impossible" for human beings to grasp, describes the way in which natural forms "unfold," or slide inward and outward into each other in overlapping sections. In the passage from "Nominalist and Realist" quoted above, Emerson criticizes "modern" art because it attempts to imitate beauty through a method of "miscellaneous" addition and not a principle of iteration, or the unfolding of a single unit into a variety of other self-similar forms. The purpose of "true art" is the same as that of "true science": to

1. Architecture from the linear neoclassical school offers an aesthetic of imposed abstractions—and is a clear counterexample of the organic proportion preferred by Emerson: "I read in Sir Christopher Wren—'Position is necessary for perfecting beauty. There are only two beautiful positions of straight lines, perpendicular and horizontal—this is from nature & consequently [the] necessity [of] no other than upright being firm. Oblique positions are discord to the eye unless answered in pairs, as in the sides of an equicrural triangle'" (*JMN*, 5:213). Wren's assumption that "this is from nature" erroneously attributes straight lines to nature, and his standard of beauty preferences modular addition—"answered in pairs"—over organic iteration.

reveal the unfolding, to emphasize the beauty of metamorphic iteration—a process, as the Poet demonstrates, first perceived by the eye and then contemplated by the mind.

But even the Poet is not always the one who "penetrate[s] bodily this incredible beauty" or the one whose "eyes are bathed in these lights and forms" of Nature (*CollW*, 3:101). Poetic insight is not dependent on position or intellectual training: "The day-laborer is reckoned as standing at the foot of the social scale, yet he is saturated with the laws of the world. His measures are the hours; morning and night, solstice and equinox, geometry, astronomy, and all the lovely accidents of nature play through his mind" (*CollW*, 3:136). In this passage from "Nominalist and Realist," Emerson's Thoreauvian day laborer, like the Poet, also "stands one step nearer to things." Even if at the foot of the social scale, the day laborer's vocational nearness to the natural world accords access to the higher scales of insight and knowledge of the true geometry of nature. In every way, he is not the university man: like someone who "does not tie his shoe without recognising laws which bind the farthest regions of nature," Emerson writes in "Nature," the common person, too, knows that "moon, plant, gas, [and] crystal, are concrete geometry and numbers" (*CollW*, 3:107). His understanding arises from a direct apprehension of the world. It is grounded in neither the Platonic abstraction of *Elements* nor the linear reductionism of *Principia Mathematica*. It allows for "happy accident" and spontaneity, thereby eschewing the iron rules of Euclidean logic and Newtonian cause and effect.

Emerson displays in passages such as the one above from "Nominalist and Realist" not only his familiar concern for holistic considerations of nature but also his deep distrust of "adding and adding" wherever it may be found— from the modular analysis of Newtonian physics to the Cartesian notion of structural equivalence classes. Indeed, Emerson sets himself apart from most, if not all, representative modes of Enlightenment thinking. Given that most intellectual historians consider the modern era to have begun with Bacon, Descartes, and Locke (and in this sense, "modern" serves to distinguish the Enlightenment from the medieval and ancient worlds), modern thinkers generally exhibit one or more of the following dominant traits: a totalizing, reductive regard for the past; a skeptical approach to theories of thought, existence, and will; a belief in a fundamentally material cosmos and its subsequent "natural laws"; and a discontent with anything as of yet "unexplained" by ordinary scientific investigation, especially those phenomena (and their moral corollaries) traditionally falling under the purview of religion. Emerson's own approach to history, psychology, physics, and faith, displayed amply throughout his work, exhibits little, if any, of these qualities.

Further, John Barrow summarizes the difference between modern and premodern by noting a crucial difference between the types of questions each age was willing to ask. "The Greek ideas of Aristotle attained a preeminence in philosophical thinking in Europe" before the Renaissance. "Aristotle laid great stress upon the purpose of things as revealing their true meaning and significance. He was interested in 'why' things happened as well as 'how'"; however, "figures like Copernicus, Galileo, and Newton," who articulated a functionalist epistemology, "tailored the objectives of science to answering the 'how' questions and not the 'why'" by filtering out medieval Christians' incorporation of Greek ideas.[2] The ascendancy of Enlightenment thinking, then, can be measured in part by the descent of Aristotelianism. Emerson, however, looks to Aristotle for a model of more balanced thinking. As he points out in the essay on Montaigne from *Representative Men*, "Every fact is related on one side to sensation, and, on the other, to morals. The game of thought is, on the appearance of one of these two sides, to find the other." The game of thought, in other words, requires that given the how, one must also ask the why, because having a balanced perception of nature requires both. The first side of every fact, which appeals to the senses, is "conversant with facts and surfaces." The second side, that of morals, is concerned with "identity," "faith," and "philosophy" (*CollW*, 4:85). To have a balanced understanding of the "mysterious principle of life" running throughout nature, Emerson suggests, one must take the two sides together. One cannot have a balanced understanding of nature by asking only the "how" questions—relying solely on "sensation" and a merely functionalist epistemology. Echoing Aristotle's explication of virtue in the *Nicomachean Ethics*, Emerson adds, "I know that human strength is not in extremes, but in avoiding extremes" (89).

Emerson calls anyone who finds the Aristotelian balance between the two sides of nature, presented in the Montaigne essay, a skeptic because such a person "labors to plant his feet, to be the beam of the balance" (*CollW*, 4:88). Thus, as Emerson notes in his journal, the "value of the skeptic is the

2. John D. Barrow, *The World within the World*, 363.

resistance to premature conclusions" (*JMN*, 2:295). An influential tradition of skepticism runs through the development of modern science, and it also claims as a goal the prevention of premature conclusions. However, Emerson's understanding of skepticism is at odds with the scientific notion of skepticism. Grounded in the principle of Ockham's razor, scientific skepticism reacts against Scholasticism and seeks the simplest answer over the complex one, focusing not just on the how without the why, but also on the simplest how. It prefers minimalism, or explanations of natural systems that use the fewest number of elements and contextual parameters. Thus it also leads to a proclivity to assume that the simplest is the most real, because that which is clear and distinct must therefore be most fundamental. For example, in the *Discourse on Method* (1637), Descartes explains his approach to epistemology by noting that "the *first* [precept] was never to accept anything for true which I did not clearly know to be such . . . and to compromise nothing more in my judgment than what was presented to my mind so clearly and distinctly as to exclude all ground of doubt." In *An Essay Concerning Human Understanding* (1690), Locke similarly argues, "We should not then perhaps be so forward . . . to raise Questions, and perplex our selves and others with Disputes about Things, to which our Understandings are not suited; and of which we cannot frame in our Minds any clear and distinct Perceptions, or whereof . . . we have not any Notions at all." And in *An Enquiry Concerning Human Understanding* (1748), Hume pushes the idea even further: "When we entertain, therefore, any suspicion that a philosophical term is employed without meaning or idea (as is too frequent), we need but enquire, *from what impression is that supposed idea derived?* And if it be impossible to assign any, this will serve to confirm our suspicion. By bringing ideas into so clear a light we may reasonably hope to remove all dispute, which may arise, concerning their nature and reality."[3] In other words, Descartes, Locke, and Hume each make an argument (appealing to and also validated by skepticism) for seeking out simple, clear, and distinct ideas about our world and ourselves, and for eschewing the complex, ambiguous, and affective. They value specialized understanding: straightforward analysis carried out in reductive contexts and resulting in minimalized, precise explanations. This

---

3. René Descartes, *Discourse on Method,* 17–18; John Locke, *An Essay Concerning Human Understanding,* 45; David Hume, *An Enquiry Concerning Human Understanding,* 20–21.

leads them as well to assume that it is possible to derive knowledge that is foundational, or fully explicit and unpolluted by human assumptions, even though so many aspects of human experience (mind, freedom, and will, for example) and the natural world (such as causation, flow turbulence, or phase transitions) do not fit into their rigorous paradigm—a fact even Hume begrudgingly acknowledged.

Because of its skepticism and minimalism, linearity resists the idea of qualitative change; it has no means of explaining natural processes except quantitatively. It explains change as a mechanical process that can be predicted by the Newtonian laws of motion, within a universe of absolute space and time, for, as Newton understood it, all matter was made up of atoms and "atoms were also impenetrable and inert, and therefore did not move, unless acted upon by outside forces." Additionally, motion "was continuous, as matter was not, and mathematically calculable. But motion brought about no sort of qualitative change, only the spatial displacement of atoms or their aggregates."[4] Such a worldview has significant consequences: it posits, in theory, a universe that is entirely deterministic, predictable, free of uncertainty, free of history, and free of novelty. But phenomena that consist of abrupt, discontinuous change—what is observed, for example, when bubbles burst, when a steady flow of water suddenly becomes turbulent, or even when someone experiences a "eureka" moment—must be described by something more complex than Newtonian laws of motion. Such phenomena point toward the qualitative dimension of the natural world.

The qualitative aspects of Nature are perhaps the most recognizable of Emersonian themes. Addressing the difference between functional and teleological explanations in the essay "Nature," Emerson highlights this issue in particular, as when he writes: "The astronomers said, 'Give us matter, and a little motion, and we will construct the universe. It is not enough that we should have matter, we must also have a single impulse, one shove to launch the mass, and generate the harmony of the centrifugal and centripetal forces. Once heave the ball from the hand, and we can show how all this mighty order grew.'—'A very unreasonable postulate,' said the metaphysicians, 'and a plain begging of the question. Could you not prevail to know the genesis of projection, as well as the continuation of it?'" (*CollW*, 3:107). The

4. Baumer, *Modern European Thought*, 460.

matter-and-motion view of the astronomers posits a universe of discrete particles impinging on one another like balls on a billiard table. It is purely functional. In this case, any notion of "causation," a qualitative category, is presumed to be false: as Hume argues in *An Enquiry Concerning Human Understanding*, what we experience as causation is instead a series of discrete states in succession, which, presumably, could develop forward or backward in time without any meaningful difference. And, if a process is fundamentally physical, and thus reversible, how can it be said to have a cause, or an origin, or even a purpose? The metaphysicians, as Emerson has framed the debate, raise a key point: where does the impetus for motion come from? Where do we look for the "one shove to launch the mass"? Might it point to a qualitative dimension to nature? In answer to this problem, Emerson writes: "Exaggeration is in the course of things. Nature sends no creature, no man into the world, without adding a small excess of his proper quality. Given the planet, it is still necessary to add the impulse; so, to every creature nature added a little violence of direction in its proper path, a shove to put it on its way; in every instance, a slight generosity, a drop too much" (107). Each thing in creation contains within it "a drop too much"; as such, its existence, role, and influence on everything else around it requires more than a linear, merely functional understanding. The very problem with the matter-in-motion worldview, Emerson believes, is that it posits an explanation that ends up being no explanation at all: "there is throughout nature something mocking, something that leads us on and on, but arrives nowhere, keeps no faith with us. . . . Every end is prospective of some other end, which is also temporary; a round and final success nowhere" (110). In other words, Nature has a qualitative dimension; everything in it possesses what Emerson calls a "small excess" of its "proper quality"—a "something mocking" that escapes simple functional explanations. Indeed, recognition of this situation becomes a defining point in "The Transcendentalist": "The materialist respects sensible masses . . . every establishment, every mass, whether majority of numbers, or extent of space, or amount of objects. . . . The idealist has another measure, which is metaphysical, namely, the *rank* which things themselves take in his consciousness; not at all, the size or appearance" (*CollW,* 1:203). Size and appearance are easily analyzed, but rank is clearly a qualitative category, one that is all but wiped out by traditional science.

As Humean skepticism prescribes a regimen of consistent and unrelenting doubt, the "real" is that which survives the rigors of suspicion. Thus, that which Hume deems "real" has been brought "into so clear a light we may reasonably hope to remove all dispute" of its being assumed to exist on self-evident grounds. Practiced in this way, then, skepticism drives toward authoritative and singular explanations, a convention that relies directly, of course, on the principles of linear philosophy to which the philosophy of flowing law is opposed. With characteristic ironic humor, Emerson dismisses reductive skepticism outright: "The cool disengaged air of natural objects, makes them enviable to us, chafed and irritable creatures with red faces, and we think we shall be as grand as they, if we camp out and eat roots; but let us be men instead of woodchucks, and the oak and the elm shall gladly serve us, though we sit in chairs of ivory on carpets of silk" (*CollW*, 3:106). Skepticism in Emerson means a refusal to settle on any one explanation as final. It implies a constant openness to broader understanding, to complex analysis, intricate contexts, and multifaceted—even contradictory—explanations. It recognizes that Nature "keeps her laws, and seems to transcend them," such that "if we look at her work, we seem to catch a glance of a system in transition" (105). Analytic expansiveness, Emerson argues, is thus able to capture best the many contexts of the whole system. Rather than truncate, Emerson advises, the true skeptic enlarges.

Humean skepticism promotes the notion that "real" knowledge is formalizable and also the notion that the only objective (that is, unbiased) experience is one that can be rendered fully explicit. As Emerson knew, such expectations are nearly always doomed to result in disappointment and eventually in anxiety about the place of human beings in the world—a natural springboard, among others, for deconstructionist analysis. John Michael's *Emerson and Skepticism* (1988) is one such that pursues the skepticism-as-doubt model. Michael argues that "skepticism in [Emerson's] early texts furnishes the means for a liberating critique of popular dogma and of institutional authority," but "skepticism also forces the doubter to seek confirmation for his inner sense of things in the external criteria of his community's judgment, in the pragmatic affirmations and refusals of practical reason and common sense." Hence, "the texts of the 1830s do not represent"—in contrast to Stephen Whicher's influential judgment—"the

triumph of Emerson as an individual and separate self; they reiterate a challenge . . . [that] is, as Emerson comes to realize, unanswerable." Michael sees
in Emerson's "oddly textured and sometimes tortuous prose" someone who,
tellingly, "is more essentially our contemporary." Thus, of the "game of
thought" presented by Emerson in his essay on Montaigne, Michael argues
that "the middle ground on which this exercise leaves the skeptic is not one
of pragmatically assured self-reliance—as critics have so often claimed—but
one in which the self is caught up by and defined in the conflict between the
opposing forces that it mediates." However, in David Jacobson's view, "It is
not enough . . . to infer from the destructive elements of Emerson's thought,
from his skepticism in general, that his theory merely overthrows meaning,
or that it leads to a prolific indeterminacy, or least of all, that it leads to some
sort of broad deconstructionist position." Jacobson's 1990 essay "Vision's
Imperative" explores Emerson's "practical imperative" and argues that "Emerson's skepticism does not function within the limits of the epistemological
project that largely defines modern philosophical thought." To assume that
it does "thus runs a sizeable risk: that of inappropriately situating Emerson's
thought in a context he would not recognize as his own."[5]

In addition to the outcomes of Humean skepticism, linearity forms a
broader intellectual context Emerson would also not recognize as his own. As
it grew in importance during the past few centuries, it directed the development of modern scientific thinking above all other intellectual systems, with
its assumptions becoming the operational premises of many different disciplines. Linear thinking is directed, rigorous, and geared toward achieving specific ends. Thus, linear equations, for example, offer single solutions based on
recognized parameters. Linear thinking places all phenomena in linear relationships: Linear relationships can be graphed via a straight line, as on a
Cartesian grid. Linear relationships are modular, meaning that the whole is
the sum of its parts and nothing more. Linear relationships describe direct
proportion, influence, and cause and effect; they describe how two or more
phenomena correlate, coordinate, or coincide. Thus, linear relationships are
easily captured by language ("the bigger, the better") and pictorial or symbolic
signs. They are easy to think about, and easy to apply for analytic purposes.

5. John Michael, *Emerson and Skepticism: The Cipher of the World*, xi–xii, xiii, 107; David
Jacobson, "Vision's Imperative: 'Self-Reliance' and the Command to See Things as They Are,"
557–58.

The most representative linear relationships are the mechanical laws of planetary motion laid out by Isaac Newton in the *Principia* (1687). In this work, Newton formalizes the mechanics of Galileo, who, in his *Two New Sciences* (1665), abandoned Aristotle's argument that causal physical explanations best describe natural phenomena, and stated instead that science should pursue description and not causation, that science should follow deductive (that is, mathematical) reasoning, and that scientific principles should be based on experimentation rather than the conclusions of the intellect. Thus, Galileo simply described what he observed and did not concern himself with, for example, *why* falling bodies accelerate; simply knowing *how* they do so was enough. Further, Galileo, like Kepler before him, regularly deferred to Euclidism, noting in *The Assayer* (1623) that the universe "is written in the language of mathematics, and its characters are triangles, circles, and other geometric figures without which it is humanly impossible to understand a single word of it; without these, one wanders about in a dark labyrinth."[6] Such characters form the basis of describing and understanding the world in terms of strict linear relationships.

Following Galileo's philosophy, Newton developed his three famous laws of motion, from which he was able to deduce the inverse square law of universal gravitation and thus combine Kepler's three laws on planetary motion (in *The New Astronomy* [1609] and *Harmony of the Worlds* [1619]) with Galileo's laws on terrestrial motion. Newton's success in accurately approximating the motion of physical bodies by means of determinative mathematical laws ensured the rise of Galilean science (strictly descriptive, mathematical, and experimental) and the standardization of Newton's own methods. Furthermore, when Kant (in *Metaphysical Foundations of Natural Science* [1786]) divided human knowledge of nature between the rational discovery of inherent, internal principles and a cataloging of mere sensory impressions, and argued that real science lay with the former, the response to "rationalize" science in the manner of Newton guaranteed the spread of the linear paradigm—even though certain significant gaps in its account of the organic natural world remained.

The oxymoron *accurate approximation* is intentional. As time and further experimentation showed that the Newtonian scheme did not account

6. Galileo Galilei, *The Assayer*, 237–38.

for all natural phenomena, those that did not fit the paradigm—various forms of chaotic behavior, for example—were attributed to experimental "error" and were considered as largely unimportant. This view came to be encapsulated by perturbation theory, the belief that the dominant behaviors of natural systems are explained by linear dynamics (Newton's laws of motion) and that nonlinearities within the systems, or so-called "weak effects," are mere perturbations, or irregularities that do not change the qualitative behavior of the whole. For example, small deviations in the expected positions of known masses in the solar system—the revelation, in other words, of discrepancies between predictions made through calculation and actual data collected from observation—were seen to require only refined calculation and did not undermine faith in the regularity and reliability of the matter-in-motion worldview.[7]

Nonetheless, until the advent of Einstein's theory of general relativity, faith in the underlying linear logic of Newtonian theory remained strong—so much so that the largest conceptual gap in Newtonian physics, the problem of *actio in distans,* or how it is that physical bodies exert influence on one another over a distance, remained unsolved. Newton's laws presuppose that actions such as motion or the application of force have physical causes, yet the effects of gravity, as Newton openly acknowledged, cannot be so explained.[8] Despite such criticism, primarily from Leibnitz and Berkeley, eighteenth- and nineteenth-century scientists ignored the issue: "They were so flushed with success in following Newton's lead that they lost sight of the problem of explaining the *physical* nature of gravitation. They resorted to the mechanical law of gravitation, and their successes . . . in deducing some known irregularities in the heavenly motions and in encompassing new phenomena were so great, so remarkably accurate, that the problem of explaining the physical action of gravitation was buried under a heap of

---

7. Such a process led, for example, to the discovery in 1846 of Neptune, the existence of which was previously inferred from unexpected anomalies observed in the orbit of Uranus. On the other hand, discrepancies were not always so easily resolved: in 1878 the existence of a new planet called Vulcan was announced (predictions of which were based on anomalies observed in the orbit of Mercury), but it later turned out not to exist.

8. General relativity explains gravity not in terms of physical attraction between masses, but in terms of curvatures in space-time. Celestial bodies orbit one another (planets around stars, moons around planets, and so on) because smaller masses are caught in depressions in space-time (or gravitational wells) created by larger ones.

mathematical papers."[9] As a result, the admittedly stunning successes of Newtonian physics allowed its failures to pass virtually without notice, such that the whole linear paradigm came to be regarded as not just comprehensive, but exhaustive.

The rise of linear philosophy to dominance was also bolstered by changes in the role and aims of an increasingly linear and abstract system of mathematics, changes that brought the "language" of science further and further away from real analogues in the natural world. On the one hand, in the world of architecture, for example, where mathematics is used for practical application, an emphasis on fundamental scales, rather than organic wholes, began to emerge. The more truly Pythagorean approach to proportion used among the ancients and medievals, in which the successive subdivisions of harmonic scales derived smaller proportions from larger ones—as in the familiar division of golden rectangles, for example—preserved the idea of unified wholes inherent to classical aesthetics. In the Renaissance, this aesthetic remained influential; however, improved building techniques and stronger materials allowed for much more expansive building projects, and structures came to be seen as assemblages of smaller units rather than divisions of larger ones. Gradually, the harmonic scale was replaced by an arithmetic one, in which the successive multiplication of a fundamental unit determined the dimensions of larger pieces. Thus, "the first, or harmonic, system was used by those seeking to develop an abstract mathematical canon of proportion, while, as in the case of the [architectural] orders, the second, or arithmetical, system was found convenient by those whose approach . . . was more empirical."[10] And on the other hand, eventually figures like David Hume, in *A Treatise of Human Nature* (1739) and *Of the Standard of Taste* (1757), and Edmund Burke, in *Enquiry into the Origin of Our Ideas of the Sublime and Beautiful* (1757), argued that concepts such as beauty, if properly understood, were only subjective truths of the perceiving individual and not objective truths intrinsic to particular entities in the world. Thus, the beautiful in architecture, as in art generally, came to be seen as having nothing to do with either harmonic calculation or the principles of Euclidean geometry, but with whatever needs and tastes may suit a particular time and

9. Morris Kline, *The Mathematical Search for Knowledge*, 231–32.
10. P. H. Scholfield, *The Theory of Proportion in Architecture*, 42; see also 39–54.

place. As Rudolf Wittkower describes it, "In this process man's vision underwent a decisive change. Proportion became a matter of individual sensibility and in this respect the [modern] architect acquired complete freedom from the bondage of mathematical ratios."[11]

Furthermore, seventeenth-century advances in astronomy and the physical sciences ensured that mathematics began to be seen less as a symbolic or mystical system revealing the deeper structures of reality and more as an abstract system that scientists invent and manipulate in order to quantify nature. Kepler is a transitional figure on this point. For example, he employed detailed empirical observations of Mars and developed a theory of elliptical, rather than circular, planetary orbits, but his thinking, as W. T. Jones has noted, was "colored by a Pythagorean mysticism that convinced him that God had created the universe in accordance with certain simple mathematical harmonies. This conviction gave him the fortitude to see the failure of one formula after another without giving up hope that there was a formula to be found." Descartes, too, felt that mathematics would offer an insight into reality, yet his analytical geometry, which made use of abstract notation (for example, $y = mx + b$), further propelled the transition from Pythagorean mysticism to nominalistic empiricism. Hobbes completed the job, notably in *De Corpore* (1655), declaring mathematics to be nothing more than a set of arbitrary and self-referential signs. "Hobbes believed that the certainty of mathematics derives from the fact that it is a knowledge of the consequences or arbitrarily chosen names, from the fact, that is, that the objects judged about are nothing but what we say they are."[12] What mathematics did retain, however, well through the nineteenth century, was its Euclidean character, which imagined a world of certain regularities—continuous curves, straight lines, discrete angles—without which Newtonian physics could not function.

In this context, Emerson's call for "a habitual respect to the whole by an eye loving beauty in details"—premised as it is in an affective consideration of reality—emerges as a clear challenge to the sensationalist rigor of Cartesian, Lockean, and Humean skepticism. And if, in 1844, "modern sculpture, picture, and poetry" were for Emerson not all they should be, certain poets and artists did seem to have hit on some, if not all, of the right ideas. In 1833, just

11. Rudolf Wittkower, *Architectural Principles in the Age of Humanism,* 153; see also 142–54.
12. W. T. Jones, *A History of Western Philosophy,* vol. 3, *Hobbes to Hume,* 95, 160.

over ten years before he wrote of "flowing law," Emerson was in England on the return leg of his first European voyage.[13] One of the many Emerson met who shared his interest in literature and science was William Wordsworth. Emerson visited the sixty-four-year-old poet at home, and Emerson's account of the meeting (*JMN*, 4:223–24) notes that the two men walked through Wordsworth's garden, along "the walk in which thousands of his lines were writ," and discussed poetry, nature, chemistry, and physics. Wordsworth also recited some lines he had been working on that day. He "had just been to Staffa & within a few days had made three sonnets upon Fingal's Cave & was making a fourth when he was called in to see me," Emerson writes. Wordsworth's sonnets focus on the "Cave of Staffa," its construction, and the effect its unique structure has on the viewer.[14] What appeals most to Wordsworth is the design of the cave with its many thousands of hexagonal basalt columns. He describes it as a place in which one might observe

> the effect
> Of those proportions where the almighty hand . . .
> Has deigned to work as if with human Art!

However, Wordsworth notes that it would be "presumptuous" to "assign / Mechanic laws to agency divine," for the cave, with its "pillared vestibule, / Expanding yet precise," indeed seems "designed to humble man, when proud / Of his best workmanship by plan and tool." Additionally, the cave appears to be a model of structural equipoise:

> Calm as the Universe, from specular towers
> Of heaven contemplated by Spirits pure
> With mute astonishment, it stands sustained

13. The trip was more a tour of Europe's most important institutions of science than anything else. Harry Hayden Clark writes, "Indeed, one is tempted to raise the question whether the greatest impact on Emerson's mind in Europe was not caused by his observations in museums of natural history, listening to scientists, and by his contemplation of religious problems in the light of science" ("Emerson and Science," 250; see also 250–53).

14. Fingal's Cave, on the Island of Staffa in County Argyll, Scotland, is the northern terminus of a wide band of densely packed hexagonal basalt columns running under the sea from what is known as the Giant's Causeway, on the coast of County Antrim, Northern Ireland. Wordsworth's four sonnets on Fingal's Cave are part of a much longer series of poems inspired by a short 1833 summer tour in Scotland.

Through every part in symmetry, to endure,
Unhurt, the assault of Time with all his hours,
As the supreme Artificer ordained.[15]

The basalt columns of the cave are "specular towers," ideal (and here idealized) examples of strength and permanence in the perfect balance of their hexagonal design.

Wordsworth shared his lines with Emerson "in great spirit," no doubt moved by the excitement of the composing process, and his enthusiasm caught Emerson as well, who found "the second & third more *beautiful* than any of his printed poems." Two phrases from the third sonnet fixed in Emerson's mind in particular: "calm as the Universe" and "as the supreme Geometer ordained," the second phrase revised by Wordsworth to "as the supreme Artificer ordained" in the finished version of the poem. As an intriguing formation, still quite mysterious to early nineteenth-century natural philosophy, the hexagonal columns at Staffa lend their weight to geometrical configurations of the natural world and a geometer god determining its design. But Wordsworth's revision to this line further reinforces his equally significant conception of God as artist and craftsman. It also helps to make the contrast between God's own artistry and that suggested by the hexagonal columns of Fingal's Cave, in which, seemingly, "the almighty hand, / has deigned to work as if with human Art." The hexagonal columns are rigid, linear, and uniformly proportioned, characteristics that make them seem out of place—seemingly unnatural yet reminiscently neoclassical—in a littoral setting otherwise characterized by the flowing curves of coast and sea.

Like Emerson, Wordsworth took keen interest in geometrical forms, and he often described nature in geometrical terms. In Book 5 of *The Prelude* (1805/1850), he celebrates Euclid's *Elements,* a text with which he was intimately familiar from his years at Cambridge and beyond, and Book 6 presents an application of geometrical ratios and proportions to descriptions of nature and natural laws. As Lee Johnson demonstrates in *Wordsworth's Metaphysical Verse: Geometry, Nature, and Form* (1982), Wordsworth regularly used geometric ratios—the golden mean, for example—in composing many of his major works, from "St. Paul's," to "Tintern Abbey," to *The*

15. William Wordsworth, *The Poetical Works of Wordsworth,* 716–17.

Excursion, to *The Prelude* and others. Wordsworth's use of continuous proportions as symbolic forms in his poetry shows, among other things, "its
propriety in representing . . . the philosophical idealism he finds in geometrical thought."[16] In other words, Wordsworth's regular use of geometrical
principles as structures for composing poetry demonstrates that his geometrical conception of nature was deeply ingrained in his thinking, and as
such, geometry provides not only a window into his mind but also an aid to
the interpretation of his work.

In Book 6 of *The Prelude* (1850), Wordsworth writes of geometry's
ordering influence on the mind:

> Mighty is the charm
> Of those abstractions to a mind beset
> With images, and haunted by herself,
> And specially delightful unto me
> Was that clear synthesis built up aloft
> So gracefully; . . .
> . . . an independent world,
> Created out of pure intelligence.

The principles of geometry are like a "clear synthesis" that is "created out of
pure intelligence." Like Platonic Forms, they exist in "an independent
world," one in which Wordsworth took refuge and solace. Wordsworth also
expresses the notion, writes Johnson, "that geometrical principles are not
derived from empirical experience but from innate ideas which reflect a
metaphysical ontology"—a concept championed, of course, by Kant as
well. However, "Wordsworth's interest in geometry was not only metaphysical but practical, and Newton was his guide to the rational apprehension of
the external universe." Like *Elements,* the *Principia* was also a major Cambridge text, and so Wordsworth's own naturalism follows the logic of Newtonian astronomy, in which abstract geometrical forms correspond to
natural forms by providing a rational basis for describing and analyzing
them. The beginnings of this process are described in the 1805 edition of
The Prelude:

---

16. Lee M. Johnson, *Wordsworth's Metaphysical Verse: Geometry, Nature, and Form,* 12.

With Indian awe and wonder, ignorance
Which even was cherished, did I meditate
Upon the alliance of those simple, pure
Proportions and relations with the frame
And laws of Nature, how they could become
Herein a leader to the human mind,
And made endeavors frequent to detect
The process by dark guesses of my own.

As Johnson's analysis skillfully demonstrates, "the most characteristically Wordsworthian attitude towards geometrical and natural forms is that the presence of one calls forth the other." But at the core of Wordsworth's exposition of geometrical and natural forms in Book 6, however, "stands geometry's essential nature as a subject which originates in infinitude and lies beyond all human passion"—a sign that the primary text informing Wordsworth's own understanding of form is indeed *Elements,* with its emphasis on ratios and continuous proportions, and its resonating Platonic overtones.[17]

The Staffa poems suggest something of a contrast to the Newtonian underpinnings of *The Prelude.* The columns of Fingal's Cave illustrate instead the notion that "mechanic laws" cannot explain "agency divine," as much as they seem examples through which to do so. Indeed, to many nineteenth-century heirs of Newton, mechanic laws promised to explain, and explain away, a great deal of divine agency. But in the poems, the hexagons of Fingal's Cave, after all, give only the appearance of being laid out as if with "plan and tool." Whether "supreme Geometer" or "supreme Artificer," God's ways ultimately remain inscrutable.

But while the Staffa poems contrast with *The Prelude,* they yet retain a Euclidian aspect in their architectural descriptions of natural form. In the poems, the cave is a temple, with "long-drawn nave," frieze, and architrave. The hexagonal columns present a "pillared vestibule" beneath a "roof embowed." The cave is clearly a natural structure—imprecise, asymmetrical, unevenly composed, amply supplied with irregular curves—but the model Wordsworth uses to describe it is Greco-Roman. A temple built in the

17. William Wordsworth, *The Prelude: A Parallel Text,* 215; Johnson, *Wordsworth's Metaphysical Verse,* 48, 50; Wordsworth, *Prelude,* 212; Johnson, *Wordsworth's Metaphysical Verse,* 51, 81.

Euclidean manner, sanctioned by Platonic idealism, serves as the formal archetype of the real cave. Wordsworth eschews an accurate description of the cave's *natural* features for a description of its *ideal* features—features a phenomenal cave only approximates but which, as items taken to be worthy of our contemplation, seem more real, even if (yet also because) they are not directly experienced. Clearly, here, as in *The Prelude*, natural forms evoke in Wordsworth's mind the "clear synthesis" of geometrical shapes that are "created out of pure intelligence." *Elements* provides Wordsworth with not just a way of thinking about form but also the very objects of his thought.

The Euclidean and Platonic model of form favored by Wordsworth presents an instructive contrast to Emersonian form theory, and there is no doubt that an Emersonian description of the Cave of Staffa, if we had one, would present a strikingly different set of assumptions regarding natural structures. Whereas Wordsworth looked to *Elements* for the ideal forms with which to describe nature and constructed much of his poetry based on the ratios he found in Euclid, Emerson looked for models in structures just as he found them out in the world. More a participant than an observer, he writes, "I go out one day & see the mason & carpenters busy in building a house, and I discover with joy the parallelism between their work & my construction of a sonnet, and come home glad to know that I too am a housebuilder" (*JMN*, 9:231). While Wordsworth looked to the golden section for indications of "pure intelligence" and used it to communicate the transcendentally incommunicable, Emerson relied on shapes, as it were, much closer to home: "A rhyme in one of our sonnets should not be less pleasing than the iterated nodes of a sea-shell" (*CollW*, 3:15). House and shell, as models for poetry, are equally significant for their rigorous domesticity, for the very fact that they are of this world and not another.

The shell also serves to show that to Emerson morphology, or the geometry of an organism's surface, is its primary distinguishing feature. It is empirically clear that the morphology of an organic form has geometrical traits. The shell, for example, comprises a closed surface in space, and despite its highly regular morphology, its shape can be manipulated only within certain physical—that is, geometrical—limits before it is no longer recognizable as a shell. Further, the intellect, Emerson writes, "always ponders" "the problem of existence," but it is a problem that concerns not "person or place" so much as it concerns form: "Nature shows all things formed and bound. The intellect pierces the form, overleaps the wall, detects intrinsic likeness between remote things, and reduces all things into a few principles" (*CollW,* 2:194). This is the very reason why Wordsworth turns to Euclid. Formal descriptions of regular geometric solids can often be reduced to a few principles: defining the infinite number of points in a parabolic curve, for example, requires very little in the way of mathematical representation. Thus, when applied to the real world, such geometrizing reduces the intrinsic likenesses in infinitely complex natural geometries to an abstract class of similars. Shells, for example, come to be seen as assemblages of cones, spirals, and helices.

On the other hand, Emerson notes not that the intellect detects intrinsic likeness between things, but between *remote* things. Implicit in his response to Nature's showing all things "formed and bound" is a recognition of the fact that the range of natural geometries is too complex to be described by means of collections of points, lines, and curves, and too fluid to be expressed with algebraic equations. Indeed, direct apprehension demonstrates conclusively that abstract geometrical classifications of morphology are of limited use. The brain is able to recognize, from a variety of perspectives and virtually instantaneously, the most complex and intricate of natural geometries—individual faces in a moving crowd, for example—without reference to simple Euclidean shapes. Thus, when one is dealing merely with abstract notions of order and stability, Wordsworth's reductive comparison of the natural geometry of the Staffa cave to a neoclassical temple serves its purpose well. But when one is looking for accurate descriptions of organic shapes—the true morphology of living objects—the Euclidean model belies the perceptive abilities of the mind. Even real temples miss their mark: while in Milan in 1833, Emerson writes, "It is in the soul that architecture exists & Santa Croce & this Duomo are poor far-behind imitations. I would rather know the metaphysics of architecture as of shells & flowers than anything else in the matter" (*JMN,* 4:75).

Many references to natural form are scattered throughout Emerson's public and private writing, underscoring his belief that the "power of form" is one of several "facts of a science which we study without book, whose teachers and subjects are always near us" (*CollW,* 6:152). Indeed, form is of such great consequence to not only the apprehension but also the comprehension of nature that Emerson begins one of his most famous essays, "The Poet," with an argument emphasizing the primacy of form:

Those who are esteemed umpires of taste, are often persons who have acquired some knowledge of admired pictures or sculptures, and have an inclination for whatever is elegant; but if you inquire whether they are beautiful souls, and whether their own acts are like fair pictures, you learn that they are selfish and sensual. . . . Their knowledge of the fine arts is some study of rules and particulars, or some limited judgment of color or form, which is exercised for amusement or for show. It is a proof of the shallowness of the doctrine of beauty, as it lies in the minds of our amateurs, that men seem to have lost the perception of the instant dependence of form upon soul. There is no doctrine of forms in our philosophy. We were put into our bodies, as fire is put into a pan, to be carried about; but there is no accurate adjustment between the spirit and the organ, much less is the latter the germination of the former. So in regard to other forms, the intellectual men do not believe in any essential dependence of the material world on thought and volition. (*CollW*, 3:3)

Elsewhere he notes, "When the poet comes into the wood . . . his form dilates" (*JMN*, 8:267–68) because he "love[s] . . . Form: believing that Form is an oracle which never lies" (*JMN*, 8:405). These thoughts, written in the years just before the publication of "The Poet," do not quite find their way toward such explicit expression in the essay; however, it is clear from Emerson's journal that form was very much on his mind while he wrote "The Poet," and it is also clear that Emerson's Poet is one who holds fast to a "doctrine of forms." The Poet's "metre-making argument," for example, "puts eyes, and a tongue, into every dumb and inanimate object" (*CollW*, 3:6, 12) because the Poet perceives "that within the form of every creature is a force impelling it to ascend into a higher form; and, following with his eyes the life, uses the forms which express that life, and so his speech flows from the flowing of nature" (12). The Poet "re-attaches things to nature and the Whole" and "sees them fall within the great Order not less than the bee-hive, or the spider's geometrical web" (11). Indeed, Emerson's reasoning throughout the entire essay hinges on the observation that the creation is held together like the hive or the web, two natural structures the integrity of which depends almost entirely on the exactness of the forms inherent to them.

Emerson's discussions of nature emphasize that form is neither static nor an end product. Rather, form has an origin, undergoes development, and is a crucial element in a larger context of cosmic forces—an idea not always easily captured in human arts, imaginative though they may be. "Sculpture," for example, "may serve to teach the pupil how deep is the secret of form, how purely the spirit can translate its meanings into that eloquent dialect. But the statue will look cold and false before that new activity"—that is, vitality—"which needs to roll through all things, and is impatient of counterfeits, and things not alive." Because it is not alive, the sculpture remains caught in its stasis. It cannot fully delineate the form of living beings and is always just a representation. Thus, "picture and sculpture are the celebrations and festivities of form. But true art is never fixed, but always flowing" (*CollW*, 2:216).

Philosophically considered, form is the structure, organization, or essential character of a thing. Form refers to both the outward shape and the internal structure of objects, but more specifically it is the intrinsic determinant of quantity, from which figure or shape is derived. Further, various types of form have been used in ancient and medieval thought to describe four different aspects of real objects. Substantial form gives a specific nature or essence to a thing, such as the form of iron, or of a shell, or of a man. Inherent form determines the material attributes of a thing, thus making, for example, a stone a stone and not, say, a leaf. Accidental form, of which inherent form is a type, makes an object quantifiable or qualifiable in some way, thus allowing one to speak of not just a tree but also a large tree, or a thin tree, or a maple tree. Last, separated form refers to something such as the human soul, which is thought to exist apart, if not entirely independent of, the matter that it actuates. A consideration of form thus opens up four different ways of talking about a thing.

Emerson refers to all four understandings of form in his writing, but he places the greatest importance on substantial form in his thinking and writing on nature. For Emerson, form is perhaps the most important way of talking about the existence of living objects in the world, but it must always be understood as something caught up in the continuous becoming that is the condition of being alive in a flow of time, an idea that only a living object, and not a sculpture, is able to communicate:

> Children delight in the summer berry lifting its polished surface a few inches
> from the ground.... 'Tis six or seven months, that the sun must make the
> tour of the heavens, every day, over this tiny sprout, before it could bear

its fruit. The sea has evaporated its countless turns of water into the atmosphere, that the rain might wet the roots of this vine. The elastic air exhaled from all live creatures, and all minerals, yielded this small pensioner the gaseous aliment it required. The earth, by the attraction of its mass, determined its form and size; and, when we think how the earth's attraction is fixed at this moment in equilibrium by the attractions on every side of distant bodies, we see that the berry's form and history are determined by causes and agents the most prodigious and remote. (*LL*, 2:145)

Emerson argues in this passage from "Moral Sense" that the development of a simple, tiny berry is a cosmic enterprise. The interactions of chemical and organic agents here on earth only partly explain its existence (that is, its becoming a berry). In a larger sense, and in a wider context, its growth is the work of galaxies. The point Emerson wishes to emphasize in this passage is that the presence of something as simple as a berry is more complex than seems at first. Like children, we also delight in the berry, but it is more than just a material thing. It has accidental form (it is a "summer" berry with "polished surface," for example) and inherent form, drawing its matter from elements of water, earth, air, and sun. But also it has substantial form: it is a "fruit" that grows out of a "tiny sprout," yet the larger context of its "form and history" make it a unique being with a singular existence. Emerson suggests that the berry is what it is in a time and place where no other thing could exist in its stead. What it has come to be is a berry and a berry only. The cosmos itself determines that this is so.

The berry's uniqueness and singularity are key elements in our knowing what it is—more so than its inclusion in a whole class of similars. In Emerson's rendering, it is not representative of an ideal type. Yet the assumption that Emerson's natural philosophy is Platonic is perhaps one of most widespread beliefs about Emerson's thought. While Plato is the first of Emerson's "representative men," Emerson's praise of Plato is certainly not unqualified: "The longest wave is quickly lost in the sea. Plato would willingly have a Platonism, a known and accurate expression for the world, and it should be accurate. It shall be the world passed through the mind of Plato,—nothing less. . . . This is the ambition of individualism. But the mouthful proves too large. . . . Unconquered nature lives on. . . . So it fares with all: so must it fare with Plato" (*CollW*, 4:43). In the *Journals*, Emerson expresses similar, and more explicit, views regarding Plato. Plato's "accuracy" is simply a measure of his individualism; it is not necessarily a claim on truth. Indeed, "in view of eternal nature, Plato turns out to be philosophical exercitations." For Emerson, the world is too large for Plato to swallow—too complex for Plato's philosophy to fully encompass: "for Plato, it would be pedantry to catalogue his philosophy, the secret of constructing pyramids & cathedrals is lost, & not less of Platonic philosophies." Learning Plato is not without value, of course, for Platonism teaches that "every whole is made of similars and in morals & metaphysics this is specially true." So, tellingly, "the fables of Plato will reward the ear" and thus give the mind something worthwhile to ponder—but Plato's fables will not, it seems, reward the eye, which takes note of the world as it really is and focuses the mind away from ideal abstractions (*JMN*, 9:223). First with the eye, and then the mind, we understand that "the berry's form and history"—as well as the form and history of any other natural object—"are determined by causes and agents the most prodigious and remote."

Plato's philosophy of form begins with the belief that form is an expression of Idea, or *eidos*—that is, an archetype or pattern of which individual objects in any natural class are imperfect copies. Platonic Forms thus have what might be called a necessary existence; they are there to be discovered, and they will exist even if no one ever thinks of them. As evidence of this fact, Socrates, in the *Meno*, engages an uneducated slave boy in a mathematical proof—taken from Euclid's *Elements*—and the boy "recollects," or rediscovers, the proof. Thus, for Plato, the proposal supported by the phenomena of geometry is that knowledge is independent of experience, language, and mind: investigation merely brings one into contact with preexisting forms. Further, Plato's *Timaeus* presents a universe ordered by geometric principles (based on Empedocles' division of matter into four elements) that link material existence to transcendent forms with an important result. Beginning with the incorporeal, two-dimensional triangle, Plato derived from it five (and only five) regular geometric solids, now called Platonic solids: the tetrahedron, the cube, the octahedron, the dodecahedron, and the icosahedron. Plato connected each of the four elements to one of these solids—fire with the tetrahedron, earth with the cube, air with the octahedron, and water with the icosahedron—and the whole cosmos to the dodecahedron. Thus, the idea that nature has a geometric basis gains firm grounding in Plato, but his geometric scheme emphasizes the unseen (and transcendent Form) over the seen: what matters most—what is most real—is something other than the actual appearance of things.

Unlike Plato, Emerson saw a great deal of perfection in the accidental forms of natural objects, as the berry passage demonstrates, and he discarded the notion of an Idea, or archetypal pattern on the Platonic model, as the metaphysical basis of natural objects. For Emerson, what is most real is firmly grounded in the actual appearance of things, in their particular, and peculiar, morphology. Further, the multiplicity of forms in the natural world, both within and across natural classes, intrigued him perhaps more than any other natural phenomenon. For example, in his account of his visit to the Jardin des Plantes in Paris (*JMN*, 4:198–200)[18]—a moment most agree was key to the development of his philosophy and his career—Emerson writes: "'Tis wise in man to make Cabinets. When I was come into the Ornithological Chambers, I wished I had come only there. The fancy-coloured vests of these elegant beings make me as pensive as the hues & forms of a cabinet of shells, formerly. . . . The limits of the possible are enlarged, & the real is stranger than the imaginary" (198–99). By noting that the real is stranger than the imaginary (a truly remarkable comment), Emerson calls attention to the actual appearance of things, to their materiality. He lends metaphysical weight, in other words, to accidental and inherent form. More than this, he is moved by the display itself, by its arrangement of natural forms according to morphological characteristics, and by the larger implications it has for our understanding of the means by which nature is organized:

> Ah said I this is philanthropy, wisdom, taste—to form a Cabinet of natural history. . . . Here we are impressed with the inexhaustible riches of nature. The Universe is a more amazing puzzle than ever as you glance along this bewildering series of animated forms,—the hazy butterflies, the carved shells, the birds, beasts, fishes, insects, snakes,—& the upheaving principle of life everywhere incipient in the very rock aping organized

18. See also *EL*, 1:7–10. The Jardin des Plantes, or Muséum d'Histoire Naturelle, presented at the time of Emerson's visit in 1833 mineral collections organized by Haüy, a menagerie and zoological cabinets organized by Cuvier and Saint-Hilaire, a shell collection organized by Lamarck, and botanical gardens organized by de Jussieu (see Brown, *Emerson Museum*, 264n1).

forms. Not a form so grotesque, so savage, nor so beautiful but is an expression of some property inherent in man the observer,—an occult relation between the very scorpions and man. I feel the centipede in me— cayman, carp, eagle, & fox. I am moved by strange sympathies. (199–200)

Here, Emerson focuses directly on substantial form, but also he notes how substantial form indicates a "strange sympathy," or principle of similarity, across classes. Each natural object in the exhibit exists according to its own specific properties, but each points more directly toward Nature's "upheaving principle of life." The series of animated forms might in its appearance be bewildering for all its variety, but it is nonetheless "organized." Like belongs with like—shells, birds, fishes, insects, snakes—but each, whether grotesque, savage, or beautiful, points to the "occult relation" up and down the whole chain of being, from scorpions to man. For Emerson, the actual appearance of things opens up the key to their mystery; further, the variety and difference of natural forms is an integral part, even an essential part, of "the cipher of the world" (*CollW*, 2:179).

In the essay "History," for example, Emerson repeats the idea of the organizing principle suggested by the Paris Muséum, but as before, the multiplicity and wide variety of the forms of natural bodies take metaphysical precedence:

> Genius detects through the fly, through the caterpillar, through the grub, through the egg, the constant individual; through countless individuals, the fixed species; through many species, the genus; through all genera, the steadfast type; through all the kingdoms of organized life, the eternal unity. Nature is a mutable cloud, which is always and never the same. She casts the same thought into troops of forms, as a poet makes twenty fables with one moral. Through the bruteness and toughness of matter, a subtle spirit bends all things to its own will. The adamant streams into soft but precise form before it, and, whilst I look at it, its outline and texture are changed again. Nothing is so fleeting as form; yet never does it quite deny itself. (*CollW*, 2:8)

On the one hand, Emerson's likening Nature unto a cloud—even the adamant streams and flows like vapor—may at first suggest an idea of the Platonic nebulae, as though the material world were merely an appearance, like shadows on the wall of a cave, and not as "real" as the "subtle spirit" igniting it. But the cloud itself is a material object here, just another example, albeit an emblematic one, of the many "troops of forms" to be found in the natural world. On the other hand, the cloud, the outline and texture of which are in a state of constant flux, may also suggest Heraclitean chaos, as though clouds and other natural objects, even if fundamentally material, never rest in any "real," or permanent, series of forms. Emerson maintains a fine balance: he articulates a position between Plato and Heraclitus. Form itself may be too fleeting to ever find expression in some Platonic ideal, but never does it become lost in a state of endless transition.

Emerson's *via media* here is primarily Aristotelian. Aristotle accepted the views of Plato and the pre-Socratics that earthly substances are complex rather than simple, but also reducible to a small set of fundamental principles or elements. He also accepted that these elements—fire, earth, air, and water—undergo transmutations, and that in themselves they are not fixed and immutable. Extending this idea, Aristotle argued that the elements, like all substances, are composites of form and matter, and that matter is capable of assuming a succession of forms. But Aristotle also saw the radical skepticism implied by assertions of unending change. He counters such Heraclitean claims of a universe existing in perpetual flux by means of a theory of form that attempts to point toward fixed and immutable principles organizing what only appears to the senses to be a chaos of perpetual change: as Emerson similarly points out in the essay "History," nothing is so fleeting as form, yet never does it quite deny itself.

Further, in *Metaphysics*, Aristotle argued that earthly objects, or substances, are comprised of form and matter. He broadly defines matter, in part, as that which has form. Form, which provides the individual thing its properties, supersedes matter in making the thing what it is; thus, matter is for Aristotle simply the passive recipient of form (an idea implied by the "summer berry" passage cited above). Particularly among natural (that is, nonsynthetic) objects, then, form plays a greater role than matter in determining an object's nature or essence, which disposes it to certain kinds of behavior. As a result, form plays a key role in placing an object in its particular species or kind, and it allows for a means of segregating, classifying, and quantifying objects based on natural properties, as suggested by the Parisian exhibits Emerson so keenly observes. Even so, Aristotle recognized that certain forms—those of living beings, for example—are imminent, that they develop internally over time and are not imposed from without the way a carpenter fashions a piece of furniture out of wood. In this sense, form is organic: it explains a thing's development, and is the intelligible structure of a thing as it proceeds through stages of development. Thus, living things grow in order to actualize successive forms, and their natural behaviors, those not resulting from chance nor caused by outside influences, are understood to be the determining factors in natural change. They are necessarily of great interest to natural philosophers. Additionally, Aristotle's definition of substance as matter and form made it possible to theorize—as did Thomas Aquinas and Duns Scotus—something unalterable and eternal (that is, form or essence) regardless of its concrete and mutable manifestation in individual objects.

Many of these Aristotelian ideas are rearticulated in Emerson's meditations on nature and form. Because he imputes metaphysical predominance to form over matter, for example, Emerson places repeated emphasis on Nature's "flowing law," the Aristotelian idea that forms are not static but continually changing according to fixed mechanisms of metamorphosis. All of nature, including humanity, participates in this metamorphosis of form. Likewise, in the essay "Nature," the natural world "publishes itself in creatures, reaching from particles and specula, through transformation on transformation to the highest symmetries, arriving at consummate results without a shock or a leap" (*CollW*, 3:104). And further, "a little water made to rotate in a cup explains the formation of the simpler shells; the addition of matter from year to year, arrives at last at the most complex forms," so there is "but one stuff . . . to serve up all [Nature's] dream-like variety. Compound it how she will, star, sand, fire, water, tree, man, it is all one stuff, and betrays the same properties" (105). In the manner of Aristotle, Emerson theorizes form in a way that points toward developmental variety and variation, but also toward fixed and immutable principles reflected in individual objects.

Additionally, Emerson's own thought process—his method of making observations of the natural world, and then describing complex systems with the information he gathers—draws much more support from Aristotelianism than from Platonism, and he is certainly not alone in this regard. As Emerson points out in *Representative Men:* "The robust Aristotelian method, with its breadth and adequateness, shaming our sterile and linear logic by its genial radiation, conversant with series and degree, with effects and ends, skilful to discriminate power from form, essence from accident, and opening, by its terminology and definition, high roads into nature, had trained a race of athletic philosophers" (*CollW,* 4:59). One of Aristotle's major criticisms of Plato is that if, in Plato's rendering, Ideas are eternal unchangeable truths, then learning becomes impossible because the world of Ideas is completely separated from the world of experience. Instead, Aristotle unites the two worlds and understands learning by claiming that forms have, on the one hand, a universal and higher *a priori* reality like Plato's Ideas, but, on the other hand, that they are also a formative principle in an individual's experience. The mind's adaptability is thus due to a meeting between the potentiality present in Ideas and the actuality of matter, creating an individual experience. Form-as-potentiality evolves into form-as-actuality. Similarly, Emerson claims in *Nature* that "by degrees we may come to know the primitive sense of the permanent objects of nature, so that the world shall be to us an open book, and every form significant of its hidden life and final cause" (*CollW,* 1:23), because, as he notes elsewhere: "In the animal frame . . . nature makes the effort to . . . change the blood into hair, horns, scales, or teeth, according to the needs of the creature. We have continually suggested to us a larger generalization, that each of the great departments of nature, chemistry, vegetation, and animal life, exhibit the same laws on a different plane; that the intellectual and the moral world are analogous to the material; that what is out there a law in matter, is in mind a sentiment; but with one cause,—astonishing us with these varieties of form" (*LL,* 2:146). By looking at the matter, then, we have a reasonable chance of deducing the ideas, or organizing principles. And the same is true for human forms as for any other animal and natural form, potentially uniting even the mind-brain dichotomy under a single principle of organization. In a clear challenge to Cartesian essentialism, Emerson pushes the metaphysical implications of natural form to their logical end: "It is certain that there is a relation . . . between the activity of my brain, & its outward figure; there is a relation, but how to find it?" (*JMN,* 9:387). Here Emerson considers the radical notion—in yet another example of his empirical idealism—that structures of mind and structures of brain exist not in separation but in reciprocity, each one dependent on, yet at the same time determining, the other. As it is with the brain, so it is with the mind, and vice versa.

There is a relation, but how to find it? Through a recognition of the iterative properties of natural form, or the principle of self-similarity by which nature is organized. For Emerson, form constitutes the basic foundation of material reality, and "the symmetry & coordination of things is such that from any one creature well & inly known, any & every other might be legitimately deduced" (*JMN*, 9:387). Further, as he notes in "The Method of Nature": "Nature can only be conceived as existing to a universal and not to a particular end, to a universe of ends, and not to one,—a work of *ecstasy*, to be represented by a circular movement, as intention might be signified by a straight line of definite length. Each effect strengthens every other. There is no revolt in all the kingdoms from the commonweal: no detachment of an individual. Hence the catholic character which makes every leaf an exponent of the world" (*CollW*, 1:125). Here, nature is a congeries of primary shapes, like the leaf, arranged in infinite replication. But as natural forms are always fleeting, these shapes are not precisely delineated. The circle, for example, is clearly an emblematic shape for Emerson, but rarely, if at all, will one find a circle in nature. Rather, one finds near-circles, ovals, round curves, and irregular curves—just as in a leaf, or in the "mutable" billows of a cloud, in which the shape of a circle is infinitely repeated, but with slight alterations in each iteration. Even so, "nature may be cooked into all shapes, & not recognized," as when "they are melted in Promethean alembics, & come out men; & then, melted again, come out words" (*JMN*, 9:357), but "genius watches the monad through all his masks as he performs the metempsychosis of nature" (*CollW*, 2:8). In other words, only the keenly perceptive mind detects the monad, or primary shape, as it is continuously reiterated through subsequent forms. "The world globes itself in a drop of dew" (*CollW*, 2:59).[19]

Like the cloud, the forms of nature, particularly the living forms of animals, are always and never the same: on certain scales, whether ontogenetic or phylogenic, all living forms bear some resemblance to each other. Thus, as Emerson writes in the essay "Compensation": "These appearances indi-

19. The monad—a distinct, unitary particle that reflects the characteristics and attributes of the whole system of which it is a part—is a term and concept taken from Leibniz, who believed the fundamental elements of the universe to be evolving units of consciousness that create continuity between the physical and psychological realms. Leibniz argues in *Monadologie* (1714) that these monads, of varying degrees of percipience, exist in all inanimate, plant, and animal matter, and that it is through their organization and harmony that one can infer the existence of God.

cate the fact that the universe is represented in every one of its particles. Every thing in nature contains all the powers of nature. Every thing is made of one hidden stuff; as the naturalist sees one type under every metamorphosis, and regards a horse as a running man, a fish as a swimming man, a bird as a flying man, a tree as a rooted man. Each new form repeats not only the main character of the type, but part for part all the details, all the aims, furtherances, hindrances, energies, and whole system of every other" (59). As the circle is a monad or primary figure, "repeated without end" and "the highest emblem in the cipher of the world" (*CollW,* 2:179), the circular cloud becomes a representation of the whole system of nature, at every scale. Even tiny "volvox globator"—a minute organism occurring in spherical colonies that rotate about a central axis—"has got on so far! He has rolled to some purpose truly" (*JMN,* 9:230). In these tiniest of creatures, Emerson finds an illustration of the whole system of nature. All of nature is interrelated through form.

In sum, one can make two important observations. First, when Emerson refers to form, he has a nonlinear, or organic, concept of form in mind, and not just a metaphoric allusion to linear (and primarily Euclidean) conceptions of shape. Second, when Emerson refers to form, he refers also to cosmic design. Form is the fundamental dimension of all reality, coequal to and manifested in the materiality of all physical objects. Thus, in referring to form as "always and never the same," Emerson theorizes an organic geometry that begins to step beyond abstract idealism and Platonic perfection toward a direct observation of nature as it really is. "The Greek letters last a little longer, but are already passing [away], and tumbling into the inevitable pit which the creation of new thought opens for all that is old" (*CollW,* 2:180). Where Plato would refer to Form as being ideal, timeless, and never changing, Emerson refers to form as always and never the same. Thus, as he argues in "The Over-Soul," just as "the soul's advances are not made by gradation, such as can be represented by motion in a straight line; but rather by ascension of state, such as can be represented by metamorphosis" (*CollW,* 2:163), so too do the forms of nature participate in dynamic and continuous processes of creation. Where Plato's geometric understanding of nature focuses on an arithmetic, or a principle of addition, Emerson's geometric understanding focuses on an algorithm, or a principle of iteration.

Form theory demonstrates that Emerson's frequent use of terms like "flowing law," "mutation," and "metamorphosis" to describe a theory of ascendancy, both material and spiritual, throughout the chain of being, is grounded in his direct observation of the natural geometries of organic objects. Although it falls squarely in the camp of readings that meet Emerson halfway—that is, only in terms of metaphor—Daniel Shea's 1975 essay "Emerson and the American Metamorphosis" nonetheless offers a well-conceived analysis of the concept of metamorphosis in Emerson's contributions to an emerging American literature. Shea writes, for example:

> Confirmed by experience, the notion of metamorphosis served Emerson well through distinctive stages of his development. His incapacity for discursive logic and the tendency of his mind to convert the Many into the One and back again regularly created the need for a metaphor both Protean in substance and prolific in implication. At various times he employs metamorphosis to mean: the soul's awakening; the perpetual miracle of nature; the leap of natural fact into spiritual fact as symbol or metaphor; simple process; process as becoming and amelioration; the dynamic of nature by which spiritual law is visibly incarnated; and, in the social order, the decay of institutions and their replacement by increasingly humane and therefore divine systems of organization.

Conceived in this way, metamorphosis provides for Emerson, as well as for others, a broad range of inroads toward writing and expressions of identity. Resting in the assumption that "metaphor [is] a problem-solving device," Shea argues, "Emerson had no mental itch to work out a philosophical consistency between the One and the Many, but as poet and rhetorician he badly needed a way of talking about two truths of perception at once. Metamorphosis, the observable process in nature by which something changes while maintaining its identity, was that way of talking."[20] Shea's logic is muddled—if truly "observable," then why must metamorphosis be only "a way of talking"?—but his reading does help illustrate a contrast in worldview. My own analysis of form in Emerson's natural philosophy shows two things: first, that his thinking on the subject is Aristotelian and not Platonic; and second, that his algorithmic, and metamorphic, understanding of natural processes emphasizes means over ends—indeed, Emerson frequently discards any notion of *ends* as useless. Metamorphosis is, then, a descriptive

20. Daniel B. Shea, "Emerson and the American Metamorphosis," 38, 41, 40.

rather than an allegorical "way of talking," and, in truth, Shea's reference to an Emersonian "incapacity for discursive logic" is in fact a refusal of discursive logic. Emerson favors intuitive logic, and to place on him a demand for discursive logic misses the point: the transmutations of form demonstrate that Nature participates in no such linear pattern. Taking his cue from this observable phenomenon—of organic objects undergoing continuous changes while still retaining their identity—Emerson does not either.

The contrast between discursive logic and Nature's metamorphosis places the issue of Emersonian form theory in its philosophical context. Emerson's 1850 *Representative Men,* in a passage cited above, makes reference to the "robust Aristotelian method . . . shaming our sterile and linear logic" that "trained a race of athletic philosophers." The phrase *athletic philosophers,* though deliberately playful, offers another clear challenge to nineteenth-century Cartesianism, a challenge that takes the unity of the human being and nature, of body and consciousness, of brain and mind, as so in accord with individual experience as to be axiomatic. The source meditation from his journal notes that "the Aristotelian method was the athletic training of the scholars of 17th Century, & a method so wide & respective of such universal relations that our education seems narrow, linear, & indigent." Clearly, Emerson equates linear thinking with narrow-mindedness and imaginative poverty. The stripping away of Aristotelianism ultimately limits the types of questions "scholars"—that is, scientists and other natural philosophers—are willing to ask. As Emerson continues, he suggests that even if a few such as "the Galileos, Keplers, Des Cartes, . . . show their rough training" in Aristotelian methods, "like Roman soldiers they were required to carry more weight in the daily discipline then they would need in war" (*JMN,* 11:157). In other words, the rise toward dominance of the linear paradigm, very rapidly approaching its zenith by 1850, ensured that the robust athleticism of the seventeenth-century past would, in Emerson's view, be rarely utilized in the ongoing struggle, or "war," to understand man's complex relationship to nature. What was intended to provide training in responding to the complex, ambiguous, and affective aspects of individual experience, Emerson observes, has been stripped away, stringently and deliberately, to our detriment and ultimate impoverishment.

The contrast between mechanical laws and divine agency—the subject of Wordsworth's Staffa poems—places Emersonian form theory more directly in its scientific context. As Emerson writes in "The Method of Nature,"

"When we are dizzied with the arithmetic of the savant toiling to compute the length of [nature's] line, the return of her curve"—an allusion to Newton—"we are steadied by the perception that a great deal is doing; that all seems just begun; remote aims are in active accomplishment" (*CollW*, 1:126). The grand question of how to define motion through space and time, Emerson implies, is just beginning to be answered. The thought very closely expresses the tenor of Emerson's conversation with Wordsworth eight years earlier: Emerson records that Wordsworth, in their discussion of chemistry and physics, "spoke of the Newtonian theory as if it might be superseded & forgotten" (a remarkable comment, suggesting that Wordsworth was imagining the possibility of a physics more advanced than Newton's).[21] The two men also discussed the atomic theory of John Dalton. Though atomism itself is an old and recurring idea, finding expression in Democritus, Epicurus, Lucretius, Ockham, and Hobbes, Dalton's theory is a formalized example of the minimalist proclivity to assume that the simple, clear, and distinct is the most real.[22] Some thirty years after his conversation on the subject with Wordsworth, Emerson notes that "chemistry takes to pieces, but it does not construct" (*CollW*, 6:150). Emerson frequently reiterates this idea in his work, that although scientists like Dalton may argue that matter is made up of discrete and inert particles—atoms that are tiny, indivisible, and indestructible units—material forms are far more complex than what the reductive claims of nineteenth-century chemistry allow for.

21. Jonathan Bishop notes that "Newton had a special meaning for Emerson's generation, which the name has lost since. For the eighteenth century, 'Newton' nicknames the mind that once and for all defined all motion in space and time, all of nature that could be conceived. He was therefore the arch- or protoscientist; and as such Newton seemed an archenemy of the imagination in the eyes of a generation that had learned from German philosophy and English poetry to blame their alienation from organic nature and from themselves on the intellectual world view Newton stood for" (*Emerson on the Soul*, 52). Emerson, like Wordsworth, clearly responds to the challenge Newton represents, but Emerson also distinguishes between the man and his theory. As an example of Man Thinking, Newton is often an object of Emerson's praise. As Bishop notes, Emerson "could redefine the Newton of the Lockists as paradoxically transcendental: as in startling fact a prime representative of just that style of active intellect that especially and crucially concerned the man of imagination" (52).

22. In 1808, Dalton, a meteorologist and discoverer of color blindness among other things, published a new atomic theory that explained how elements combine with one another in fixed ratios and in multiples of those ratios. Unlike earlier philosophical speculations, Dalton's theory was supported by his careful chemical measurements, and it remains, with certain significant emendations following the discovery of subatomic particles, the conceptual foundation of modern chemistry.

More broadly stated, Emerson argues that nature holds secrets beyond the reach of scientific scrutiny, enigmas that are impermeable to the analytic reductionism of Enlightenment science, and it is another point to which he frequently returns. Commenting on biology, for example, in "The Method of Nature," Emerson asserts: "In all animal and vegetable forms, the physiologist concedes that no chemistry, no mechanics, can account for the facts, but a mysterious principle of life must be assumed, which not only inhabits the organ, but makes the organ. How silent, how spacious, what room for all, yet without place to insert an atom,—in graceful succession, in equal fullness, in balanced beauty, the dance of the hours goes forward still. Like an odor of incense, like a strain of music, like a sleep, it is inexact and boundless. It will not be dissected, nor unraveled, nor shown" (*CollW*, 1:125). Emerson's position here, that animal and vegetable forms are beyond scientific scrutiny, is radical: it denies, without qualification, the central goal of modern science—indeed, its very raison d'être. Dissection, perhaps the quintessential act of nineteenth-century biological inquiry, proposes to break down natural systems in modular fashion (a process applicable across the sciences, whether directed toward atoms, animal bodies, or planetary orbits) by laying out and isolating component parts and exposing their attendant functions to scrutiny. For Emerson, some "mysterious principle of life"—almost ineffable, it not only inhabits but *makes* the thing what it is—always eludes capture in such an act.

The natural forms of Fingal's Cave as Wordsworth presents them are Platonic. But even though the hexagonal columns are mineral and not biological, Wordsworth too undoubtedly intimated "remote aims in active accomplishment" in his contemplation of them. Despite the differing conceptions of form to be found in each man's work, what struck them, in their discussion of the cave's hexagonal columns—in what one might literally call their poetic philosophizing about them—is that indeed "no mechanics can account for the facts": lining themselves up "in graceful succession, in equal fullness, in balanced beauty," these columns cannot be fully explained. Their mystery cannot be dissected, unraveled, or shown. Of course, there *is* a geologic explanation as to why these unusual crystalline solids should come into being,[23] and even though an advanced geologic understanding was unavailable to

---

23. Basalt is an igneous rock made up of labradorite and pyroxene found in lava flows and minor intrusions, so intense subterranean temperatures, massive volcanic pressures, shifts in the earth's crust, and an eon of erosion all play a role the creation of the Cave of Staffa.

Wordsworth and Emerson in 1834, neither man likely would have doubted its validity if it had been available. But what is missing in such an explanation is a "law in the mutations," the idea that, as Emerson expresses it in *Conduct of Life*, "Beauty is the moment of transition, as if the form were just ready to flow into other forms. Any fixedness, heaping, or concentration on one feature . . . is the reverse of the flowing, and therefore deformed. Beautiful as is the symmetry of any form, if the form can move, we seek a more excellent symmetry. . . . If we follow it out, this demand in our thought for an ever-onward action, is the argument for the immortality" (*CollW*, 6:155–56). Here Emerson displays another instructive contrast to Wordsworth, who writes of Fingal's Cave that it

> stands sustained
> Through every part in symmetry, to endure,
> Unhurt, the assault of Time with all his hours.

Wordsworth sees immortality communicated by the hard, immutable stasis of the columns, the forms of which seem to him impervious and permanent. Emerson wants a much wider context: solid rock has clearly flowed into these regular forms, these hexagonal columns, but what other forms will this (or any other) rock flow into? The "more excellent symmetry" to be found in an explanation of this or any other phenomenon would tell us not just how it came to be, but also what it may become. "These geologies, chemistries, astronomies, seem to make wise, but they leave us where they found us" (*CollW*, 6:150). If such astonishing regularity emerges from the surrounding irregularities of cave, coastline, and sea, what can be said of the relationship, through form, between structure and chaos, or of order within disorder?

As evidenced by the general context provided by figures discussed so far, the linear sciences that emerged during the early modern era promoted certain fundamental ideas (Newton's laws are only one example) that, by the nineteenth century, were widely accepted as true. More importantly, however, is the fact that the claims of linear science were so pronounced, and so vehement, that linear modes of thought became themselves the parameters for defining consciousness, reason, and other mental processes *as such*, even though the Enlightenment's tendency to schematize all phenomena tended to undermine its own capacity for critical self-reflection. Because of its emphasis on ends over means, linear thinking tempts us with the certainty of a one-to-one correspondence between questions and answers, and thus it implies the possibility of being free of error. Emerson was, of course, well aware of the attractiveness of linear thought and the comforts it purports to provide. Indeed, the restless tone of "Experience" arises from a contrast between the lure of linearity, or our "natural" tendency toward linear thinking, and Emerson's own intuitive, even if commonsensical, insight that the creation follows a different course:

> How easily, if fate would suffer it, we might keep forever these beautiful limits, and adjust ourselves, once for all, to the perfect calculation of the kingdom of known cause and effect. In the street and in the newspapers, life appears so plain a business, that manly resolution and adherence to the multiplication-table through all weathers, will insure success. But ah! presently comes a day, or is it only a half-hour, with its angel-whispering,—which discomfits the conclusions of nations and of years! Tomorrow again, [however,] everything looks real and angular, the habitual standards are reinstated, common sense is as rare as genius . . .—and yet, he who should do his business on this understanding, would be quickly bankrupt. (*CollW,* 3:39)

Here, Emerson expresses what became the crux of modernist anxiety in the early decades of the twentieth century, and it is likely for this reason that "Experience" has commanded such wide appeal. To the passively seeing eye, the world looks "real": it is fundamentally material, governed by interactions of the seen and not the unseen. It is also "angular": obeying the strict rule of cause and effect, it is as linear, ordered, and predictable as a multiplication table, no matter what alternate views might be evidenced by the weather. And yet the actively seeing eye—even if only for a brief half-hour—admits of a different world, one that knows no such limits, however "beautiful" they might seem to be. Certainly "there is more beauty in the morning cloud than the prism can render account of" (*JMN,* 4:95), but more than this, the weather makes us cognizant of a storm of change: nonlinear systems of the highest order, weather patterns remind us of a world that is inordinately complex, unpredictable, and constantly fluctuating. "Experience" teaches that, in the face of both sunshine and rain, linearity, like he who should do his business on such understanding, is bankrupt. Linear philosophy presents a historically contingent, narrowly construed way of thinking that need not be generalized to the status of a foundational, ahistorical norm. "Power keeps quite another road . . . , namely, the subterranean and invisible tunnels and channels of life" (*CollW,* 3:39)—routes that linear thinking cannot without great difficulty follow.

In the next chapter, I delve more deeply into the problem of cognition and its relation to language, as well as analyze how certain tenets of nonlinear science infuse Emerson's vision of the whole of nature. Certainly nonlinear science—including nonlinear dynamics, or the so-called chaos theory—raises significant questions about the presence of order within disorder and about the relationship between perception and intuition, both of which are principal Emersonian themes. Nonlinearity offers a description of nature that has been frequently summarized as "orderly disorder." Unlike linear relationships, nonlinear relationships are not easy to think about, as they are not easily captured by language or pictorial representation. Nonlinear equations do not offer single solutions, nor even any discrete solution, and they often deal with unknown parameters, or parameters so numerous as to defy calculation. Nonlinear relationships often cannot be graphed, even in three dimensions. Nonlinear relationships are not modular, as the elements and conditions acting on them can change over time. But more particularly, nonlinear functions force us to think about the world in unexpected ways. They suggest that small causes—in weather systems, for example—can give rise to enormous effects. They allow that the measurement of irregular forms—as in the length of coastlines—will not converge to a set limit but will increase without limit as measurement scales decrease. They point toward recursive symmetries (or deep structures) between scale levels—describing turbulent flow, for example, as swirls within swirls. And they make use of feedback loops, or iteration, in which output is reincorporated as input and a system becomes characterized by certain self-sustaining behaviors. So if nonlinear science is conducive to thinking about Emerson, the reverse is also true: Emerson forces the reader to rethink the connection between definitions of order and definitions of consciousness—that is, the mind's acts of composition, and the way that mind itself is composed. The result is a philosophy of nonlinearity that aims to raise our wonderment and awe of the seeming complexity, yet remarkable simplicity, of the inner workings of nature.

5

ON THE BROW OF CHAOS

How idle to choose a random sparkle here or there, when the indwelling
necessity plants the rose of beauty on the brow of chaos, and discloses
the central intention of Nature to be harmony and joy.

—Ralph Waldo Emerson, "Fate," *The Conduct of Life* (1860)

Thus far I have emphasized the Aristotelian components of Emerson's
rather eclectic philosophy of nature in order to distance my arguments
from those more heavily focused on Plato and Bacon, whose respective
shadows fall over many twentieth-century studies of Emerson's work. In
Chapter 4, I argued that Emerson looked to Aristotelian models of intellect
and form theory in order to bridge the mind/matter divide created by the
linear abstractions of Enlightenment science. And in Chapter 2, I made
note of how Emerson criticizes Baconian science as being too reductive in
its strict materialist approach toward scientific investigations of the world.
In the present chapter, I change tack somewhat by emphasizing Emerson's
distance from Aristotelian teleology (in which final cause is expressed by an
action principle—admittedly a major theme in Emerson's thought) in
order to suggest some of the ways in which Emerson was thinking beyond
Aristotle in this regard. This chapter explores more particularly his speculations on the behavior of natural systems as they develop over time.

On the one hand, I wish to close out the argument I have been making
throughout that Emerson's natural philosophy is nonlinear and harmonic, in

sharp contrast to the linear and modular understanding passed down from the Enlightenment. On the other hand, what emerges in the broader context of my discussion is a theory of Mind, as it emerges in Emerson's work, that focuses more on the mind's "software" than its "hardware." By moving away from the standard ontological approaches to knowledge typical of laboratory science (those that assume physical models of natural systems represent nature as is, such that scientific inquiry consists chiefly of manipulating the model) and toward an epistemic or knowledge synthesis approach (one that assumes physical models of natural systems are incomplete and focuses instead on examining the conceptual mechanisms of our thought processes), I wish to explore not simply Emerson's way of representing nature, but also his way of thinking about it—in essence, his way of seeing it from a particular point of view so as to derive new insights into its inner workings. To that end, I confine the scope of my discussion of the growth of knowledge to the cognitive explanations favored by Emerson, in contrast to the explanations of simple logic, which argue that new knowledge is derived from old, and social explanations, which point to hierarchical organization, power structures, economic necessity, networking relationships, mutual interests, and so forth, to explain the emergence of new knowledge. Cognitive theories point to the mental structures and procedures of thought available to the conscious mind, a favorite topic to which Emerson turns again and again.

Physical models of nature can work in both ontological and epistemic directions. For example, when Emerson walked through the protoevolutionary exhibits at the Jardin des Plantes in 1833, he was introduced not just to an organizing principle (morphological classification, as discussed in Chapter 2) used to interpret Nature ontologically, but also to a novel means of physical modeling that sought to organize not only the things themselves (plants, animals, shells, and so on) but also our knowledge about those things, that is, the ways people talk about and understand them. And since Emerson thought of Nature as an analogue for Mind—one of the lessons of Paris— talking about principles of Nature became for him a way of talking about both. As I discussed in Chapter 3 with regard to Emerson's assumptions about the influence of sight on cognition, the brain/body hardware (typified by the functions of the eye) integrates so nicely with the hardware of Nature that the Mind of humans and the Mind of Nature come together, at the deepest levels, seemingly without need of intercession by either brain or body.

And yet, the intercessory function of brain/body hardware cannot be ignored, as it is through the body that we come to know the world around us. But knowledge is not something to be grasped like a tool; it is made up of concepts, or mental states (an idea, a feeling, an intuition, and so forth), that bear particular relationships to some feature of the world at large. Indeed, this is the very premise behind Emerson's arguments in *Nature* that "words are signs of natural facts," "particular natural facts are symbols of particular spiritual facts," and "Nature is the symbol of spirit" (*CollW*, 1:17). As Emerson reminds us, then, language and embodiment are thus never far apart. It is one of the "use[s] of the outer creation, to give us language for the beings and changes of the inward creation"; thus it is that the Poet exploits sensory modes of access and "puts eyes, and a tongue, into every dumb and inanimate object" (1:18, 3:12)—not only making the world known but also making us known to ourselves. Indeed, the power of language to maximize knowledge acquisition, especially when spoken under the proper conditions of active seeing (discussed in Chapter 1), initiates us into what Emerson calls the "science of the real" (3:8). Thus, while what we know is a product of what sort of sensory input comes into the body, the ways in which we talk about that information are a collective index to our understanding—to what we know about what we know.

But if poetic insight, like scientific insight, puts a tongue into every dumb object, the task is nonetheless difficult, Emerson argues, because the necessary words are simply not available. Observation does not always lead directly to precise description. "But when the fact is not yet put into English words, when I look at the tree or the river and have not yet definitely made out what they would say to me, they are by no means unimpressive. I wait for them, I enjoy them before they yet speak" (*CW*, 12:5). And even when one's available language is adequate to the task of describing Nature, one's usage may not convey ideas clearly and concisely: "whenever we are so finely organized that we can penetrate into that region where the air is music, we hear those primal warblings, and attempt to write them down, but we lose ever and anon a word, or a verse, and substitute something of our own, and thus miswrite the poem" of understanding (*CollW*, 3:5–6). Thus on the one hand, Nature does not provide for ready use all the words needed to describe her mysteries, and on the other, in most ordinary attempts to explain Nature's wonders, "adequate expression is rare" because "the great majority of men seem to be . . . mutes, who cannot report the conversation they have had with nature." It seems that Nature's "rays or appulses have sufficient force to arrive at the senses, but not enough to reach the quick, and compel the reproduction of themselves in speech" (4–5).

Qualitatively speaking, language itself may be part of the problem, insofar as words function merely as tools for describing human perceptions and as such do not provide a useful enough means of expanding the boundaries of those perceptions. Emerson wanted language that was both accurate and imaginative, but by the nineteenth century it was widely presumed that these two qualities were categorically exclusive. In separating physics and metaphysics from each other, Descartes, in his *Discourse on Method* (1637), in effect divided language into two major sets of representation: physical and teleological signification. His preference for mathematics as the best language for science—rational, certain, self-evident, descriptive—was a hallmark of the coming Newtonian age, which valued abstraction and linearity most of all. Enlightenment literature followed suit: "When the novel appeared it was guided by the rules of empirical description and linear cause and effect. Novelistic characters, like the billiard balls of Newtonian physics, were subject to the laws of action and reaction. . . . European poets and, later, novelists turned from the richly complex linguistic textures of Renaissance poetry and narrative to what they supposed were neoclassical virtues . . . [but their] literary language was constrained by a 'neoclassical decorum' that had as much to do with mathematical abstractions and linear description as the 'classical' qualities of Greek and Latin literature." The Romantic response to neoclassicism only further encouraged the separation of descriptive, linear language from imaginative, spiritual language. In the well-known fourteenth chapter of *Biographia Literaria* (1817), Samuel Coleridge, while discussing the poems of Wordsworth, defines poetry in terms of its opposition to science—the one written in the pursuit of pleasure, the other of truth: "A poem is that species of composition, which is opposed to works of science, by proposing for its *immediate* object pleasure, not truth; and from all other species (having *this* object in common with it) it is discriminated by proposing to itself such delight from the *whole*, as is compatible with a distinct gratification from each component *part*." Coleridge's division of the factual language of science from the merely emblematic language of literature persists through the nineteenth and twentieth centuries. "'Literature' in its familiar modern sense was thus born the moment poetry renounced claims to any but 'fictive' truth."[1]

Another problem with language is the apparent arbitrariness of words, in their role as signs of natural facts. Following up on Bacon's program for stripping the mind of speculation, which included reducing language to a system of transparent signs, John Locke argued in *An Essay Concerning Human Understanding* (1690) that the function of language was to provide signs for our ideas and knowledge, that in this role its words were derived from our sensory perceptions, and that its greatest value lay in its usefulness for efficient and direct communication. As such, words themselves he considered to be arbitrary, having no direct connection to the objects and ideas they describe. Further, Locke suggested that whatever meaning words contain is dependent on sociological, historical, and political context: words have no essential or inherent meaning themselves but only that commonly agreed upon in any particular time or place by those who use them. Despite the fact that Locke's theory is based upon highly abstract, idealized, and unrealistic assumptions about Mind, the influence of ideas like his can be seen from the nineteenth century's biblical criticism to today's postmodern culture wars. By stripping words of any nonfunctional value, Locke throws the meaning of imagination and insight into irresolvable conflict. Thus, "just as [Emerson] had to reject the scientific methodology of his fellow Americans, he also had to throw off their notions of words. Bacon's reign extended not only over science but also language. Inflected through Locke and [Dugald] Stewart, Bacon's dreams of a transparent language stripped of figure had firm control over language theory in Emerson's America."[2] For Emerson, the difficulty for the Poet was compounded: not only was he to serve as an Adamic namer of things previously unperceived, drawing on the premise that "words are signs of natural facts," but also he was to instruct others on how to perceive. Both tasks are rendered futile, it seems, in the wake of Locke: within the Lockean paradigm, imaginative language is a contextual mirage.

Rhetorically, then, Emerson's ultimate desire as a speechmaker—to see the Poet whom he describes reflected in the faces of his audience—is

1. Philip Kuberski, *Chaosmos: Literature, Science, and Theory*, 18; Samuel Taylor Coleridge, *Biographia Literaria; or, Biographical Sketches of My Literary Life and Opinions*, 13; Kuberski, *Chaosmos*, 20 (see also 15–22).
2. Wilson, *Emerson's Sublime Science*, 100.

doomed to fail under the conditions of language Locke describes: auditors will not follow where they think words cannot go. Further, because of the Cartesian and Coleridgean division of literary language and scientific language, the writer who aims to describe the actual while adhering to modes of thought traditionally bound to the imaginary—the sort of thing Marianne Moore later cited as "imaginary gardens with real toads in them"—faces an uphill battle.[3] The result is that today Emerson's understanding of Nature, and the ways he sees and perceives of Nature, more often than not come to be interpreted as the subjects of a private rather than a communal vision. His writings are read through the lens of personality, and his words, albeit highly descriptive, sensory, and precise, come to be seen as evidence of metaphorical ruminations on private thoughts, private complexes, and continuously slippery notions of art, culture, and power. For example, in her discussion of Emerson and evolution in *Spires of Form* (1951), Vivian Hopkins calls attention to the metamorphosis of natural forms throughout the biological orders of which Emerson was so keen. She argues that Emerson conceives of nature "as repeating the same process on different planes, from plant, to animal, to man," not because of what Emerson knew to be an observationally demonstrable principle of iteration at work in the natural world, but because "optimism governs this theory."[4] The example may be dated, but it is representative of a trend. As I pointed out in Chapters 1 and 2, this kind of linguistic transference is one of the norms of Emerson criticism, not the exception—a way of avoiding what Emerson was really talking about, often because his observations are not considered to be "scientific."

Emerson thought of Nature as an open book waiting to be read, but it was a book without words and written in a language few could understand. In "The Poet" he writes, "We know the secret of the world is profound, but who or what shall be our interpreter, we know not" (*CollW*, 3:7). That secret was undeniably there to be read, however. In "The Uses of Natural History," Emerson refers to "this natural alphabet, this green and yellow and crimson dictionary" on display at the Jardin des Plantes in Paris, "where grows a grammar of botany" (*EL*, 1:8). But while he often affirmed, on the one hand,

---

3. Marianne Moore, *Complete Poems*, 267.

4. Vivian Hopkins, *Spires of Form: A Study of Emerson's Aesthetic Theory*, 123; see also page 3: "Optimism controls Emerson's idea of the circle becoming a spiral, ever rising even as it revolves upon itself."

that "Nature furnishes the nouns which must be of use whenever & where-ever" (*JMN*, 13:376), Emerson also struggled with the problem, on the other hand, that "Nature never troubles herself with the difficulty which Language finds in expressing her" (*JMN*, 8:69). Simply put, natural language and man-made language are two distinct entities, existing, often at odds, for different uses and ends. While Nature's language contains all things—"I believe in Omnipresence & find footsteps in Grammar rules, in oyster shops, in church liturgies, in mathematics, and in solitudes & in galaxies" (*JMN*, 10:35)—human language does not contain enough: "One who looks at the clouds or the aspect of a tree sees how rude & initial our language is, we cannot yet begin to describe these things" (*JMN*, 8:372). Indeed, for Emerson human language did not contain enough even to describe man to himself—for even that which he could make sense of with the mind and eye often escaped the grasp of words: "The manners of the eye reveal all the interiors of the man[,] yet is our language inadequate to paint them" (*JMN*, 11:151).

Contemporary science offered a vocabulary for talking about nature, but as Emerson argues, it too offered little in the way of providing access to the untranslated language of Nature. "I wish I knew the nomenclature of botany & astronomy. But these are soulless both, as we know them; vocab-ularies both. . . . We must hold our science as mere convenience, expectant of a higher method from the mind itself" (*JMN*, 13:374). Such comments are common in Emerson's work, and the fundamental point he argues through them is that maximizing knowledge is not about accumulating facts and figures, in the manner of conventional science, but about maxi-mizing language—about expanding both the modes and means of expres-sion we have for talking about nature, of finding new and insightful ways to think about natural systems and the various roles of the elements within them. "The love of nature [—] what is that but the presentiment of intelli-gence of it: nature preparing to become a language to us" (*JMN*, 7:412).

In addition, this language was to Emerson more than mere words. He describes knowledge acquisition on a continuum from the senses to the higher powers of the mind. It begins with "the daily accidents which the senses report, and which make the raw material of knowledge." In this first form, "it was sensation; when memory came, it was experience; when mind acted, it was knowledge; when mind acted on it as knowledge, it was thought" (*CW*, 8:24). Language exists on the high plane of thought, where its inventiveness, playfulness, and ingenuity make possible the mind's insight into the lower domains of consciousness—our sensation, experience, and raw knowledge of the world. But this language can be expressed in many forms: "I think that he only is rightly immortal to whom all things are immortal; he who witnesses personally the creation of the world; he who enunciates profoundly the names of Pan, of Jove, of Pallas, of Bacchus, of Proteus, of Baal, of Ahriman, of Hari, of Satan, of Hell, of Nemesis, of the Furies, of Odin, & of Hertha;—knowing full well the need he has of these, and a far richer vocabulary; knows well how imperfect & insufficient to his needs language is; requiring music, requiring dancing, as languages; a dance, for example, that shall sensibly express our astronomy, our solar system, & seasons, in its course" (*JMN*, 9:452). Here, language is sound and action as well as words, both of which Emerson considered, like an earlier age of science, to be a kind of naming for natural processes, from the movement of heavenly bodies to the change of seasons. All levels of experience, both verbal and nonverbal, give insight into Nature's language, which is, like dancing, about conceptualizing development and change through time and space.

As Emerson argued, we arrive at knowledge through the modes of perception available to us, primarily through seeing and speaking, and not through the manipulations of a formal model assembled according to some set of physical laws. "Nature is a language & every new fact that we learn is a new word; but rightly seen, taken all together it is not merely a language but the language put together into a most significant & universal book." He argues that language creates a space in the mind for new knowledge, not the other way around: "I wish to learn the language not that I may know a new set of nouns & verbs but that I may read the great book which is written in that tongue" (*JMN*, 4:95).[5] In the Lockean and Baconian model of science, the expansion of knowledge domains—as seen in the disciplinary flowering of nineteenth-century science: ecology, geology, chemistry, meteorology, psychology, evolution, electrodynamics, and the like—drives the growth of language, or as Emerson would say, the creation of "vocabularies." An alternate model claims the opposite, that the expansion of language—not so much in the number of words but in the ways we use them to talk about the world—opens the mind for new knowledge.

---

5. See also "The Uses of Natural History," *EL*, 1:26.

In their initial, conceptual stages, new disciplines often proceed in this manner, positing an array of new ideas, many of which may not stand the test of time, but many of which do. For example, in coining the phrase "arrested and progressive development" in an early delivery of "Poetry and Imagination," the first essay in *Letters and Social Aims*, Emerson provided his auditors a startling new way of thinking about the methods of evolutionary process, one which had not been widely accepted and one which Charles Darwin would later (independently) expand on.[6] But for relatively well-developed sciences, such as astronomy, Emerson found that the ways of talking about things had become habitual and limited, which is to say that the Newtonian model of the universe was no longer a means of expanding conceptual understanding but of controlling it. In his essay on Swedenborg in *Representative Men,* Emerson argues, for example, that although "gravitation, as explained by Newton, is good," there is "a sort of gravitation operative also in the mental phenomena," one that draws the analytic Newtonian mind into an endless tabulation of facts and figures. In such a state, the mind loses sight of broader interdisciplinary concepts. Indeed, "what we call gravitation, and fancy ultimate, is one fork of a mightier stream for which we have yet no name. Astronomy is excellent; but it must come up into life to have its full value, and not remain there in globes and spaces." By not using language to explore new ideas and open up wider avenues of thought, the "grand rhymes or returns in nature" go unexplored, and science reduces itself to "an aimless accumulation of experiments" (*CollW*, 4:62). Indeed, the mightier stream or unified theory Emerson imagines here has yet to be found.[7]

6. Emerson attributes the phrase to John Hunter, but he himself coined it to summarize some of Hunter's key ideas. See Allen, *Waldo Emerson,* for an account of the lecture and Moncure Conway's effort to identify Emerson's sources in the works of Hunter, Erasmus Darwin, and Robert Chambers (574–75). See also *CW*, 8:359–60n7.

7. The main obstacle in the way of a grand unified theory involves reconciling the physical laws of general relativity with those of quantum mechanics, a problem to which Einstein unsuccessfully devoted his later life. M-theory offers the best potential candidate for a unified theory of the universe at present. However, even though its ability to unite general relativity, quantum mechanics, and the various string theories under the same umbrella has proved to be conceptually useful in opening up new ways of thinking about the universe, M-theory, like the string theories, is untestable, and so it remains a specialized branch of philosophical mathematics, not a proper science. While supercolliders are being used to look for evidence of strings at the quantum level, their general acceptance by most physicists has yet to occur.

In his introduction to the 1854 essay "Poetry and Imagination" (*CW*, 8:1–75),[8] throughout which cognition is a running theme, Emerson makes a clear distinction between two types of knowledge, both of which are assumed by Darwinian evolutionary theory. In broad terms, Darwin's theory is an account of the historical growth and development of knowledge in individuals and species. More particularly, evolution is a process of knowledge acquisition, in which information about the environment is incorporated into the ontogenetic and phylogenic development of organisms by means of a continuous, oftentimes cognition-based, procedure of adaptation. That is, information is acquired through experience, expressed (in most cases) through behavioral traits, and then passed on to the species at large through the long-term processes of reproduction and natural selection. What develops over time, then, are two kinds of knowledge bases, endosomatic knowledge, or information acquired through species-wide adaptation and subsequent genetic transmission to future generations, and exosomatic knowledge, or information behaviorally encoded through an individual's contact with the environment. Exosomatic knowledge provides for a localized knowledge base that is made up of site-specific information about real-world systems. This type of knowledge includes the kind of data generated by individual experience, as well as that produced by empirical observation, an awareness of uncertainty, and various types of experimentation (whether controlled or trial-and-error). It is time- and place-dependent. Additionally, while exosomatic knowledge will have varying degrees of applicability across locations, times, or situations, information in this knowledge domain, as is the case with a street map of New York City for example, will be highly context-dependent. Eventually, localized knowledge with the greatest degrees of applicability becomes encoded, through the evolutionary process, as endosomatic knowledge. Among humans, endosomatic knowledge allows for a general knowledge base, made up of various constructs having broad-based, across-the-board validity: the stuff of general scientific theories, physical laws, or simple Euclidean equations, for example. This knowledge base exists independently of time and place.[9]

8. In the following discussion of "Poetry and Imagination," all quotations from the essay may be found on pages 1–25.

9. For more detailed discussions of evolutionary epistemology, in which these ideas are explored more fully, see Gerard Radnitzsky and W. W. Bartley III, eds., *Evolutionary Epistemology, Rationality, and the Sociology of Knowledge* (LaSalle, Ill.: Open Court, 1993), and Alvin Goldman, *Epistemology and Cognition* (Cambridge: Harvard University Press, 1986).

The Origin of Species was not published in the United States until 1859. By distinguishing between endosomatic and exosomatic knowledge domains, as well as by exploring the evolutionary relationship between them, Emerson anticipates the Darwinian account of knowledge acquisition, although very broadly and in limited ways. The opening sentence of "Poetry and Imagination" sets forth the argument, "The perception of matter is made the common sense." Without specifically referring to adaptation, Emerson nonetheless notes how a certain kind of fundamental contact with nature (the perception of matter) becomes transferred into the general knowledge base, what he refers to in the essay as the common sense. "This [transfer] was the cradle, this the go-cart, of the human child. We must learn the homely laws of fire and water; we must feed, wash, plant, build. These are ends of necessity, and first in the order of Nature." Indeed, this type of knowledge, made up of the rules and laws governing the most basic processes of organic life, appears to have such a terrific force of self-evidence that even the tempering influence of self-awareness cannot induce us to imagine otherwise: "The intellect, yielded up to itself, cannot supersede this tyrannic necessity." What develops from this first assumption, then, is the further assumption that information contained within the common sense or general knowledge base unerringly points to the world as it really is. Thus, within this knowledge domain, the force of thousands of years of human experience tells us that we, as a species, live in a world that—when seen from a perceptual, biological, and behavioral point of view—offers limited alternatives. In other words, we, as a species, have adapted to it: "The common sense which does not meddle with the absolute, but takes things at their word,—things as they appear,—believes in the existence of matter, not because we can touch it or conceive of it, but because it agrees with ourselves, and the universe does not jest with us, but is in earnest, is the house of health and life. In spite of all the joys of poets and the joys of saints, the most imaginative person never makes with impunity the least mistake in this particular,—never tries to kindle his oven with water, nor carries a torch into a powder-mill, nor seizes his wild charger by the tail. We should not pardon the blunder in another, nor endure it in ourselves." It is because of the existence of a general knowledge base, tied at the most rudimentary level to the inheritance of our genes, that we believe in the existence of matter and "things as they appear"—not because we touch matter or have language to conceive of it, but because we know in some instinctual way, for example, that fire and wild horses can be inherently dangerous. Our behavioral adaptations,

Emerson suggests, give us the obvious advantage of a greater chance of survival, so much so that, as he writes, we would neither pardon nor endure the blunder of acting in a manner that does not accord with our instincts.

What arises from our response to this knowledge base, then, is a science of ontology—the belief that it is possible to know, to use Emerson's phrase, "things as they appear." In other words, what you see is what you get: the idea that models of natural systems—that is, analytical representations of "reality"—can be constructed so as to describe nature as it really is, stripped down to fundamental particles and processes, has become the driving force behind the ontological approach of conventional science. This basic empirical assumption finds its oldest support in Aristotle's definition of human beings as rational animals, as well as in Socrates' belief in the works of Plato that one cannot possess knowledge of a thing (beauty, justice, piety, and so on) without first giving a formal account of it. But it finds its most recognizable appeal in various forms of eighteenth-century mathematical formalism, from Newton to Hobbes.

Of course, good models must also account for the passage of time and the development of systems through time. The idea of process in ontological modeling has been understood both before and after the Enlightenment as being primarily physical (though some, like Hobbes, questioned the mind's ability to "know" process at all). Premodern definitions retained, though increasingly discarded, a strong notion of divine agency as well as strict kinetic interaction, as found in Aristotle's explanation, in the *Physics,* of force in terms of direct contact and a prime mover, but Galileo's experiments with acceleration and Newton's theory of gravitation refined the idea of process to more strictly material terms. Additionally, the numerous variational principles of conventional science support the idea that the energies contained within complex systems range from minimum to maximum potentials that average out to steady variational states,[10] supporting a widespread understanding of nature as a central stillness. And in a nineteenth-

10. This is the principle of minimum potential energy, which states that the average energy for a system in any quantum state must be at least as large as the lowest energy state, or ground state, of the system. The discovery of the variational principle is generally attributed to de Maupertuis, who cited the principle of least action as evidence of rationality in a divine creation; however, the oldest forms of the variational principle can be traced back to Aristotle. Euler, Lagrange, and others formalized the variational principle in the eighteenth century, but the ultimate reason why it holds true in nature is still unknown.

century evolutionary context, in which various evolutionary theories emerged against a backdrop of increasing interest in historiography (as seen, for example, in Comte's organization of past and present into culminating developmental stages), there also emerges in the conventional ontological approach to modeling a genetic hypothesis, which claims that knowing a thing fully is to know its origins.[11] Thus understood, even the most vast and complex of natural systems come to be seen as closed and self-contained— well outside the influence of forces such as divine agency, or, as Hume rigorously argued in *An Enquiry Concerning Human Understanding* (1748), the purview of the miraculous, or even, as Newtonian astrophysics claims, the spontaneous emergence, seemingly *ex nihilo*, of the random and chaotic. Collectively, these penchants for materialism, experimental isolationism, and reductionism in ontological science helped produce a very strange situation, one in which the model itself (including the laboratory) replaces the reality it is meant to describe. Conventional ontological science assumes that not only can we know by observation, but also we can know, by means of analytical prediction (if our models are good enough), what we do not observe. While the results of such predictions must be independently replicated to become accepted as fact, such procedural redundancy is as likely to verify only the self-evidence of the model as it is to confirm new truths about nature. Emerson expresses his frustration with this state of affairs clearly in *The Conduct of Life:* "What a parade we make of our science, and how far off, and at arm's length, it is from its objects!" (*CollW,* 6:150).

In "Poetry and Imagination," Emerson describes the creation of the endosomatic knowledge base—"things as they appear"—as an inductively motivated process: certain repeated perceptions of the world lead to generalized understandings of natural phenomena, and thus to what is taken to be a "common sense" view of the world. But his main concern is that this common sense underlying the conventional ontological approach to modeling natural systems is not complete. Emerson's main point is that "whilst

---

11. The problem of origins also plays a role in definitions of consciousness, ranging from reductionism in Hobbes, who argued that consciousness is an illusionary epiphenomenon, to essentialism in Huxley, who argued that it is a distinct human trait and thus evidence of our superiority over sheer "cosmic process." I do not explore the influence of this debate here, but it does have wider relevance to my discussion of the epistemological problems associated with endosomatic and exosomatic knowledge bases.

we deal with this [the common sense] as finality, early hints are given that we are not to stay here . . .—a warning that this magnificent hotel and conveniency we call Nature is not final." In other words, the solution set offered by an ontological approach to systems analysis—a description of closed systems, made up of primary units and predictable, cause-and-effect processes existing in fundamental equilibrium to one another—does not, by itself, fully account for our everyday experience of reality, in which things like randomness, spontaneity, and agency regularly alter the character and quality of events and natural systems. The conclusions of conventional science, he argues, are not necessarily universal—"Nothing stands still in Nature . . . the creation is on wheels, in transit, always pressing into something else, streaming into something higher"—nor are they always correct. For example, Emerson points out that "matter is not what it appears": instead of fundamental particles and primary units, "the supposed little cubes or prisms of which all matter was built up" and the mainstay of a Newtonian cosmos, "we should not find cubes, or prisms, or atoms, at all, but spherules of force"—an idea confirmed by twentieth-century quantum physics.[12] It is not that the seemingly universal truths of ontological science—the bias toward materialism, for example—turn out from time to time not to be true, such that one need only replace one ontological belief with another that is more refined. Rather, "something more subtle" is at work. Nature is not a central stillness—not simply an assemblage of closed systems existing in equilibrium—but is always "streaming into something higher." What is required is a method of problem solving that offers not only new data and new words but also new concepts and new languages entirely.

Emerson notes in "Poetry and Imagination" how the inadequacy of ontological modeling is made apparent by the "innuendos, then broad hints, then smart taps" given by Nature that the common-sense scientific view is "only provisional." He also argues that Nature, and each particle in it, is "steeped in thought." Evidence of the mind of Nature was most obviously evident to him in biological metamorphosis—in the evolutionary growth of forms, observed across the scale of being, driven not only by

12. See also Chapter 2, wherein this passage is cited more fully. Emerson makes these comments in reference to Faraday, whose experiments in electromagnetism, electrolysis, chemistry, light, and the physics of flames were well known, although his ideas about the "new" force of electromagnetism were not proven until many decades after he first proposed them.

environmental stimuli but also by an internal principle or law of self-generation: "Thin or solid, everything is in flight. I believe this conviction makes the charm of chemistry,—that we have the same avoirdupois matter in an alembic, without a vestige of the old form; and in animal transformation not less, as in grub and fly, in egg and bird, in embryo and man; everything undressing and stealing away from its old into new form, and nothing fast but those invisible cords which we call laws, on which all is strung." What Emerson believes we begin to understand from the observation of the metamorphosis of forms throughout the natural world is the presence of some fundamental law at work that a disciplinarily fractured approach to science can observe and catalog and describe, but not synthesize into an encompassing theory. Therefore the common sense arising from the conventional ontological approach of traditional science begins to seem, as Emerson says, "a makeshift." Because standard empirical science relies "on the clearest and most economical mode of administering the material world, considered as final"—that is, because it reduces our basic understanding of nature to a description of sheer matter in motion—"everything is compromised." As a result, our knowledge of the true Nature falls short. Rather than know Nature as it really is, we know more instead about the models created to describe it. Eventually, the realization that the models are inadequate "sets the dullest brain in ferment."

Nature is, Emerson knew, fundamentally uniform: Nature's "secret codes or laws show their well-worn virtue through every variety, be it animal, or plant, or planet." As Goethe argued, the fundamental unity of Nature suggests that vast and complex natural systems cannot be properly modeled, as in the laboratory, when separated from their real-world contexts. For this reason, Emerson believed Nature itself provided the strongest argument against the fracturing of science into isolated disciplines. The fact that each of those disciplines can justify itself by producing such great quantities of data and a specialized vocabulary is mere solipsism: while a disciplinarily fractured science is able to say much about the categorical parts of complex natural systems—the specific biomechanical mechanisms driving the development of an embryo into an adult mammal, for example—it cannot say why similar processes appear to be at work in so many other domains of being. A true knowledge, and a better kind of science, would say why such "invisible chords which we call laws" appear to exist everywhere; a better kind of science would not be broken into so many parts. Therefore, Emerson argues, the scientific mind should seek the same level of uniformity for itself. That is to say, he believes we must reconsider not simply the means by which we model and analyze complex systems. Rather, we must also reevaluate the conceptual mechanisms of our thinking, the habits of mind, both individual and hardwired, that allow us to understand things as we do: "Whilst the man is startled by this closer inspection of the laws of matter, his attention is called to the independent action of the mind; its strange suggestions and laws; a certain tyranny which springs up in his own thoughts, which have an order, method and beliefs of their own"—ones which, it turns out, are "very different from the order which this common sense uses."

It may at first appear that Emerson simply advocates a remingling of science and metaphysics, which the Enlightenment mind, particularly among the Scottish Realists, fought so hard to disentangle. In the first lecture of his *Mind and Manners* series, for example, Emerson implies as much when he notes how the disciplinary "narrowness" of "foolish scholars" shows how "a whole Scotland of argumentation does not really help us" (*LL,* 1:150). However, Emerson sees metaphysics as merely another order in the whole domain of knowledge, and his main focus in "Poetry and Imagination" is on epistemological considerations. Emerson expresses what is fundamentally an epistemic and cognition-based theory of knowledge acquisition: a description of knowledge tied not to the manipulation of ontologically "correct" models but to the conceptual mechanisms of thought driving our inquiry. Indeed, the evolutionary observation that "the creation is on wheels, in transit, always passing into something else," leads Emerson to a much bolder speculation about the modeling problem, "that under chemistry [is] power and purpose; power and purpose ride on matter to the last atom. It [Nature] [is] steeped in thought; that, as great conquerors have burned their ships when once they were landed on the wished-for shore, so the noble house of Nature we inhabit has temporary uses, and we can afford to leave it one day. . . . Then we see that things wear different names and faces, but belong to one family; that the secret codes or laws show their well-known virtue, be it animal, or plant, or planet, and the interest is gradually transferred from the forms to the lurking method." Because Nature is steeped in thought—existing most fully, and fundamentally, in the form

of organizing principles—the objects of scientific study are not as important as "the lurking method" behind it all. In this way, Emerson presents
the modeling of natural systems as a knowledge synthesis problem. It is
important to note that Emerson does not express a Platonic view here;
rather, the salient contrast is between data contained in the site-specific
knowledge base of the sciences (in this case, chemistry) and the principles
of thought found in the general knowledge base of humans as rational animals—between our awareness of the phenomena of Nature and our conceptual understanding of what propels them, developmentally, through
space and time.

Emerson describes a process of gradual awareness, a moving away from
inadequate models that produce a lot of descriptive data and toward an
epistemic consideration of cognitive process. "Such currents . . . exist in
thoughts," he notes, "that as soon as one thought begins, it refuses to
remember whose brain it belongs to."[13] Indeed, "one of these vortices or
self-directions of thought is the impulse to search resemblance, affinity,
identity, in all its objects, and hence our science,"—taken as a whole—
"from its rudest to its most refined theories." Emerson identifies one major
principle of knowledge synthesis, the principle of parallelism or the ability
of the mind to readily identify resemblances between otherwise differing
objects. Thus it is we know that "identity of law, perfect order in physics,
perfect parallelism between the laws of Nature and the laws of thought
exist"[14]—because an epistemic consideration of cognitive process leads us
to expect, and observation confirms, that such is the case. And the principle
holds, Emerson suggests, across disciplines:

13. This is an early expression of one of the main principles in contemporary meme theory, which analyzes the spread of self-propagating pieces of cultural information in both
evolutionary and genetic terms. Such information includes behaviors particularly, but also
phrases, ideas, melodies, skills, values—anything that can be learned as a contained unit and
passed on.

14. This is what has commonly been called correspondence theory in Emerson studies,
following his use of the term elsewhere. In "Poetry and Imagination," Emerson reiterates the
idea in saying, "Walking, working or talking, the sole question is how many strokes vibrate
on this mystic string,—how many diameters are drawn quite through from matter to spirit;
for whenever you enunciate a natural law you discover that you have enunciated a law of the
mind." However, the "parallelism" to which Emerson refers ought not be taken to refer to a
linear construct, in the sense of set ratios or cause-and-effect relationships; rather, Emerson
defines correspondence as referring to a relationship between differing scales of experience
and of contact with nature.

> In botany we have the like, the poetic perception of metamorphosis,—
> that the same vegetable point or eye which is the unit of the plant can be
> transformed at pleasure into every part, as bract, leaf, petal, stamen, pistil
> or seed. In geology, what a useful hint was given to the early inquirers on
> seeing in the possession of Professor Playfair a bough of a fossil tree which
> was perfect wood at one end and perfect mineral coal at the other. Natural
> objects, if individually described and out of connection, are not yet
> known, since they are really parts of a symmetrical universe, like words of
> a sentence; and if their true order is found, the poet can read their divine
> significance orderly as in a Bible. Each animal or vegetable form remem-
> bers the next inferior and predicts the higher.

Our "reading" (meaning *understanding*) of Nature depends on how we talk
about what we observe. If it is from the point of view of seeing that complex
forms grow out of simpler ones, then natural objects (in this case, biological forms) appear like the words in a sentence: they will be fairly meaningless and arbitrary if taken separately but capable of expressing complex
ideas if taken collectively, or "in series" as Emerson often puts it.

Additionally, Emerson argues that "there is one animal, one plant, one
matter, and one force," implying that therefore there must be one science:
"The laws of light and of heat translate each other;—so do the laws of sound
and color; and so galvanism, electricity and magnetism are varied forms of
the selfsame energy." An expansive, interdisciplinary approach opens the
mind to ever greater sentences in the language of the natural world:

> While the student ponders this immense unity [in the laws of Nature], he
> observes that all things in Nature, the animals, the mountain, the river, the
> seasons, wood, iron, stone, vapor, have a mysterious relation to his
> thoughts and his life; their growths, decays, quality and use so curiously
> resemble himself, in parts and in wholes, that he is compelled to speak by
> means of them. His words and his thoughts are framed by their help.
> Every noun is an image. Nature gives him, sometimes in a flattered like-
> ness, sometimes in caricature, a copy of every humor and shade in his
> character and mind. The world is an immense picture-book of every pas-
> sage in human life. Every object he beholds is the mask of a man.

In this passage, Emerson presents knowledge acquisition as language
acquisition, with the clear implication that we know only as much as we

can speak. To repeat: representing nature, practically and conceptually, for the purpose of scientific inquiry is, Emerson argues, an epistemic problem, not an ontological one. That is to say, the breadth of our knowledge depends on cognitive issues, not on how well we can model nature as is. The "common sense" understanding, such as that arising from the ontological approach of empirical science, misses the mark in this regard. As noted above, it "takes things at their word" and "believes in the existence of matter," but not much more; it never calls for a reexamination of the conceptual mechanisms of scientific thinking. Thus, "chemistry, geology, hydraulics, are secondary science," and the solutions they produce are of value only to the scientist who finds his or her own beliefs reinforced by them. Emerson notes, for example, that "the atomic theory is only an interior process *produced,* as geometers say, or the effect of a foregone metaphysical theory"—one that does not leave room for adventuring beyond the ontological biases limiting science to data collection through the measurement of matter in motion. "Mountains and oceans we think we understand;—yes, so long as they are contented to be such, and are safe with the geologist,—but when they are melted in Promethean alembics and come out men, and then, melted again, come out words, without any abatement, but with an exaltation of power!"

From a cognitive point of view, the problem with common sense is that it often relies on belief, and belief is notoriously unreliable, often wrong, and certainly an inadequate means of advancing knowledge of the world. Knowledge is made up of concepts (mental states that bear a particular relationship to some aspect of the world at large), and concepts are derived from perception or postulation, or as the products of a reasoning process. A belief is a complex mental structure that organizes concepts in a specific way. Beliefs, however, are not derived from their own role in a reasoning process; they are derived from the way they use concepts. Concepts alone play the primary role in valid reasoning, and not the various possible beliefs (more strictly, prejudices) in which those concepts happen to be contained. In other words, beliefs have a stake in the outcome of reasoning and problem solving, which may threaten to overturn them. Further, beliefs are culturally determined and, if powerful and widespread enough, culturally determining. Their effect is to channel and close the mind, rather than open it. Newtonian linearity is one such example:

By the 1720s Newtonianism had become identified with specific technological programs, with "pure" scientific research, with the institutionaliza-
tion of scientific inquiry under the auspices of Newton's presidency of the
Royal Society, and with the broader sociopolitical implications of Britain's
efforts to "apply" its scientific and technological expertise to a variety of
areas: navigation, trade, manufacturing, mining, and so on. Newtonianism, therefore, must be seen not simply as a form of empirical science or
specialized research but as an ideological structure of beliefs that integrated scientific research into the political and economic operations of
eighteenth-century British society.[15]

By the end of the eighteenth and the beginning of the nineteenth centuries,
the ideological structure of beliefs represented by Newtonianism had taken
hold in America as well. Indeed, it is from a recognition of the effects of such
rising tides of abstraction that Emerson begins his defense of "The American
Scholar": "The state of society is one in which the members have suffered
amputation from the trunk, and strut about so many walking monsters,—a
good finger, a neck, a stomach, an elbow, but never a man" (*CollW,* 1:53).

Empirical science holds to the belief that natural objects can be separated from their environments—that a laboratory is just as good, and perhaps even better, a place to learn about the world as is nature. Expressing
this belief is the widespread scientific practice of controlled experimentation, which allows the researcher to isolate particles, processes, and so forth,
in order to exclude unwanted or unintended causes or agents from having
an effect on the mechanism being studied. Supporting this belief is a deeper
assumption that all systems are modular, that is, they are mere sums of their
parts and nothing more—even though, in their natural environments, natural systems are subject to a huge array of impinging forces and nonphysical processes that a laboratory environment fails to account for. But the very
idea of creating a laboratory as a locus of explanation is bound up in widespread notions regarding a human being's role as observer, rather than participant, in the natural world. Emerson categorically disagreed with this
idea. In "Poetry and Imagination" he writes, "Science was false by being
unpoetical. It assumed to explain a reptile or mollusk, and isolated it,—

15. Robert Markley, "Representing Order: Natural Philosophy, Mathematics, and Theology in the Newtonian Revolution," 141–42.

which is hunting for life in graveyards. Reptile or mollusk or man or angel only exist in system, in relation." The problem is that certain concepts—in this case, *relation*—are preemptively discarded by dogmatic beliefs. Thus, Emerson calls science "unpoetical" because a belief in disciplinary and experimental isolationism does not allow the idea that shellfish, human beings, and spirits might be interrelated in some way to enter into its investigations of the world. To Emerson, this bias was absurd on its face: "We use semblances of logic until experience puts us in possession of real logic." Elsewhere Emerson writes, "true knowledge of the world teaches to hold fast to that which falls not, even whilst we behold the fall of that which taught us it" (*LL,* 1:151).

In addition to its being unpoetical, Emerson also believes that "Science does not know its debt to imagination."[16] The main argument in "Poetry and Imagination" is that imagination is more suited than belief or common sense to extending the frontiers of knowledge. Working without the self-preserving demands of belief, imagination reorders old concepts and invents new ones. Clearly, Emerson defines knowledge from an epistemic and cognitive point of view. As he notes, "The primary use of a fact is low; the secondary use, as it is a figure or illustration of my thought, is the real worth. First the fact; second its impression, or what I think of it." Facts are one kind of concept, and what we think of them another. Both types are subject to either the demands of common sense/belief or the freedoms of imagination. "Whilst common sense looks at things or visible Nature as real and final facts, poetry, or the imagination which dictates it, is a second sight, looking through these, and using them as types or words for thoughts which they signify."

But just as arguments can be valid or invalid, sound or unsound, yet still believed in by minds incognizant of the structure of their logic, so too can the imaginative faculty prematurely range into unwarranted enthusiasm about a false concept.[17] So while imagination is free to move beyond received ideas and conventional beliefs, Emerson does not allow it to be

---

16. Emerson defines imagination as "the vision of an inspired soul reading arguments and affirmations in all Nature of that which it is driven to say" (*CW,* 8:28).

17. In such a case, Emerson explains, the mind is not using Imagination per se; when it "at leisure plays with the resemblances and types, for amusement, and not for its moral end, we call its action Fancy."

haphazard or anarchistic in its approach to knowledge synthesis. Imagination must be confirmed by experience and contact with the world: "A happy symbol is a sort of evidence that your thought is just. I had rather have a good symbol of my thought, or a good analogy, than the suffrage of Kant or Plato. If you agree with me, or if Locke or Montesquieu agree, I may yet be wrong; but if the elm-tree thinks the same thing, if running water, if burning coal, if crystals, if alkalies, in their several fashions say what I say, it must be true."[18] Thus, while the products of imagination might be confirmed by other rational minds, their final affirmation comes from direct observation and the study of Nature's forms—that is, from the way in which the imagination is able to assemble concepts and the mental structures containing them into a kind of language that is agreeable to Nature.

So while "the world exists for thought," the purpose of which "is to make appear things which hide," the best use of the imagination comes from seeking out correspondences between natural forms: "all thinking is analogizing, and it is the use of life to learn metonymy." The metonym is the most important kind of concept, the most meaningful unit of knowledge. A metonym, as Emerson describes it, is any concept denoting the visible part for the invisible whole, or "seeing the same sense in things so diverse"—the change from larva to pupa to adult butterfly, understood as a figure for the principle of metamorphosis at work throughout the natural world, for example. "The endless passing of one element into new forms, the incessant metamorphosis, explains the rank which the imagination holds in our catalogue of mental powers," because "the imagination is the reader of these forms." What we know about the forms themselves (Nature's facts, which science attempts to collect and analyze) is not as important as what we know about what those facts signify, the way in which we talk about them, and the extent to which we apply the principles we uncover across all disciplines. "The poet"—simply, one who uses the imagination instead of relying on common sense or belief—"accounts all productions and changes of Nature as the nouns of language, uses them representatively, too well pleased with their ulterior [meaning] to value much their primary meaning." As Emerson shows in "Poetry and Imagination," the illumination of

18. See also the second lecture in Emerson's *Mind and Manners* series, "Intellect and Natural Science," in which he repeats this passage almost identically, in an expanded discussion of the role of imagination in scientific inquiry (*LL*, 1:163).

conceptual mechanisms and cognitive structures is the real worth of any new knowledge.

So far my discussion has focused on the cognitive basis of (and justification for) my analysis of Emersonian naturalism in terms of nonlinear theory. I have approached the issue in terms of knowledge synthesis. In many essays and lectures, but particularly in "Poetry and Imagination," Emerson strongly emphasizes the inadequacies of laboratory science as a kind of science that replaces the study of real nature with the study of artificial models of nature. The principal problem with such an approach, as Emerson sees it, is that this sort of ontological modeling uses linear paradigms to interpret nature. These paradigms are useful only for knowing the model, whereas real nature is fundamentally nonlinear and thus too complex to be explained by linear modeling. One consequence of this problem, a consequence Emerson laments most of all, is that the scientific mind becomes trained to think in ways that distance it from the mind of Nature. Just as linear modeling inadequately describes natural processes, so too does linear thinking inadequately give access to the laws governing those processes. In order to see them correctly, Emerson argues, we must retrain our minds and establish patterns of thinking that replicate the natural patterns we can actually observe, an activity Emerson frequently refers to as rhyming: "Rhymes. The iterations or rhymes of nature are already an idea or principle of science, & a guide. The sun & star reflect themselves all over the world in the form of flowers & fruits & in the human head & the doctrine of series which takes up again the few functions & modes & repeats them with new & wondrous result on a higher plane.... Then, as I have written before, Astronomy is not yet astronomy, until it is applied to human life; & all our things are to be thus exalted or echoed & reechoed in finer & higher rhymes" (*JMN*, 11:153–54).

Because scientific knowledge is something generated at the human level—as opposed to something handed down from a higher source—Emerson understands scientific inquiry as a knowledge synthesis problem, which explains why he often describes the mind as a kind of plant. The point is not simply that human beings have an epistemologically reliable point of view on the world, but that the human mind is itself, both as brain and cognitive faculty, yet another site in which nature's principle of iterative growth can be observed. In the second lecture from *Mind and Manners*, Emerson explains:

> Thus the idea of Vegetation is irresistible in considering mental activity. Man seems a higher plant. What happens here in mankind, is matched by what happens out there in the history of grass and wheat: an identity long ago observed or, I may say, never not observed, suggesting that the planter among his vines is in the presence of his ancestors, or, shall I say, that the orchardist is a pear raised to the highest power? . . . This curious resemblance to the vegetable pervades human nature, and repeats, in the mental function, the germination, growth, state of melioration, crossings, blights, parasites, and, in short, all the accidents of the plant. (*LL*, 1:156)

"The analogy is so thorough," Emerson writes, and one cannot help but take notice of it. And by doing so, one can free the mind to think organically, according to its own natural tendencies, without reference to or reliance on artificial linear dogmas. "Intellect agrees with nature. Thought is a finer chemistry, a finer vegetation, a finer animal action. The act of imagination is an obedience of the private spirit to the currents of the world" (163). Therefore, what is needed—and this is the crucial point—is a kind of science that starts with direct observation of natural systems and then deduces their properties without first constructing an underlying model. As it happens, nonlinear science does just that.

The more he recognized the cognitive issues defining the differences between linearity and nonlinearity, the more Emerson placed his faith in a nonlinear worldview. By noticing and contemplating the many nonlinear characteristics of the natural world, Emerson was simply exploring the margins of scientific knowledge. He was neither a maverick nor any particular kind of exceptional genius for doing so (especially as many of his ideas originate in seventeenth-century cosmology and organicism), but his philosophy of nature stands as an exception to the general rule of the day. Katherine Hayles argues in *Chaos Bound* (1990) that even though nonlinear philosophy appears to be a "new," or late-twentieth-century paradigm, the only difference between the present age and earlier eras of scientific theory is a change in emphasis. As Hayles writes, "Presumably observations confirming the extent of nonlinearity in the natural world could have been made at any time; the point is they were not." While some did notice problems in linear paradigms, the majority of scientists in the nineteenth century overlooked evidence contradicting them, because "the emphasis in Newtonian paradigms on long-term prediction directed attention away from the issue, making it seem like a nonissue."[19] Taken as a general theory, there is no reason why nonlinearity could not have emerged as a major nineteenth-century paradigm, except that Newtonian paradigms (and the cultural forces motivating their acceptance) directed scientific inquiry elsewhere.

Emerson made many observations confirming the extent of nonlinearity in the natural world, and I now turn more specifically to the main ideas he developed and the ways in which he expressed them. In what follows, I demonstrate more clearly certain points of union between Emerson's theory of flowing law, introduced in Chapter 4, and the fundamental suppositions of nonlinear theory. My approach is descriptive, taking a cue from the notion that "a geometrical figure, whether upon the blackboard, or the printed page, or in a block of wood, or a set of stretched threads, is incontrovertible evidence that a geometer has been expressing, by this means, a geometrical thought."[20] Even if he never wrote an essay devoted solely to nonlinear philosophy, an array of statements, impressions, and suppositions throughout his work (and throughout his life) suggest that Emerson was undoubtedly thinking in this direction. I turn to the contemporary science of chaos, the so-called chaos theory arising from nonlinear dynamics, not only for examples of nonlinear modes of thinking but also for the use of certain terms and definitions. My task is simply to point out and characterize the main points of emphasis in Emerson's nonlinear approach to nature, with an aim toward alerting readers to their suggestiveness and depth.[21]

Additionally, one must be open to the suggestiveness of Emerson's language. As he comments in the *Natural History of the Intellect*, "We find ourselves expressed in Nature, but we cannot translate it into words" (*CW,*

---

19. Hayles, *Chaos Bound,* 144.

20. Thomas Hill, *Geometry and Faith; A Supplement to the Ninth Bridgewater Treatise,* 3. Emerson owned the first (1849) edition of Hill's *Geometry and Faith.*

21. Several studies of creative literature and nonlinear philosophy have been written. See, for example, Hawkins's study of Shakespeare and Milton, *Strange Attractors;* Ira Livingston, *Arrow of Chaos: Romanticism and Postmodernity* (Minneapolis: University of Minnesota Press, 1997); Thomas Jackson Rice, *Joyce, Chaos, and Complexity* (Urbana: University of Illinois Press, 1997); Robert L. Nadeau, *Readings from the New Book on Nature: Physics and Metaphysics in the Modern Novel* (Amherst: University of Massachusetts Press, 1981); Susan Strehle, *Fiction in the Quantum Universe* (Chapel Hill: University of North Carolina Press, 1992); N. Katherine Hayles, *Cosmic Web: Scientific Field Models and Literary Strategies in the Twentieth Century* (Ithaca: Cornell University Press, 1984); and William R. Paulson, *The Noise of Culture: Literary Texts in a World of Information* (Ithaca: Cornell University Press, 1988).

12:37). The vocabulary of modern nonlinear philosophy was not available to Emerson, even though many similar concepts were: again and again, Emerson describes natural systems in terms of their chaotic qualities, but the language he uses is characterized by the free range of his imagination. Finally, in drawing on the terms of nonlinear philosophy to explicate Emersonian naturalism, it is nonetheless necessary to be selective. Nonlinearity, or chaos theory, refers to a wide-ranging interdisciplinary paradigm, the roots of which developed in the nineteenth and early twentieth centuries and branched out into contemporary fields such as nonlinear dynamics, fractal imaging, irreversible thermodynamics, meteorology, and epidemiology; it encompasses broad fields of study, each in its own way developing in different directions toward differing ends. In general terms, nonlinearity can be defined as a way of thinking that departs from traditional Euclidean-Newtonian linear science; it is the study of complex natural systems in which irregularities, perturbations, and other so-called anomalies are seen as integral features of a system rather than bothersome deviations from linear notions of causality. More specifically, nonlinear dynamical systems are algorithms that are both deterministic and unpredictable. By focusing attention on complexity as a key to understanding the unusual behavior of natural systems, nonlinearity offers an alternate perspective for understanding the basic elements of nature. As Emerson continually held, it is in those places where nature is surprising and bizarre, where it subverts expected norms, that we see the most: "Nature is a tropical swamp in sunshine, on whose purlieus we hear the song of summer birds, and see prismatic dewdrops,—but her interiors are terrific, full of hydras and crocodiles" (*LL*, 2:147).

As a way of thinking about the interrelatedness of order and disorder, the science of chaos is quite old. One of the earliest studies of the meaning of chaotic systems occurs in *De Rerum Natura,* written by Lucretius in 50 BC, which provides a comprehensive exposition of Epicurean natural philosophy. While today common usage of the word suggests the premundial void of Genesis, *chaos* in its original sense, as *De Rerum Natura* explains, does not mean complete disorder or the absence of order. Epicurus imagined a universe that was materialistic, consisting of fundamental particles (atoms) physically interacting with each other. He believed that these interactions occurred entirely by chance, without regard to goals or final causes, but he also concluded that the world as we know it—bodies, minds, ideas, gods—is simply an ongoing cosmic event, a never-ending coupling and uncoupling of atoms that results in the gradual emergence of entire new worlds and the gradual disintegration of old ones. In this sense, chaos means order and disorder each emerging from the other: "Although in contemporary nonscientific usage 'chaos' has come to denote confusion and disorder, in contemporary understandings of science the word has an affinity with the original Greek: it suggests the paradoxical state in which irregular motion may lead to pattern and disorder and order are linked. Indeed, in engineering, chaos theory is called stability theory—that is, the study of stability as implicit in disorder and instability, though some scientists remind us that, conversely, disorder is implicit in order."[22] In *Chaos Bound,* Katherine Hayles points out two general emphases in chaos theory, emphases that map out two different points of view regarding randomness in nature. The first is that "chaos is seen as order's precursor and partner, rather than as its opposite. The focus here is on the spontaneous emergence of self-organization from chaos." Such "dissipative structures" "arise in systems far from equilibrium, where entropy production is high"—stressing the idea that entropic systems make possible rather than obstruct the emergence of spontaneous singularities. The second general emphasis is the idea that "hidden order . . . exists *within* chaotic systems." Chaotic systems are distinct from truly random systems because they develop according to underlying rules. In particular, "whereas truly random systems show no discernible pattern when they are mapped into phase space"—that is, when rates of change in certain variables are plotted onto coordinate planes—"chaotic systems contract to a confined region and trace complex patterns within it," examples of which can be found in the behavior of such diverse systems as lynx fur returns, outbreaks of diseases such as measles, the rise and fall of the Nile, and the eye movements of schizophrenics. This branch of chaos theory remains attentive to systems that stay chaotic but are nonetheless bounded: "the focus is on the orderly descent into chaos rather than on the organized structures that emerge from chaos." As Hayles elsewhere observes, chaos is a force enabling self-organization: "It envisions a world that can renew itself rather than a

22. Gordon E. Slethaug, *Beautiful Chaos: Chaos Theory and Metachaotics in Recent American Fiction,* xxiii.

universe that is constantly running down, as nineteenth-century thermody-
namicists believed."[23]

Both emphases identified by Hayles echo very clearly Romantic notions
about Nature being both pleasingly organic and impulsively wild, but Emerson also makes note of other cases in which the relationship between order
and disorder can be observed. Recalling a drawing exercise from his child-
hood, for example, Emerson writes, "When a boy . . . I discovered . . . the
charm of drawing vases by scrawling with ink heavy random lines, & then
doubling the paper, so as to make another side symmetrical,—what was
chaos, becoming symmetrical" (*JMN*, 16:263). These ersatz Rorschach
drawings suggest the appearance of order from randomness; in this case,
chaos precedes order. The example is also instructive in that Emerson dou-
bles the paper to achieve the effect that charms him: when his random ink
lines become part of a recursive process, structure and meaning emerge
from it, and the system (such as it is) becomes a stable and self-contained
whole. In other instances, Emerson sees chaos as a creative force in its own
right. For example, war has long been understood as a destructive and anni-
hilating force. When considering the effect of the Civil War on society, Emerson often recognized the ruin combat leaves in its wake, but he also detected
the way in which war organizes some structures even while tearing others
down: "All decomposition is recomposition. What we call consumption is
energetic growth of the fungus or whatever new order. War disorganizes, but
it also organizes[;] it forces individuals & states to combine & act with larger
views, & under the best heads, & keeps the population together, producing
the effect of cities; for camps are wandering cities" (*JMN*, 15:353). If a peace-
time society represents one kind of order, a wartime society is another. Both
represent differing states of the same overall system, which decomposes
from one state to recompose into another. In this instance, war represents an
orderly descent into chaos, from which singularities, or "wandering cities,"
can be seen to emerge according to the underlying rules, or "larger views,"
controlling the system. Last, however, meteorological systems frequently
offer the best examples of the relationship between chaos and order. Storms
are particularly good examples of systems displaying order within disorder:
despite their unpredictability and frequent destructiveness, they build up,

23. Hayles, *Chaos Bound*, 9–10; Hayles, "Introduction: Complex Dynamics," 12.

expend themselves, and dissipate according to very definite physical rules. They also show that, in a larger sense, "order" may simply be a matter of definition—or, more accurately, a matter of preference. Remarking on the effect on the mind of fair weather after a storm, Emerson writes: "After the storm, come perfect days, neither hot nor cold, when it is a joy to live: and the equilibrium of the elements is then felt by all to be the normal state, & the hurricane the exception" (*JMN*, 15:319). But what is normal? As Emerson implies, perhaps the disorder represented by the storm is the more fundamental, or "normal," state of nature—the point at which the elements within the system are far from equilibrium and entropy production throughout is high.

Emerson recognized the fundamentally chaotic nature of Nature in other ways as well. Eric Wilson's 2000 essay "Emerson's *Nature*, Paralogy, and the Physics of the Sublime" reinterprets Emerson's vision of the sublime as something not transcendental (in a Platonic, Burkean, and Kantian sense) but paralogical, that is, not unifying but chaotic. Drawing on Jean-François Lyotard's *The Postmodern Condition: A Report on Knowledge* (1984), Wilson argues that "sublime energies are 'paralogical'—beyond *(para)* logic, reason, and word *(logos)*—and thus liberating. They counter the 'master' values of the West—unity, homogeneity, and predictability—with difference, heterogeneity, creativity: the muses of the agitated poet and the iconoclastic scientist." More particularly, Wilson analyzes Emerson's interest in sciences such as electrodynamics and magnetism—fields of inquiry "that challenged the Western narratives out of which transcendental aesthetics emerged"—to argue that "these emerging sciences of electricity suggested to Emerson that nature resists unity, that it is paradoxical, paralogical: it is simultaneously discernible matter and polarized energy, static and dynamic, substantive and transitive. Beyond logic and representation, this volatile universe is indeed sublime, but not in the transcendentalist sense. Rather than inspiring a vision of a spiritual whole, it challenges the mind to represent unpresentable *physical* forces: evanescent currents, fluxional patterns, polarized strife."[24] Indeed, evanescent currents, as the famous first chapter of *Nature* testifies, formed the very basis of Emerson's perceptual experience of nature, but variational quantities—the defining element of dynamic systems—were all around him, as physical reality. Such "fluxional quantities" or "fluxions," which "treat of

24. Eric Wilson, "Emerson's *Nature*, Paralogy, and the Physics of the Sublime," 39–40.

flowing numbers, as, for example, the path through space of a point on the rim of a cartwheel," held great appeal because they point to the cyclical, harmonic character of natural phenomena, the "flowing or varying" quality of things as well as ideas: "Most of my values are very variable" (*JMN*, 15:166). More importantly, the dynamic universe revealed by matter and polarized energy provided a model of the dynamic mind, a polarizing force all its own. "The thoughts, no man ever saw, but disorder becomes order where he goes" (*CW*, 10:75).

Fluxional or dynamic systems are systems having interrelated properties that change through time. A common move in nineteenth-century scientific thinking was to point to variational principles as proof that a mechanical universe remained, fundamentally, in a state of equilibrium. Emerson suggests as much, for example, early in his professional career, in his sermon on astronomy.[25] Dynamic systems, however, can easily fall out of equilibrium and still remain stable, the main difference being that they display chaotic motion, which is nonperiodic rather than periodic. For instance, to draw on Emerson's example of fluxional quantities cited above, the movement of a point on the rim of a turning cartwheel can be described in terms of the dynamic relationship between vertical and horizontal position (assuming a stable axis of rotation, the path of the point is a circle), one which (assuming constant motion) repeats as a closed loop of constant but discrete states. This type of system displays what is called a periodic attractor: in this instance, no matter how quickly the wheel is turning (that is, no matter how much energy is in the system), both the vertical or horizontal positions of the point on the rim will at any given moment in time be somewhere between interdependent extreme values (up/down, left/right) clearly defined by the radius of the wheel.[26] In addition, their relationship is linear:

25. See *The Complete Sermons of Ralph Waldo Emerson*, 4:157: "It is the glory of La Grange to have demonstrated that all the irregularities which take place in our system are periodical, an error on one side being compensated by an exactly equal error on the other, and fluctuate between fixed and impassible limits, that there is no ungoverned orb, no loose pin, no lawless particle through all the heights and depths of the City of God." This sermon was first delivered in 1832. See also *LL*, 2:384 for a similar passage in "The Rule of Life," first delivered in 1867.

26. A dynamic system, particularly a dissipative system (one that loses energy), generally tends to develop toward one or more specific states, or attractors. A damped pendulum, for example, will come to rest at a single point. This type of system displays a fixed-point attractor. Other examples of attractors include periodic-point attractors, that is, limit cycles or finite-length repeating loops of discrete states (for example, a beating heart, or a program-

at every given time in the rotation of the wheel, height equals width. If viewed from above or from the side, the path through space of the point on the rim of the wheel will appear to move back and forth in a straight line, much like an undamped pendulum moves: its motion is periodic and predictable. If we turn the wheel upright (now it spins laterally, not vertically) and allow the radius of the wheel to vary, the system becomes even more like a pendulum; that is, the path of the point of interest becomes ellipsoidal, and it will trace out a pattern much like that of a child's toy Spirograph. If we imagine the plane of the wheel to be shaped like a bowl, rather than a plate, then the system is exactly like a pendulum. The trajectory of the point of interest will be the same as that traced out by a bob swinging freely from a fixed point. Now the system is more complex, but it remains periodic and linear, governed by a periodic attractor, as was the original wheel.

Something interesting happens when the arm of the pendulum becomes elastic, or a swinging spring. It can exhibit both linear and nonlinear motion, depending upon the initial conditions of the system. In a low-energy state, in which the bob swings below the fixed point of the pendulum, the motion of the swinging spring remains linear, tracing out a periodic and predictable path through space. But in a high-energy state, in which the bob moves with enough force to swing all the way around the fixed point of the pendulum, the motion of the swinging spring becomes nonlinear, tracing out a nonperiodic and unpredictable path through space.[27] That is, it never repeats itself exactly. At any given time the path of the bob through space will appear to be random (nonperiodic), and its position will be impossible to measure accurately.[28] However, the system is still deterministic: the bob must fall somewhere within the bounds imposed by the limit sets defining the system (the maximum length of the spring, the

---

ming bug that causes a computer to fall into an infinite loop); spatial attractors, which are periodic but spatially extended (for example, an audience wave in a sports arena, or the burn cycle of an unmanaged forest); and strange attractors, the most common type, which govern chaotic motion, as defined below.

27. For further explanation of the behavior of elastic pendulums and animated illustrations of regular and chaotic motion in swinging springs, see Peter Lynch's Swinging Spring Web page: http://www.maths.tcd.ie/~plynch/SwingingSpring/SS_Home_Page.html.

28. Even if the limit points of attractors are discretely known, the values between them will contain irrational numbers. Consider, for example, the impossibility of discretely defining a point on the rim of a wheel if the radius of the wheel is some multiple of π units long.

mass of the bob, the force of gravity, and so on). Thus, the motion of the system is chaotic: it is nonperiodic and unpredictable, but it develops according to underlying rules. Such systems display strange attractors, and they exist everywhere in nature.[29]

A weather system, for example, is nonperiodic and unpredictable, never repeating in exactly the same way, but its behavior is nonetheless bounded: winds may blow, but they will never become absolutely still nor accelerate to the speed of sound; summers will be hot and winters cold, but never so much as to melt lead or liquefy oxygen. Thus, attractors are confined states toward which dynamic systems develop, and as such they are indicators of underlying rules governing those systems. Attractors are particularly salient points of interest in Emerson's study of nature because they are the things by which seemingly random systems can be shown to be deterministic. The example above of the strange attractor in the elastic pendulum comes from an artificial system, but several examples of natural attractors present themselves in Emerson's writing. Some of the most important are the forms living bodies will take as they develop.

In Chapter 4, I argue that Emersonian naturalism holds as its central thesis the idea that form has an origin, undergoes development, and is a crucial element in a larger context of cosmic forces. Based on his reading of Goethe and Guillaume Oegger,[30] for example, Emerson imagines in his essay on Swedenborg a way of understanding bodies based on the idea that "nature iterates her means perpetually on successive planes" (*CollW*, 4:60), a process visibly illustrated in the natural world in the way mature, complex

29. Chaotic motion is not always as visibly apparent as that of a swinging spring; it may instead be a behavior associated with properties within the system as they change over time. One way to model this behavior is to construct a phase space. A phase space is a graphic representation of the relationship between two or more properties of a system (position and velocity, for example) at a specific instant in each cycle of the system. Thus, the orbits created in phase space provide a map of changes in the system's behavior during repeated cycles, and not of trajectories through actual space. Further, the particular dynamic relationship displaying chaotic motion can have fractional, or "fractal," dimensions. For example, rather than one, two, or three dimensions, as in Euclidean geometry, a system may have some number of dimensions between the integers, such as 0.8, 1.7, or two and two-thirds.

30. In 1835, Emerson read Elizabeth Peabody's translation of Oegger's *Le Vrai Messie*, or *The True Messiah* (1829). Oegger was a French Catholic priest who converted to Emanuel Swedenborg's New Church. Oegger's ideas on the correspondence between nature and the spiritual world, the dependence of the individual consciousness on God, and the spiritual language of nature inspired Emerson a great deal. See *JMN*, 5:66–67, 77–78.

forms develop recursively from basic ones: "In the plant, the eye or germinative point opens to a leaf, then to another leaf, with a power of transforming the leaf into radicle, stamen, pistil, petal, bract, sepal, or seed. The
whole art of the plant is still to repeat leaf on leaf without end, the more or
less of heat, light, moisture and food determining the form it shall assume"
(61). In this example, the germinative point of the plant body (a rudimentary leaf) possesses a fundamental shape—that is, an attractor—toward
which the system develops in each stage of its growth. That is, no matter
how long the system develops, or in what ways, it always tends toward the
properties and characteristics of its initial state. This fundamental shape is
also a strange attractor. Heat, light, moisture, and nutrients are the variables
that influence the system, providing, most importantly, the initial conditions of each stage in its growth cycle; they determine the actual shape
toward which an individual plant will grow. And as Emerson suggests, as
they vary, so too does the final form of the plant, in which case no two
plants of a species are exactly the same. But there is still an underlying rule
(the strange attractor) that keeps this unpredictable system within certain
bounds: "the whole art of the plant is still to repeat leaf on leaf without
end," ensuring that as the system progresses through successive iterations,
we can know for certain that leaves and leaves only—rather than, say, gills
or fingers—will emerge as structures within it.

The motion displayed by the development of plants is, as Emerson
describes it, chaotic: comparing plant with plant within a given species, we
see that the progress of the system is nonperiodic, that the stages of actual
growth within any given development cycle are dependent on initial conditions, and that the system is predictable only to the extent that its development is bounded (that is, it has a strange attractor). Each of these are
defining properties of chaotic systems. Of course, Emerson does not confine these qualities to plants only. Animal bodies follow a similar pattern of
design, one that also explains growth in terms of iteration: "In the animal,
nature makes a vertebra, or a spine of vertebrae, and helps herself still by a
new spine, with a limited power of modifying its form,—spine on spine, to
the end of the world" (*CollW*, 4:61). Again, the system has "limited power"
to modify itself; it will not stray far from its attractor, in this case the form
of a vertebra. The type of body it develops into, or the number of spines
that will develop from the system, is also dependent on initial conditions:

sometimes the system becomes a single spine, but at other times it becomes multiple spines. Referring to Oegger, Emerson writes:

> A poetic anatomist, in our own day, teaches that a snake, being a horizontal line, and man, being an erect line, constitute a right angle; and between the lines of this mystical quadrant all animated beings find their place: and he assumes the hair-worm, the span-worm, or the snake, as the type or prediction of the spine. Manifestly, at the end of the spine, Nature puts out smaller spines, as arms; at the end of the arms, new spines, as hands; at the other end, she repeats the process, as legs and feet. At the top of the column she puts out another spine, which doubles or loops itself over, as a spanworm, into a ball, and forms the skull,—with extremities again: the hands being now the upper jaw, the feet the lower jaw, the fingers and toes being represented this time by upper and lower teeth. (61)

In this passage, the system Emerson describes develops into a human being, within which, "on a higher plane, all that was done in the trunk repeats itself": "The mind is a finer body, and resumes its functions of feeding, digesting, absorbing, excluding and generating, in a new and ethereal element. Here in the brain is all the process of alimentation repeated, in the acquiring, comparing, digesting and assimilating of experience. Here again is the mystery of generation repeated. In the brain are male and female faculties: here is marriage, here is fruit. And there is no limit to this ascending scale, but series on series. Everything at the end of one use is taken up into the next, each series punctually repeating every organ and process of the last. We are adapted to infinity" (61). Emerson envisions the human being as merely one possible stage (albeit a very advanced one) in a much larger recursive process, one that can go through perpetual iterations.

As he did that of the plant, Emerson describes the dynamic system of the animal body in terms of chaotic motion. The animal body displays many iterative characteristics, from its growth and development, to its vital biological functions, to its powers of cognition. On all of these planes of development, Emerson argues, the attractor is indicated by the form of a vertebra unfolding into a spine. Over time, individual distinctiveness will emerge (including speciation as well as unique traits among individuals of a given species), thus creating nonperiodicity in the system (sometimes a snake, sometimes a human, sometimes a form in between), and this distinctiveness will depend on any number of variables defining the initial conditions of each stage in the development of the system. But, as in the plant body, the animal body, as a dynamic system, has set limits. In other words, its infinite complexity is controlled by a simple, underlying rule: "Creative force, like a musical composer, goes on unweariedly repeating a simple air or theme, now high, now low, in solo, in chorus, ten thousand times reverberated, till it fills earth and heaven with the chant" (62).

Elsewhere Emerson extends the function of strange attractors into a general rule. In "The Method of Nature," he writes, "Not the cause, but an ever novel effect, nature . . . is unbroken obedience" (*CollW*, 1:124). He argues that nature has underlying laws such that natural systems will develop within particular set limits, but beyond that, "creative force," as he writes in his essay on Swedenborg, reverberates throughout the universe with any number of results. Thus, nature is "an ever novel effect"—that is, it is nonperiodic and unpredictable—even if it is nonetheless governed by "unbroken obedience" to certain rules. In other words, the whole of nature is a chaotic system, seemingly random and unpredictable, but at the same time deterministic. Against this backdrop of universal volatility, order emerges from disorder when creative forces coalesce around sites of attraction. For example: "What agencies of electricity, gravity, light, affinity combine to make every plant what it is, and in a manner so quiet that the presence of these tremendous powers is not ordinarily suspected. . . . The ripe fruit is dropped at last without violence, but the lightning fell and storm raged, and strata were deposited and uptorn and bent back, and Chaos moved from beneath, to create and flavor the fruit on your table to-day. The winds and the rains come back a thousand and a thousand times" (*CW*, 10:70–71).[31] In this passage from "Perpetual Forces," Emerson argues that, in contrast to the master narratives most widely circulated in his day—the spontaneous, *ex nihilo* reifications of biblical creationism versus the accidental, *ex materia* collisions of Newtonian gravitational physics—the form of the fruit is itself an attractor, a node of convergence (among countless trillions in the universe) toward which cosmic forces inevitably flow. This flowing is an ongoing and perpetual event ("the winds and the rains come back a thousand

---

31. See also *LL*, 2:290–91; the Bosco and Myerson edition alters and omits key passages from "Perpetual Forces" as it is arranged by James Elliot Cabot in the edition cited here. A similar passage from the lecture on "Moral Sense" is discussed in Chapter 4 (see *LL*, 2:145).

and a thousand times"), but within its cycles, singularities arise, not just the plant and its fruit, but every other object and phenomenon in the universe, according to their own specific attractors. In "The Method of Nature," for example, Emerson observes, "An individual man is a fruit which it cost all the foregoing ages to form and ripen. . . . The history of the genesis or the old mythology repeats itself in the experience of every child. He too is a demon or god thrown into a particular chaos, where he strives ever to lead things from disorder into order" (*CollW*, 1:127–28).[32] In this passage, Emerson folds the Western myths of creation into a larger story of what he implies is a new mythology: an account of nature in which chaotic motion, made known by the perpetual iterations of cosmic forces, is its most fundamental quality. While order exists within the disorder and greater and greater complexity can be defined by scientific investigation, an endpoint will never be reached.

By and by, one begins to see the fruitfulness of the comparison: if "an individual man" is but one of the fruits of creation, then all nature's fruits must share fundamental characteristics in common, whether of form or of function. "It is true, there is a striking, and, if you will, a certain ridiculous resemblance between a man and woodchuck; between a man and a pineapple; between a man and a sponge; or whatever natural creature. The gentleman stands in his garden by his vines; gentleman and vine: the one can make a railroad, or a Canton voyage, or an oration; the other can make a watermelon. Each is a caricature of the other, the man of the vine, the vine of the man. A sort of Hudibrastic rhyme. Well, the man discovers that resemblance in all things he looks at,—the sun, the moon, or the salt, or metal, in his crucible" (*LL*, 1:159–60). Emerson explores the issue of "ridiculous resemblance" in his lecture "Intellect and Natural Science." One way of explaining these resemblances is to suggest that they are evidence of transcendent forms copied into the material universe. Thus, the similarities the mind notices are simply intimations of more perfect forms, of which actual things are merely imperfect copies. "That is Plato's doctrine, *that*, the souls [of all things] learned it all long ago by experience; have been everywhere; and are soaked and saturated with nature, and, in short, have quite

32. Examples of the order so created include anything making up "some particular language": "if not into a picture, a statue, or a dance,—why, then, into a trade, an art, a science, a mode of living, a conversation, a character, an influence" (*CollW*, 1:128).

sucked the apple of Eden" (160). However, this explanation is unsatisfactory to Emerson and not the one he accepts. Instead, he turns to a principle of recursive symmetry: "fire is made of little fires; and water, of little waters; and man, of manikins; drops make the ocean, sands compose its shores." The problem with the Platonic theory is that it has no appreciation of scale; it has no way of relating the microscopic to the cosmic. However, as Emerson argues, resemblances among natural objects reveal a principle of universality in the way large-scale features relate to small-scale details and vice versa. Complex, chaotic systems undergo a process of iteration, in which each cycle builds on the last. But at the same time, they are recursive: the larger structures within those systems replicate, and are replicated by, the smaller structures within them. Thus "a drop of water and a grain of sand give you the whole economy" of Nature (160)—or, as Emerson writes in the essay "Nature," "The whirling bubble on the surface of a brook, admits us to the secret of the mechanics of the sky. Every shell on the beach is a key to it. A little water made to rotate in a cup explains the formation of the simpler shells; the addition of matter from year to year, arrives at last at the most complex forms" (*CollW*, 3:105). Within organic objects and processes, recursive symmetries can be found across all scales.

Such symmetries exist, Emerson speculates, because complex forms and structures, from the shape of organic bodies to the unfolding of natural processes, share a fundamental sameness at the atomic level: "A man is a developed animalcule; animalcule is an arrested Man, but animalcule, again, is made up of atoms, the same atoms of which water, fire, or sand are composed, and, on each atom, the whole atomic power is impressed." Further, these atoms behave in the same way: when "the whole atomic power is impressed" on an atom, "a violence of direction is given to it, a genius belongs to it, which, in all its career of combination, it never loses, but still manages to express in a man, in an orange, in a ruby, in a peacock, in a moss: it is still atom, and holds hard by the honest manners and aims of atom" (*LL*, 1:160). Thus: "It is certain that however we may conceive of the wonderful little bricks of which the world is builded, we must suppose a similarity, and fitting, and identity in their frame. It is necessary to suppose that every hose in nature fits every hydrant; that every atom screws to every atom. So only is combination, chemistry, vegetation, animation, intellection, possible. Without identity at base, chaos must be forever" (161). Because all matter shares an "identity at base," Emerson argues, nature itself can be seen as an integrated whole, else disorder would completely overtake order.

Importantly, Emerson notes that atoms have a "violence of direction": they are unpredictable even though we know something of how they move and interact. They also have "a genius" that ensures they remain atoms, no matter how they interact. In one way of seeing matter, the "genius" of an atom might simply be tabulated as a function of chemical properties; in another, it might be understood as a kind of quantum attractor, a possibility Emerson raises when he writes, "Identity at the base. It need not be atoms: Modern theory sets aside atoms as unphilosophical, and the first of English physical philosophers, Faraday, propounds that we do not arrive at last at atoms, but at spherules of force. But, in the initial forms or creations, be they what they may, we must find monads that have already all the properties which in any combination they afterwards exhibit" (*LL,* 1:161). Monads—whether material particles (atoms), as classical physics claimed, or spherules of force, as twentieth-century quantum theorists discovered—are systems unto themselves. They are bounded by limits governing their properties and how they interact, and yet they are fitted for infinite variety in their ability to combine and recombine. They contribute these qualities to whatever greater systems they join. Summing up these ideas, Emerson states: "Every drop of blood has great talents; the original vesicle, the original cellule, seems identical in all animals, and only varied in its growth by the varying circumstance which opens now this kind of cell and now that, causing in the remote effect now horns, now wings, now scales, now hair; and the same numerical atom, it would seem, was equally ready to be a particle of the eye or brain of man, or of the claw of a tiger" (171). The animal body is a system that may develop in any number of directions, depending, importantly, on "the varying circumstance" or initial conditions of the system. But each part and particle within the system is fitted to develop into any other part, as those circumstances vary, because each original vesicle or cellule shares identical properties in every instance (individual to individual, species to species) of the system. "The symmetry and coordination of things"—both structural principles of organization—"is such that from any creature well and inly known the law of any other might be legitimately deduced" (171). Because we can observe certain properties on the "original" or atomic scale, Emerson believes, we can assume such properties to be repeated on all scales; because we can see them echoed in the structural organization of one variation of the animal body, we will see them repeated in the structural organization of each scale level in the system throughout Nature.

The key insight in these passages from "Intellect and Natural Science" is that the meaning one derives from natural systems can vary according to the scale of interest. Katherine Hayles explains in *Chaos Bound* that

> Newtonian paradigms focus on individual particles or units. The assumption is that if these units are followed through time, their collective actions will add up to the system's behavior. . . . It is a foundationalist approach, infused with assumptions about the integrity and autonomy of the individual. The fundamental assumption of chaos theory, by contrast, is that the individual unit does not matter. What does matter are recursive symmetries between different levels of the system. . . . The regularities of the system emerge not from knowing about individual units but from understanding correspondences across scales of different lengths. It is a systemic approach, emphasizing overall symmetries and the complex interactions between microscale and macroscale levels.[33]

Similarly, Emerson argues that the "resemblances in all things" one observes on the human (perceptual) scale can be inferred to exist because of resemblances on the atomic scale. The exact nature of individual units is not as important as their properties, which allow for resemblance or recursive symmetry, across scales and systems. Emerson argues that while, at the human level, resemblance can be explained as simply a "Hudibrastic rhyme" or Platonic imitation, at more refined levels another picture emerges, one in which complexity is a kind of movement seen over time. Natural systems observable on the human scale do not exist because they drop down from transcendental ether wholly formed, so much as they rise up from greater and greater complexities emerging and falling away as systems operating on smaller scales combine and recombine. Thus, complexity itself is not to be seen as an end result or highest state in a given system, especially at the macroscale; rather, complex structure and detail can also be found at the microscale, or in the presumably simpler modules or rudimentary stages of a system. For example, Emerson writes in "Compensation," "the microscope cannot find

33. Hayles, *Chaos Bound*, 169–70.

the animalcule which is less perfect for being little. Eyes, ears, taste, smell, motion, resistance, appetite, and organs of reproduction that take hold on eternity,—all find room to consist in the small creature" (*CollW*, 2:59–60). And indeed, working in the other direction, as Emerson does in "The Over-Soul," we see that structure and meaning on the transcendental scale—that stage or order of development beyond the physical plane—are also properties that rise upward rather than drop down: "And so, always, the soul's scale is one; the scale of the senses and the understanding is another. . . . After its own law and not by arithmetic is the rate of [the soul's] progress to be computed. The soul's advances are not made by gradation, such as can be represented by motion in a straight line; but rather by ascension of state, such as can be represented by metamorphosis,—from the egg to the worm, from the worm to the fly" (*CollW*, 2:162–63). Here, in an example of his correspondence theory practically applied, Emerson takes what he knows to be true of the animal body to make inferences about the soul, or the transcendental body, concluding that both develop according to the same rules. Linearity provides a model of gradation, a description of smooth change from one discrete state to the next. If one uses it to study only small units of a total system, it might prove to be useful. But when a system is taken as a larger whole, with a view toward resemblances across scales, an altogether different mode of modeling is needed, one that can account for an "ascension of state," or qualitative change from one scale or stage to the next. And finally, as Emerson writes in "The Poet," "Men have really got a new sense, and found within their world, another world, or nest of worlds; for, the metamorphosis once seen, we divine that it does not stop" (*CollW*, 3:17). All of nature participates in this scaling function. Once we take note of recursive symmetries, rather than focus on individual units, Emerson argues, a nest of worlds comes into view.

Recursive symmetry, or structure within structure and pattern within pattern, describes the development of natural forms throughout scale levels, such that, paradoxically, "The highest simplicity of structure is the last & requires the most composite" (*JMN*, 10:145). While the finished form, in other words, might suggest simplicity and unifying wholeness, it is yet made up of seemingly infinite variety, a composite of other wholes. This principle, Emerson argues, organizes not just nature, but an individual's life as well: "But you say that so moving & moved on thoughts & verses gathered in different parts of a long life you sail no straight line but are perpetually distracted by new & counter currents, & go a little way north, then a little way north east, then a little north west, then a little north again; & so on. Be it so; Is any motion different? The curve line is not a curve but an infinite polygon. . . . See the line from a sufficient distance & it straightens itself to the average tendency" (*JMN*, 7:216–17). Emerson applies the idea of irregularity to a general rule of motion, a typical trajectory of which he likens to a curving line. Scaling shows that at one level of measurement, a curving line appears to be smooth. But at successively smaller scales of measurement, Emerson argues, a curve becomes irregular, made up of smaller segments that may deviate from the average tendency in any number of directions. Like the length of a coastline, the length of a curve depends, ultimately, on the size of one's measuring stick. In this way, Emerson's example of an infinite polygon suggests a fractal form.[34]

This principle of movement is also a principle of structure. While the modeling of actual fractals requires computers, and so would not have been available to Emerson's scrutiny, natural fractal-like shapes, and the fractal property of scale-dependence they exhibit, were available for study. Like infinite polygons, fractals are scale-dependent: measurement of their size on scales of smaller and smaller length does not converge to a limit but rather increases toward infinity as scale decreases. The static coastline of an island, to take a common example, is bounded, but the shorter the measuring stick one uses to measure its length (a mile, a yard, an inch, a micron, etc.), the more toward infinity its length increases; it is a natural shape that, like trees, clouds, shells, river and circulatory systems, or developing bodies, appears at successively smaller scales to be made up of structure within

---

34. The term *fractal* (from the Latin *fractus* or "broken") was coined in 1975 by Benoît Mandelbrot to describe geometric shapes in the complex plane that are irregular on all scales of length, possess infinite detail, and contain self-similar structures as a result of generation by a recursive or iterative algorithm. Such shapes and the iterated functions producing them have been studied since the late nineteenth century, when mathematicians first attempted to measure the size of objects of fractional dimensionality. Such objects lie beyond the analytical reach of traditional Euclidean geometry or calculus, but also cannot be fully modeled without the aid of modern computers, so they were not studied in great detail until the last half of the twentieth century. Because a fractal possesses infinite detail, no natural object can be a fractal in a pure mathematical sense, but natural objects can display fractal-like properties within a bounded range of scales. Trees, clouds, mountains, river networks, circulatory systems, coastlines, and time-dependent harmonic processes, such as turbulent flow, weather patterns, or predator-prey population ratios, are just a few of the many natural phenomena displaying chaotic motion with fractal properties.

structure. As demonstrated by numerous passages on the development of bodies cited above, Emerson understood that this scale-dependence arises as a result of recursive symmetry and self-similarity across scales.

All of these ideas about chaotic motion and nonlinear dynamics are summed up in a remarkable passage from "The Method of Nature," in which Emerson describes the holistic qualities of Nature: "The wholeness we admire in the order of the world, is the result of infinite distribution. Its smoothness is the smoothness of the pitch of the cataract. Its permanence is a perpetual inchoation. Every natural fact is an emanation, and that from which it emanates is an emanation also, and from every new emanation a new emanation. If anything could stand still, it would be crushed and dissipated by the torrent it resisted, and if it were a mind, would be crazed; as insane persons are those who hold fast to one thought, and do not flow with the course of nature" (*CollW*, 1:124). The flow of the course of nature is a torrent: how apt that Emerson should make use of the imagery of turbulence. By doing so, he suggests that the course of nature is complex, dynamic, and nonlinear, a system characterized by perpetual motion and development rather than fundamental stillness or static equilibrium. It does not hold fast to one thought, but expresses itself through continuous variety—a permanence of perpetual inchoation, the very essence of strange attractors. As such it is a system always in development; it is dissipative. It is also nonperiodic and unpredictable, and yet we can see that it obeys deeply encoded rules of organization. Structure emerges from structure, emanation from emanation, such that within each part of the system, even more fundamental levels of complexity are at work. Emerson's description evokes the defining characteristics of fractals, or recursive symmetries across scales: larger structures replicate, and are replicated by, smaller structures within them, a process that arises from the iteration and self-organizing properties of the algorithms driving the system. Taken collectively, the wholeness in the order arising from these chaotic processes is the result of infinite distribution—not a distribution throughout space so much as a distribution across all scales, from the infinitely small to the infinitely large, from one emanation into the next, expanding and contracting everywhere in nature even while it remains a perpetual inchoation. Finally, the smoothness of the order of the world is that of the pitch of a cataract, another image of turbulent flow suggestive of nonlinear dynamical systems, but this time evocative of motion as seen in phase space, or in the relationships between dynamic properties. Taken from a wide perspective, a cataract indeed appears to be smooth—a continuous variational curve. Seen from a closer vantage point, a picture of infinite variety and complexity emerges, such that the pitch of the cataract is not smooth at all, but full of irregularity and randomness. And we can also see that while the whole moves inexorably toward a series of known limits —one state of organization giving way to another as river careens over precipice toward rocks and pools below—its interiors are the very picture of chaos: flow within flow, swirls within swirls, cataracts all.

Emerson draws out the major implications of such nonlinear dynamics most fully in his reading of Swedenborg, in which scaling is the main theme of his *Representative Men* essay. Emerson takes as a general, empirically confirmed rule that "nature iterates her means perpetually on successive planes," from which follows the corollary, "Nature is always self-similar" (*CollW*, 4:60–61). It is "the fine secret that little explains large, and large, little," such that "the unities of each organ are so many little organs, homogeneous with their compound: the unities of the tongue are little tongues; those of the stomach, little stomachs; those of the heart are little hearts. This fruitful idea furnishes a key to every secret" (60, 64–65). In contrast to the modular explanations of traditional science, in which complexity in dynamic systems is explained in terms of the whole being a combination or successive addition of several discrete units, Emerson prefers the nonlinear explanation in which units are "homogeneous with their compounds," or replications of the same structure on different scales. Thus it is possible to infer properties on one scale based on what one knows of another: "What was too small for the eye to detect was read by the aggregates; what was too large, by the units" (*CollW*, 4:80). This insight is profound, as it explains why one need not dissect a system in order to understand it.[35]

35. As influential as Swedenborg was on Emerson's understanding of the fractal properties of scaling and scale dependence, Emerson found his application of the idea to science and theology disturbingly lacking in expressiveness. Thus he feared that Swedenborg's ideas, as significant as they were, would have little impact on mainstream science and natural philosophy, which was in fact the case. Emerson writes, "It is remarkable that this man, who, by his perception of symbols, saw the poetic construction of things, and the primary relation of mind to matter, remained entirely devoid of the whole apparatus of poetic expression, which that perception creates. He knew the grammar and rudiments of the *Mother-Tongue*,—how could he not read off one strain into music?" (*CollW*, 4:80).

As Emerson frequently argued, the typical method of linear science—dividing a system into static parts, from which static ontological models are constructed—loses sight of the whole. In sharp contrast, scaling explains how the principles of growth, development, and change operating on one scale replicate throughout the system. In the "Natural History of the Intellect," Emerson develops this idea as a general theory of intellect and scientific inquiry: "I might suggest that he who contents himself with dotting a fragmentary curve, recording only what facts he has observed, without attempting to arrange them within one outline, follows a system also,—a system as grand as any other, though he does not interfere with its vast curves by prematurely forcing them into a circle or ellipse, but only draws that arc which he clearly sees, or perhaps at a later observation a remote curve of the same orbit, and waits for a new opportunity, well assured that these observed arcs will consist with each other" (CW, 12:11–12). Laboratory-based experimental modeling is a means of forcing complex systems—Nature's vast and complex curves—into artificial linear forms. Such action is premature, Emerson argues, because it closes off further avenues of expression or inquiry that do not fit the model; as was frequently the case, irregularity, perturbation, and spontaneity—that is, anything that did not fit within the closed and delimited circle or ellipse of linear paradigms—was assumed simply not to exist. In contrast, nonlinear inquiry is content to observe the fragmentary curve, knowing that principles of iteration, recursive symmetry, and scaling will allow one to make inferences between the properties of a system at one scale (a "fragmentary curve") and those at another (a "remote curve of the same orbit"). Additionally, this mode of intellect "waits for a new opportunity," and, because it does not rely on ontological modeling, it more easily incorporates new ideas and new observations into its knowledge base. Knowledge, he argues, should not be cold and clinical, like a tabulation of facts, but something warm and vital: "What we say however trifling must have its roots in ourselves or it will not move others. No speech should be separate from our being like a plume or a nosegay, but like a leaf or a flower or a bud through the topmost & remotest, yet joined by a continuous line of life to the trunk & the seed" (JMN, 4:36–37). Emerson thus theorizes a way of doing science in which every part, and every individual, is understood to have a deep and meaningful connection to the whole of life.

In this and previous chapters, I have laid out a case for reinterpreting Emerson's natural philosophy along phenomenological and epistemic grounds. More particularly, I have shown how his understanding of science (knowledge) and cognition (perception) was at odds with the linear paradigms dominating nineteenth-century thought. In one regard, Emerson's understanding of matter and motion, the bedrock categories of classical physics, is somewhat Newtonian in that he concedes to each attributes of absoluteness. For there is no doubt that Emerson thinks of matter in atomistic terms, that is, as made up of discrete particles existing in fundamental, or atomic, units. He even uses an atomistic metaphor to describe interpersonal relationships in his essay "Experience." But if Emerson understands nature as being made up of atomic units (whether actual atoms or, on occasion, monads), even so he does not see fundamental scales in nature. Linear science claims that natural systems each have fundamental scales, and that one can quantify them with fundamental units of space and time. Nonlinear science, on the other hand, argues that many natural systems are scale dependent, in which structures observed on one scale repeat themselves on ever smaller and ever larger scales. A smooth and continuous process, or an "average tendency," is in truth an illusion. Viewed on a closer scale, it becomes an infinite polygon, full of emerging detail and internal structure.

Additionally, Emerson does not see motion as continuous and mathematically calculable, no matter where it is observed: "Nature hates calculators; her methods are saltatory and impulsive. Man lives by pulses; our organic movements are such; and the chemical and ethereal agents are undulatory and alternate; and the mind . . . never prospers but by fits" (*CollW*, 3:39). Further, unlike Newton, Emerson gave supreme metaphysical importance to motion. Whereas Newton lent no qualitative weight to both motion and differences in successive states, Emerson believes that motion imbues material objects—whether animate or inanimate—with specific emergent properties. For example, beauty:

> Beauty is the moment of transition, as if the form were just ready to flow into other forms. . . . This is the charm of running water, sea-waves, the flight of birds, and the locomotion of animals. This is the theory of dancing, to recover continually in changes the lost equilibrium, not by abrupt and angular, but by gradual and curving movements. . . . To this streaming or flowing belongs the beauty that all circular movement has; as, the

circulation of waters, the circulation of the blood, the periodical motion
of planets, the annual wave of vegetation, the action and reaction of
nature: and, if we follow it out, this demand in our thought for an ever
onward action, is the argument for the immortality. (*CollW*, 6:155–56)

In this instance, form and motion blend into one another—with form sig-
naling a kind of becoming, or emergence, that moves, expands, and develops over time. It is "ever-onward action" that, in this passage, transcends
matter in its importance, becoming an argument for immortality. But it is,
in its essence, nonlinear: cyclical in kind, replete with iteration, yet uncertain, unpredictable, and abounding with novelty—all properties of a
strange attractor.

It is striking that Emerson should come to the conclusions he does, given
the dominance of Newtonian science in his day. Indeed, Emersonian naturalism—his theory of "flowing law"—seems itself something of a cultural
perturbation; like Romanticism generally, it had virtually no effect, after all,
on the directions mainstream natural science would pursue in the five or six
decades after 1850. Emerson, however, was willing to look beyond the foregone conclusions of the culture of linear science. In some remarks on Plato,
he notes: "For we do not listen with much respect to the verses of a man
who is only a poet, nor to the calculations of a man who is only an algebraist[,] but if a man is at the same time acquainted with the geometrical
foundations of things & with their moral purposes & sees the festal splen-
dour of the day, his poetry is exact; & his arithmetic musical. His poetry &
his mathematics accredit each other" (*JMN*, 11:148–49). Calling himself a
Professor of the Joyous Science, Emerson was often dismayed to meet "very
accomplished persons who betray instantly that they are strangers in
nature." Yet it was readily apparent to him that this separation occurs as a
result of epistemological limitations: "The poet[,] the true naturalist . . . is
in the chain of magnetic, electric, geologic, meteorologic phenomena & so
he comes to live in nature & extend his being through all: then is true science" (*JMN*, 7:181–82). The Poet, like the Joyous Scientist, is a naturalist
who unites his poetry with what he knows of its geometrical foundations.
Then "his poetry is exact; & his arithmetic musical." And because he is an
Aristotelian, Emerson's Poet-Scientist will limit himself only "with the
anticipation of law in the mutations,—flowing law," because no matter how

clear and distinct one assumes an explanation to be—that is, no matter how *objective* it may seem—"the universe is like an infinite series of planes, each of which is a false bottom, and when we think our feet are planted now at last on the adamant, the slide is drawn out from under us" (*JMN*, 9:295). The assumptionless, foundational, fundamental, minimal rationalizations of the traditional secular scientist are not adequate tools, in Emerson's mind, for interpreting the flowing law connecting all things.

Finally, it should be clear that Emerson's principle of flowing law has profound moral consequences. I have focused only on the material dimension— or more specifically, the structural import—of Emersonian naturalism, as a way of entering into the means and methods by which Emerson perceived and understood the natural world. The moral dimension, or teleological import, of nonlinear nature as Emerson understood it is beyond the scope of this study. But the nonlinear ways in which he thinks about physical laws bear directly on the ways he thinks about culture and morality. Emerson repeatedly expresses Kant's belief that the world is highly cultivated and civilized but not yet moralized; both see a dichotomy between culture and civilization on the one hand and morality on the other. Emerson frequently takes note of the ways in which our advanced civilization has not necessarily produced the best culture. The major premise of "Self-Reliance," for example, is that "society everywhere is in conspiracy against the manhood of every one of its members" (*CollW*, 2:29). In response to this problem, Emerson calls for a new morality—one based in the physical laws that he believes translate directly into moral laws. If Emerson had one aim, it was to show, in a deliberate and scientifically grounded manner, how Nature instructs us always to be open to the new and unknown, and how the mind can emerge from beneath the tyranny of dogma to its own freedom. As Emerson knew, each age bears its stamp: "Much more obviously is history and the state of the world at any one time, directly dependent on the intellectual classification then existing in the minds of men. The things which are dear to men at this hour, are so on account of the ideas which have emerged on their mental horizon, and which cause the present order of things as a tree bears its apples" (*CollW*, 2:184). But at the same time, moving within the bounds of its particular time and "present order," "an individual soul . . . is a fixation or momentary eddy in which certain affections, sciences, & powers of immaterial Force are taken up, & work & minister, in petty circles & localities, &

then, being released, return to the Unbounded Soul of the World" (*JMN*, 11:159). As locations within the same chaotic system of Nature, these two scales of experience—the global marked by notions of self-evident order, the local by turbulent flow—are not opposites so much as similars, each arising from and transforming the other. It is a notion both exhilarating and unsettling in its implications for contemporary beliefs about free will, autonomy, and personal identity, for it suggests that we are free agents only to the extent that we are cogs in a much greater wheel—a condition that twentieth-century schools of neither existentialism nor totalitarianism were willing to accept. If Emerson was able to look on this paradox with appreciation and pleasure, surely this is where his continued importance at the dawn of the twenty-first century lies.

BIBLIOGRAPHY

Allen, Gay Wilson. "A New Look at Emerson and Science." 1975. Reprinted in *Critical Essays on Ralph Waldo Emerson*, ed. Robert E. Burkholder and Joel Myerson, 434–48. Boston: G. K. Hall, 1983.

―――. *Waldo Emerson: A Biography.* New York: Viking Press, 1981.

Barrow, John D. *The World within the World.* Oxford: Clarendon, 1988.

Baumer, Franklin. *Modern European Thought: Continuity and Change in Ideas, 1600–1950.* New York: Macmillan, 1977.

Bishop, Jonathan. *Emerson on the Soul.* Cambridge: Harvard University Press, 1964.

Brown, Lee Rust. "Emerson, Paris, and the Opening of the Scientific Eye." *Prospects* 19 (1994): 315–47.

―――. *The Emerson Museum: Practical Romanticism and the Pursuit of the Whole.* Cambridge: Harvard University Press, 1997.

―――. "Emersonian Transparency." *Raritan* 9, no. 3 (1990): 127–44.

Browne, Thomas. *Religio Medici.* London, 1642. Early English Books Online. Walter Royal Davis Library, Chapel Hill, N.C.

Buell, Lawrence. *Literary Transcendentalism: Style and Vision in the American Renaissance.* Ithaca: Cornell University Press, 1973.

Chai, Leon. *The Romantic Foundations of the American Renaissance.* Ithaca: Cornell University Press, 1987.

Clark, Harry Hayden. "Emerson and Science." *Philological Quarterly* 10, no. 3 (July 1931): 225–60.

Coleridge, Samuel Taylor. *Biographia Literaria; or, Biographical Sketches of My Literary Life and Opinions.* 1817. Ed. James Engell and W. Jackson Bate. Princeton: Princeton University Press, 1983.

Cox, James. "R. W. Emerson: The Circles of the Eye." In *Emerson: Prophecy, Metamorphosis, and Influence,* ed. David Levin, 57–81. New York: Columbia University Press, 1975.

Dant, Elizabeth. "Composing the World: Emerson and the Cabinet of Natural History." *Nineteenth-Century Literature* 44 (1989): 18–44.

Descartes, René. *Discourse on Method.* 1637. Trans. John Veitch. Chicago: Henry Regnery, 1949.

Duncan, Jeffrey L. *The Power and Form of Emerson's Thought.* Charlottesville: University Press of Virginia, 1973.

Edgerton, Samuel Y. *The Heritage of Giotto's Geometry: Art and Science on the Eve of the Scientific Revolution.* Ithaca: Cornell University Press, 1991.

Emerson, Ralph Waldo. *The Collected Works of Ralph Waldo Emerson.* 6 vols. Ed. Alfred R. Ferguson et al. Cambridge: Harvard University Press, Belknap Press, 1971–2003.

———. *The Complete Sermons of Ralph Waldo Emerson.* Vol. 4. Ed. Wesley T. Mott. Columbia: University of Missouri Press, 1992.

———. *The Complete Works of Ralph Waldo Emerson.* 12 vols. Concord Edition. Boston: Houghton, Mifflin, 1903–1904.

———. *The Early Lectures of Ralph Waldo Emerson.* 3 vols. Ed. Stephen E. Whicher, Robert E. Spiller, and Wallace E. Williams. Cambridge: Harvard University Press, Belknap Press, 1959–1972.

———. *Essays and Lectures.* New York: Library of America, 1983.

———. *Essays and Poems.* New York: Library of America, 1996.

———. *The Journals and Miscellaneous Notebooks of Ralph Waldo Emerson.* 16 vols. Ed. William H. Gilman et al. Cambridge: Harvard University Press, Belknap Press, 1960–1982.

———. *The Later Lectures of Ralph Waldo Emerson.* 2 vols. Ed. Ronald A. Bosco and Joel Myerson. Athens: University of Georgia Press, 2001.

Field, J. V. *The Invention of Infinity: Mathematics and Art in the Renaissance.* Oxford: Oxford University Press, 1997.

Fulford, Robert. "Canadian Science Writing Undernourished, Inferior." Editorial. *Globe and Mail,* August 19, 1998, http://www.robertfulford.com/ScienceWriting.html.

Gablik, S. *Progress in Art.* London: Thames and Hudson, 1976.

Galilei, Galileo. *The Assayer.* 1623. In *Discoveries and Opinions of Galileo,* trans. Stillman Drake, 229–80. New York: Doubleday Anchor, 1957.

Glanvill, Joseph. *The Vanity of Dogmatizing; or, Confidence in Opinions. . . .* London, 1661. Early English Books Online. Walter Royal Davis Library, Chapel Hill, N.C.

Gleick, James. *Chaos: Making a New Science.* New York: Penguin Books, 1988.

Greenberg, Robert M. *Splintered Worlds: Fragmentation and the Ideal of Diversity in the Work of Emerson, Melville, Whitman, and Dickinson.* Boston: Northeastern University Press, 1993.

Harries, Karsten. *Infinity and Perspective.* Cambridge: MIT Press, 2001.

Hawkins, Harriett. *Strange Attractors: Literature, Culture, and Chaos Theory.* New York: Prentice Hall, 1995.

Hayles, N. Katherine. *Chaos Bound: Orderly Disorder in Contemporary Literature and Science.* Ithaca: Cornell University Press, 1990.

———. "Introduction: Complex Dynamics in Literature and Science." In *Chaos and Order: Complex Dynamics in Literature and Science,* ed. N. Katherine Hayles, 1–33. Chicago: University of Chicago Press, 1991.

———. "Turbulence in Literature and Science: Questions on Influence." In *American Literature and Science,* ed. Robert J. Scholnick, 229–50. Lexington: University Press of Kentucky, 1992.

Hill, Thomas. *Geometry and Faith; A Supplement to the Ninth Bridgewater Treatise.* 3d ed. Boston: Lee and Shepard, 1902.

Hopkins, Vivian. *Spires of Form: A Study of Emerson's Aesthetic Theory.* Cambridge: Harvard University Press, 1951.

Hume, David. *An Enquiry Concerning Human Understanding.* 1748. La Salle, Ill.: Open Court Publishing, 1958.

Jacobson, David. *Emerson's Pragmatic Vision: The Dance of the Eye.* University Park: Pennsylvania State University Press, 1993.

———. "Vision's Imperative: 'Self-Reliance' and the Command to See Things as They Are." *Studies in Romanticism* 29 (1990): 555–70.

James, Henry. *Partial Portraits.* London: Macmillan, 1888.

James, William. *Psychology.* New York: Henry Holt, 1905.

Johnson, Lee M. *Wordsworth's Metaphysical Verse: Geometry, Nature, and Form.* Toronto: University of Toronto Press, 1982.

Jones, W. T. *A History of Western Philosophy.* Vol. 3, *Hobbes to Hume.* 2d ed. New York: Harcourt Brace Jovanovich, 1969.

Kemp, Martin. *Geometrical Perspective from Brunelleschi to Desargues: A Pictorial Means or an Intellectual End?* Proceedings of the British Academy 70 (1984). London: Oxford University Press, 1985.

Kepler, Johannes. *Joannis Kepleri Astronomi Opera Omnia.* 8 vols. Ed. Christian Frisch. Frankfurt: Heyder and Zimmer, 1858–1871.

Kline, Morris. *The Mathematical Search for Knowledge.* New York: Oxford University Press, 1985.

Koyré, Alexandre. *From the Closed World to the Infinite Universe.* New York: Harper Torchbook, 1958.

Kuberski, Philip. *Chaosmos: Literature, Science, and Theory.* Albany: State University of New York Press, 1994.

Kubovy, Michael. *The Psychology of Perspective and Renaissance Art.* Cambridge: Cambridge University Press, 1986.

Leer, David Van. "Nature's Book: The Language of Science in the American Renaissance." In *Romanticism and the Sciences,* ed. Andrew Cunningham and Nicholas Jardine, 307–21. New York: Cambridge University Press, 1990.

Levine, Stuart. "Emerson and Modern Social Concepts." In *Emerson: Prospect and Retrospect,* Harvard English Studies 10, ed. Joel Porte, 155–78. Cambridge: Harvard University Press, 1982.

Locke, John. *An Essay Concerning Human Understanding.* 1690. Ed. Peter H. Nidditch. Oxford: Clarendon Press, 1975.

Markley, Robert. "Representing Order: Natural Philosophy, Mathematics, and Theology in the Newtonian Revolution." In *Chaos and Order: Complex Dynamics in Literature and Science,* ed. N. Katherine Hayles, 125–48. Chicago: University of Chicago Press, 1991.

Massumi, Brian. "Sensing the Virtual, Building the Insensible." *Architectural Design: Hypersurface Architecture* 68, nos. 5–6 (May–June 1998): 16–24.

Matthiessen, F. O. *American Renaissance: Art and Expression in the Age of Emerson and Whitman.* London: Oxford University Press, 1941.

Michael, John. *Emerson and Skepticism: The Cipher of the World.* Baltimore: Johns Hopkins University Press, 1988.

Moore, Marianne. *Complete Poems.* 1967. New York: Macmillan, 1994.

Neufeldt, Leonard N. *The House of Emerson.* Lincoln: University of Nebraska Press, 1983.

———. "The Science of Power: Emerson's Views on Science and Technology in America." *Journal of the History of Ideas* 38 (1977): 329–44.

Newton, Isaac. *Philosophiae Naturalis Principia Mathematica.* 1687, 1713. Trans. Andrew Motte, ed. Mortimer J. Adler. Chicago: William Benton, 1952.

Olsen, Taimi. *Transcending Space: Architectural Places in the Works of Henry David Thoreau, E. E. Cummings, and John Barth.* London: Associated University Presses, 2000.

Oriard, Michael. *Sporting with the Gods: The Rhetoric of Play and Game in American Culture.* Cambridge: Cambridge University Press, 1991.

Panofsky, Erwin. *Perspective as Symbolic Form.* 1927. Trans. Christopher S. Wood. New York: Zone Books, 1991.

Paul, Sherman. *Emerson's Angle of Vision: Man and Nature in American Experience.* Cambridge: Harvard University Press, 1952.

Porte, Joel. "The Problem of Emerson." In *Romanticism: Critical Essays in American Literature,* ed. James Barbour and Thomas Quirk, 59–81. New York: Garland, 1986.

Richardson, Robert D., Jr. *Emerson: The Mind on Fire.* Berkeley: University of California Press, 1995.

Robinson, David M. "Emerson's Natural Theology and the Paris Naturalists: Toward a Theory of Animated Nature." *Journal of the History of Ideas* 41 (1980): 69–88.

———. "Fields of Investigation: Emerson and Natural History." In *American Literature and Science,* ed. Robert J. Scholnick, 94–109. Lexington: University Press of Kentucky, 1992.

Rossi, William. "Emerson, Nature, and Natural Science." In *A Historical Guide to Ralph Waldo Emerson,* ed. Joel Myerson, 101–50. New York: Oxford University Press, 2000.

Rusk, Ralph L. *The Life of Ralph Waldo Emerson.* New York: Charles Scribner's Sons, 1949.

Ruskin, John. *The Stones of Venice.* 1853. Ed. J. G. Links. New York: Farrar, Straus and Giroux: 1960.

Scholfield, P. H. *The Theory of Proportion in Architecture.* Cambridge: Cambridge University Press, 1958.

Schweighauser, Charles. "'Know Thyself, Study Nature': The Contemporary Scientist's Dilemma." In *The Delegated Intellect: Emersonian Essays on Literature, Science, and Art in Honor of Don Gifford,* ed. Donald E. Morse, 109–24. New York: Peter Lang, 1995.

Shea, Daniel B. "Emerson and the American Metamorphosis." In *Emerson: Prophecy, Metamorphosis, and Influence,* ed. David Levin, 29–56. New York: Columbia University Press, 1975.

Siegfried, Tom. *Strange Matters: Undiscovered Ideas at the Frontiers of Space and Time.* Washington, D.C.: Joseph Henry Press, 2002.

Slethaug, Gordon E. *Beautiful Chaos: Chaos Theory and Metachaotics in Recent American Fiction.* Albany: State University of New York Press, 2000.

Steele, Jeffrey. *The Representation of the Self in the American Renaissance.* Chapel Hill: University of North Carolina Press, 1987.

Strauch, Carl. "Emerson's Sacred Science." *PMLA* 73, no. 3 (1958): 237–50.

Thoreau, Henry David. *Walden.* Ed. J. Lyndon Shanley. Princeton: Princeton University Press, 1971.

Walls, Laura Dassow. *Emerson's Life in Science: The Culture of Truth.* Ithaca: Cornell University Press, 2003.

Whicher, Stephen. *Freedom and Fate: An Inner Life of Ralph Waldo Emerson.* Philadelphia: University of Pennsylvania Press, 1953.

Wilson, Eric. "Emerson's *Nature,* Paralogy, and the Physics of the Sublime." *Mosaic* 33, no. 1 (2000): 39–58.

———. *Emerson's Sublime Science.* London: Macmillan, 1999.

Wittkower, Rudolf. *Architectural Principles in the Age of Humanism.* London: Alec Tiranti, 1962.

Wordsworth, William. *The Poetical Works of Wordsworth.* Cambridge Edition. Ed. Paul D. Sheats. Boston: Houghton Mifflin, 1982.

———. *The Prelude: A Parallel Text.* Ed. J. C. Maxwell. New Haven: Yale University Press, 1981.

———. *The Prose Works of William Wordsworth.* Vol. 1. Ed. W. J. B. Owen and Jane Worthington Smyser. Oxford: Oxford University Press, 1974.

INDEX

Abbott, Edwin: *Flatland,* 64
Alberti, Leon Battista: *De Pictura,* 84
Architecture: contrast between Gothic and Renaissance, 69–72; Euclidean influence on, 4; Pythagorean influence on, 4; relationship to geometry, 3–4; and space, 82–83
Aristotle: criticism of Plato, 133; and form theory, 131–32; and infinity, 97; *Metaphysics,* 131–32; *Physics,* 97, 154; and space, 81; and teleology, 109. *See also* Emerson, Ralph Waldo: and Aristotle
Attractors. *See* Dynamic systems

Bacon, Francis, 37, 108; *Novum Organum,* 51, 52, 57; and scientific method, 51–52
Berkeley, George, 97
Browne, Thomas: and sense of sight, 5–6
Burke, Edmund: *Enquiry into the Origin of Our Ideas of the Sublime and Beautiful,* 117
Butler, Joseph: *The Analogy of Religion,* 45–46

Carus, Titus Lucretius, 25, 138, 168; *De Rerum Natura,* 168
Chambers, Robert, 65
Chaos, 168–71
Chaos theory. *See* Nonlinear science
Civil War, 44, 170

Coleridge, Samuel Taylor: and language, 146–47
Comte, Auguste, 155
Copernicus, Nicolaus, 80
Correspondence theory: defined, 16; and nonlinearity, 182

Dalton, John, 138
Darwin, Charles: and evolution, 65, 151; *The Origin of Species,* 153
Democritus, 138
Descartes, René, 108, 110; *Discourse on Method,* 146; and language, 146; and mathematics, 118, 146
Dynamic systems: characteristics of, 172–74, 184. *See also* Emerson, Ralph Waldo: and dynamic systems

Einstein, Albert, 81, 116
Emerson, Ralph Waldo: and active seeing, 9–10, 11–12, 16–17, 26, 77–78; and aesthetics, 77n7, 106–8, 125–26; and angle of vision, 96; and apprehension of nature, 16, 18–19, 59, 72, 108; and architecture and nature, 71–72; and architecture and organicism, 71–72; and Aristotle, 131–33, 137, 188; and astronomy, 40, 111, 165, 172; and atomic chemistry, 138, 156; and atomic physics, 65–66, 179–80; and beauty, 72, 92, 103, 106–7, 140, 187–88; and causation, 56, 58, 111–12; and classification,